CHILDREN'S
ILLUSTRATED
FACT
FINDER

CHILDREN'S
ILLUSTRATED
FACT
FINDER

JEAN-PAUL DUPRÉ

World
HORIZONS

This edition published 1992 in Great Britain by World International Publishing Limited, an Egmont Company, Egmont House, PO Box 111, Great Ducie Street, Manchester M60 3BL.

World Horizons is an imprint of World International Publishing Limited.

First English-language edition published 1989 by Barron's Educational Series, Inc.

A catalogue record for this book is available from the British Library.

Printed in Singapore.

ISBN 0 7498 0757 1

Illustrators

Tudor Banus
Rick Blakely
Christine Michaud
Lorna Tormei
André Vial
François Vincent
Steve Wilson
Pascale Wirth
Clarie Witt
Miro Zupancic

Contents

LANGUAGE AND ITS USES

MATHEMATICS

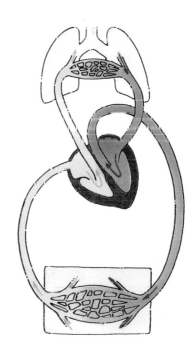

ENGLISH GRAMMAR

ARITHMETIC

PERIODS OF HISTORY

INDEX

How to Use This Book

The Children's Illustrated Fact Finder is a *reference book*. That means you can use it in two different ways.

The Fact Finder is full of interesting information about a wide range of subjects. The *Contents* list at the front of the book tells you the topics that are covered. They are listed in the same order as they appear in the book. By reading quickly through the Contents or skimming through the book itself, you will soon find something to interest you. You will learn a lot from dipping into the book in this way, and you may well find the facts and illustrations so fascinating that you read through most of the book!

You can also *refer* to the book when you want to answer a particular question or find out more about one subject. For this you will need to use the *Index* at the back of the book. This is a list of the subjects covered in the book arranged in alphabetical order. Think of the key word that best describes the subject you want to find out about and look it up in the Index. For example, if you are interested in Chinese history, you could look up 'China' in the Index. The entry for China suggests five page numbers where information may be found. By turning to those pages, you could start to learn more about China at different times in history.

With practice, you will quickly be able to find what you are looking for – and much more besides!

Early Life on Earth

4,500 million years ago
The Earth was at first a fused mass from which toxic gases escaped. Life did not exist. A long period of cooling began. It rained for millions of years.

3,000 million years ago
The first signs of life. The first living cells appeared in the oceans. They resembled *bacteria*.

600 million years ago
The appearance of *invertebrates* (*trilobites* were the most abundant) and of animals with shells.

bacteria

1,000 million years ago
The ocean was full of life – *algae, worms, sponges* and *jellyfish*. They multiplied.

jellyfish

trilobite

480 million years ago
The first *vertebrates* appeared – fish. The first fish, known as *eusthenopteron*, had no jawbones. Its body was protected by a shell.

eusthenopteron
(0.75m (2.5ft) long)

ichthyostega
(amphibian)

200 million years ago
A period of extreme cold caused the disappearance of most large reptiles. Only the most resistant ones were able to adapt to the environment. Their blood became warmer. For about 130 million years, *dinosaurs* occupied the Earth. After them, *birds* and *mammals* spread over the land.

tyrannosaur
(the largest carnivorous dinosaur)

brontosaur
(giant herbivorous dinosaur
20m (65ft) long, weighing up to 39 tonnes)

300 million years ago
From sea to land. The first
vertebrate ventured out of the
water. It was an *amphibian*. The
ichthyostega breathed with lungs
and crawled on the ground. It
had to return to the water to lay
its eggs. Amphibians were
succeeded by *reptiles*.
Dimetrodon was a carnivore. The
pterodactyl was a flying reptile.

In 1974, the
skeleton of an
Australopithecus was
found in Africa.
'Lucy' was about 1m
(39in) tall and walked
with her back
hunched. Her brain
was a third the size of
ours.

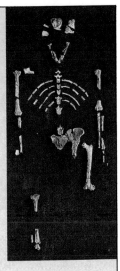

70 million years ago
Dinosaurs disappeared. Mammals and birds
multiplied. With the first *primates* the slow
evolution towards human beings began.

pterodactyl
(5.5–8m (18–26ft) long)

woolly mammoth
(hunted by humans
300,000 years ago)

dimetrodon
(2–3m (6–10ft)
long)

pantothere
(ancestor of the

marsupial and placental
mammal – the size of a
rodent)

Machairodus
(sabre-toothed
tiger, with
awesome teeth)

Australopithecus

Homo sapiens (hominid)

3 million years ago
Australopithecus was the first primate that walked almost
upright. He made and used a tool, the *chipped stone*, to
kill animals and to defend himself against carnivorous
mammals.

The evolution of
hominids continued.
Slowly, humans took
on the appearance
they have today.

11

An Overview of History

The timeline
This coloured strip shows various periods in the history of humans.

It is divided into *millennia* (thousand-year periods) and into *centuries* (hundred-year periods).

In countries that have adopted Christianity, years are counted from the birth of Christ.

1,000,000 years ago

The first people lived in Asia, Africa and Europe. They made tools from chipped stones and lived by hunting, fishing and gathering fruit and seeds.

800,000 years ago
They discovered fire and slowly learned to use it.

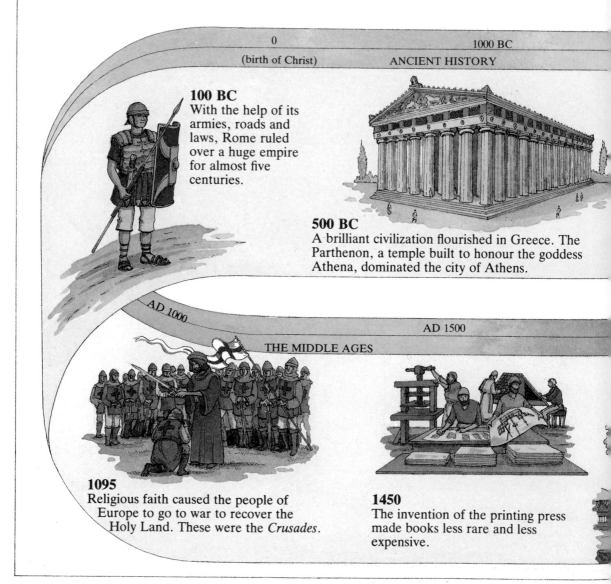

0
(birth of Christ)

1000 BC

ANCIENT HISTORY

100 BC
With the help of its armies, roads and laws, Rome ruled over a huge empire for almost five centuries.

500 BC
A brilliant civilization flourished in Greece. The Parthenon, a temple built to honour the goddess Athena, dominated the city of Athens.

AD 1000

AD 1500

THE MIDDLE AGES

1095
Religious faith caused the people of Europe to go to war to recover the Holy Land. These were the *Crusades*.

1450
The invention of the printing press made books less rare and less expensive.

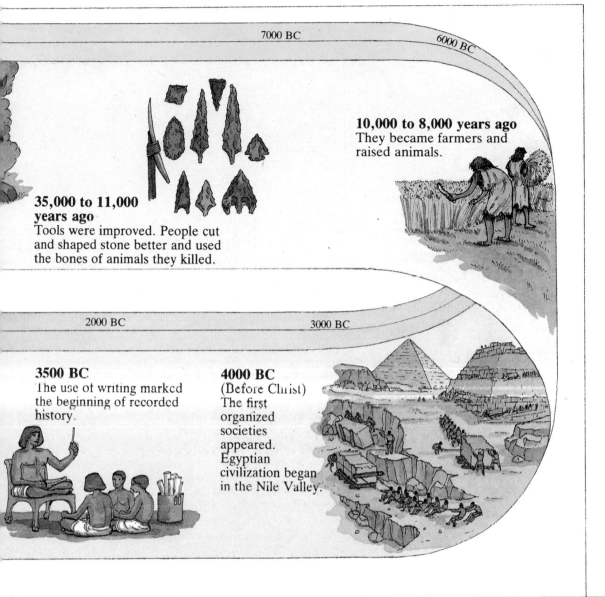

7000 BC

6000 BC

35,000 to 11,000 years ago
Tools were improved. People cut and shaped stone better and used the bones of animals they killed.

10,000 to 8,000 years ago
They became farmers and raised animals.

2000 BC

3000 BC

3500 BC
The use of writing marked the beginning of recorded history.

4000 BC
(Before Christ)
The first organized societies appeared. Egyptian civilization began in the Nile Valley.

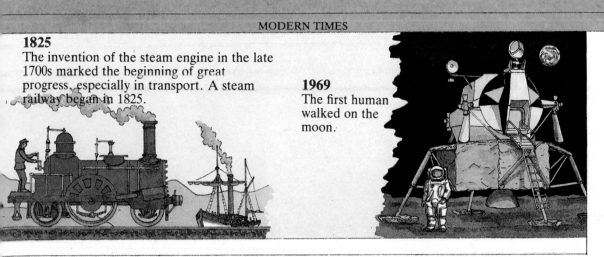

MODERN TIMES

1825
The invention of the steam engine in the late 1700s marked the beginning of great progress, especially in transport. A steam railway began in 1825.

1969
The first human walked on the moon.

Cave Dwellers

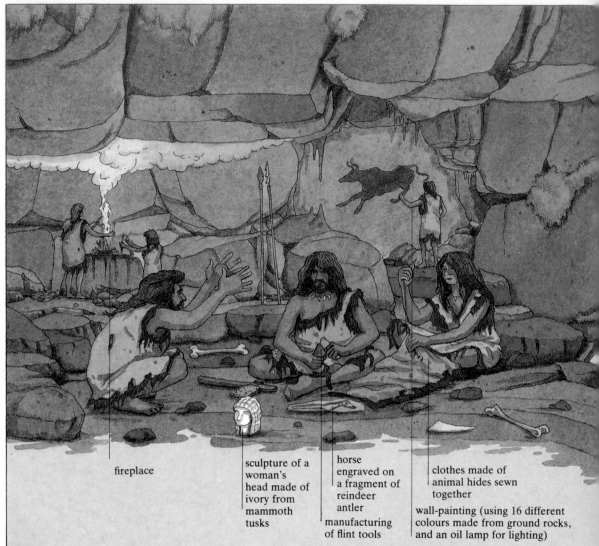

fireplace

sculpture of a woman's head made of ivory from mammoth tusks

horse engraved on a fragment of reindeer antler

manufacturing of flint tools

clothes made of animal hides sewn together

wall-painting (using 16 different colours made from ground rocks, and an oil lamp for lighting)

The term 'prehistory' refers to the long period of time between the appearance of humans on Earth and the invention of writing. The Old Stone Age or Paleolithic period goes back about one million years.

Life in the caves

Paintings and sculptures, mostly representing animals, have been found in many caves in France and Spain. The purpose of these beautiful, lifelike cave paintings is not known. However, it is generally thought that they had some religious significance and may have been part of rituals to bring success in hunting.

Caves were used for shelter only in winter. Their entrance was often marked by a small stone or by animal hides.

The first artists

With the help of very simple tools, prehistoric men and women made sculptures and engravings. By stringing shells, small bones and animal teeth, they made the first necklaces and bracelets.

Weapons and tools

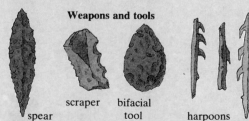

spear

scraper

bifacial tool

harpoons

Human beings were nomads

They moved from place to place and lived by hunting (mammoths, bears, reindeer, horses), fishing and gathering nuts, berries and roots. They first carved their weapons and their tools from wood and flint, and then they became skilled enough to use the tusks and antlers of animals they killed to make spears, harpoons for fishing, and even needles for sewing animal hides.

At that time, people lived in groups of about ten persons.

Hunting the woolly mammoth
With primitive weapons, hunters were not afraid to attack these powerful animals that provided them with most of the necessities of life. They hunted in groups

During their trips, hunters camped underneath tents made of hides and supported by branches or mammoth tusks. A fireplace dug in the ground was kept burning at the campsite.

They conquered fire

Between 800,000 and 500,000 years ago, the life of early humans was transformed by the discovery of fire. They learned how to start and use it. In addition to protecting them against the cold, fire was also used for lighting, for cooking food and for protection against wild animals.

Villages in Prehistoric Times

The New Stone Age or Neolithic period: 10,000 years ago

A real revolution

During this period, human beings made great progress. Tools and weapons were more precisely shaped by polishing. People learned how to work the soil, to grow wheat and to raise cattle and sheep.

polished stone axes

Stones were polished by rubbing. The *polisher* was a hard rock, often of *sandstone*.

The first villages

Humans were no longer nomads but *settled* in permanent villages. In these early villages, the various activities were distributed among the people. Some farmed or raised livestock, while others made tools. Still others wove baskets or made sheep's wool into cloth. Some created the first pottery for storing, heating and carrying food.

At the top of the hut, an opening was made for the escape of smoke produced by the central fireplace.

Sheep, beef cattle, pigs and goats were raised.

New tools (sickles, hoes) were needed for agriculture.

the first pottery

fishing with nets

Monuments

Dolmens and *menhirs* date from the age of polished stone. Dolmens were perhaps tombs and menhirs were certainly built for the worship of gods, but we do not know *how* they were used.

The word *dolmen* comes from two words in Breton: 'table' and 'stone'. Dolmens weighed between 10 and 100 tonnes.

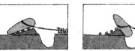

The secret of the menhirs

At Carnac in Brittany (France) stand 3,000 menhirs. The picture above shows how Neolithic people transported and built them.

dolmen

On Salisbury Plain in England there is a great circle of standing stones called Stonehenge. Each stone weighs nearly 30 tonnes. Although it was probably also used for religious ceremonies, Stonehenge is only about 3,500 years old.

Metals

At the end of the Neolithic period, *metallurgy* (the refining and use of metals) was begun. People made increasingly hard and efficient tools. They used copper, bronze and then iron. For protection against

Comparison of the duration of the various ages.

1 Age of chipped stone
2 Age of polished stone
3 Age of metals

the new metal weapons, they invented helmets and armour.

Baskets were woven from reeds and rushes and used for transporting goods.

In rivers, fish (carp, turbot, salmon, pike) were abundant.

Ancient Egypt

The gift of the Nile

Egypt is divided by a very long river, the Nile. Every year, from June to October, the Nile overflows, producing a flood that waters the adjacent lands. The Egyptians have cultivated this area of fertile land for a very long time.

The pharaoh – king and god

Egypt was ruled by a supreme master, the pharaoh. High priest and military chief, he was worshipped by his people as a god, equal to the Sun. Gifts were brought to him and he offered them to the gods. The people built a tomb for him, decorated by magnificent wall paintings and containing precious and familiar objects – everything that would make his afterlife pleasant.

During the course of Egyptian history, there were many pharaohs. Two of them have remained particularly famous:

Amenhotep IV, or Akhenaton, introduced the worship of one god, the Sun.

Ramses II, the conqueror and builder of many monuments, ruled for 66 years!

The gods

Egyptians believed that everything was a gift from the gods, who must be worshipped endlessly. These gods resembled both humans and animals. The most important were Re, the Sun god, Horus, protector of the pharaoh, and Osiris, king and judge of the dead.

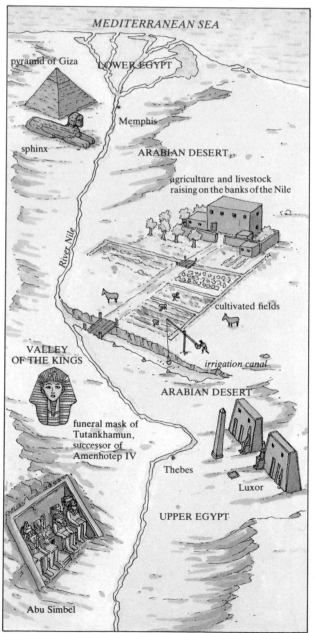

MEDITERRANEAN SEA

pyramid of Giza

LOWER EGYPT

Memphis

sphinx

ARABIAN DESERT

agriculture and livestock raising on the banks of the Nile

River Nile

cultivated fields

VALLEY OF THE KINGS

irrigation canal

ARABIAN DESERT

funeral mask of Tutankhamun, successor of Amenhotep IV

Thebes

Luxor

UPPER EGYPT

Abu Simbel

temple of the pharaoh Khafre

hieroglyphics carved on an obelisk (solar symbol)

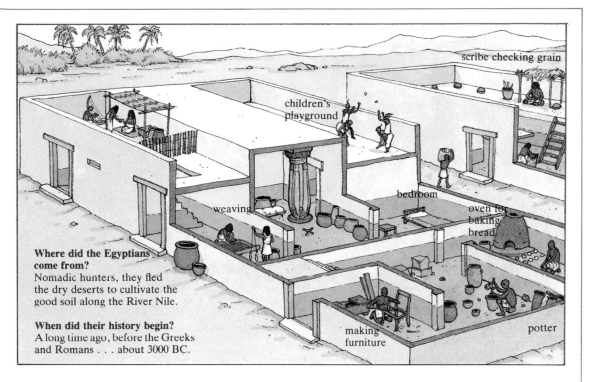

scribe checking grain

children's playground

weaving

bedroom

oven for baking bread

Where did the Egyptians come from?
Nomadic hunters, they fled the dry deserts to cultivate the good soil along the River Nile.

When did their history begin?
A long time ago, before the Greeks and Romans . . . about 3000 BC.

making furniture

potter

3,000 years of history

The Old Kingdom, founded about 3200 BC, had its capital in Memphis. During this age, great pharaohs such as Khufu (Cheops), Khafre (Khefren) and Menkure ruled.

The capital of the Middle Kingdom (2052–1770 BC) was Thebes. The economy began to develop.

During the New Empire (1580–1085 BC), Egypt was more powerful than ever during the dynasties of the Ramses. The pharaohs conquered Syria and Palestine. However, gradually, the empire fell first to the Assyrians, then to the Persians, the Greeks, and, finally, to the Romans during the first century BC.

Hieroglyphics
Egyptians knew how to write. Therefore, we have been able to learn about their long history. They did not invent the alphabet. Instead, they drew sacred images called *hieroglyphics*. Scribes (writers) wrote on sheets of papyrus, a kind of paper made of reeds.

Pyramids – tombs of pharaohs
These huge monuments were each built for only one pharaoh, who had a funeral chamber inside. The pharaoh's body was preserved by treating it with spices. The tomb was filled with furniture, clothes, food and even models of servants!

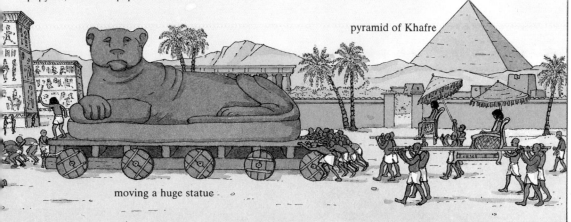

pyramid of Khafre

moving a huge statue

The Oldest Civilizations

The Sumerians – inventors of the wheel

Sumerian civilization began between the Rivers Tigris and Euphrates in Asia, about 3500 BC.

Sumerians were the first to use writing. They knew how to cultivate the soil, how to spin and weave. They were experienced sculptors. They also knew how to melt and work metals. They founded cities. They divided the hour into 60 minutes and the minute into 60 seconds.

They invented the wheel.

The Cretans – sailors

Cretan civilization started around 3000 BC on Crete, an island in the Mediterranean Sea. Its geographic location allowed contacts with other advanced civilizations from Egypt and the Near East.

Cretans excelled in architecture and decoration. Their art influenced the Greek world. They were outstanding sailors.

They invented a system of writing in about 2000 BC.

The Indians – gold- and silver-workers

Indian civilization started in the Indus Valley in about 2500 BC.

Their writing appeared in about 2300 BC as pictographs (symbols).

Indians farmed and raised livestock. They knew how to work metals (gold, silver) and were the first to use the potter's wheel.

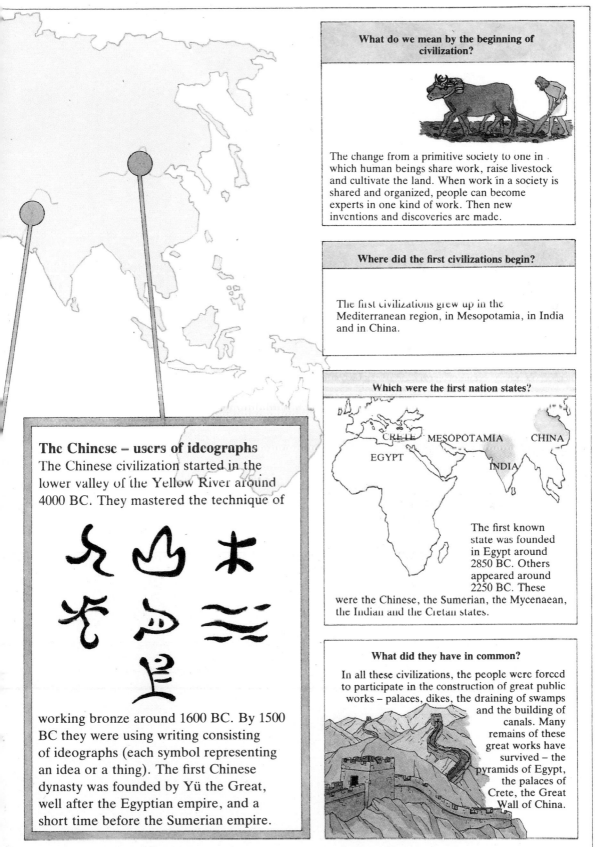

What do we mean by the beginning of civilization?

The change from a primitive society to one in which human beings share work, raise livestock and cultivate the land. When work in a society is shared and organized, people can become experts in one kind of work. Then new inventions and discoveries are made.

Where did the first civilizations begin?

The first civilizations grew up in the Mediterranean region, in Mesopotamia, in India and in China.

Which were the first nation states?

CRETE   MESOPOTAMIA   CHINA

EGYPT   INDIA

The first known state was founded in Egypt around 2850 BC. Others appeared around 2250 BC. These were the Chinese, the Sumerian, the Mycenaean, the Indian and the Cretan states.

What did they have in common?

In all these civilizations, the people were forced to participate in the construction of great public works – palaces, dikes, the draining of swamps and the building of canals. Many remains of these great works have survived – the pyramids of Egypt, the palaces of Crete, the Great Wall of China.

The Chinese – users of ideographs

The Chinese civilization started in the lower valley of the Yellow River around 4000 BC. They mastered the technique of working bronze around 1600 BC. By 1500 BC they were using writing consisting of ideographs (each symbol representing an idea or a thing). The first Chinese dynasty was founded by Yü the Great, well after the Egyptian empire, and a short time before the Sumerian empire.

Athens: the Greek Miracle

Athens

The city, surrounded by mountains, faces the Mediterranean Sea. It was founded during the tenth century BC. At that time it was nothing more than a rock called the *Acropolis*, surrounded by twelve rival cities.

Athens was named after the goddess Athena, daughter of Zeus, and protector of the city. Athenian citizens, born of an Athenian mother and father, were the only people able to take part in political life and to own land. The foreigners, or *metics*, were often merchants. Many slaves lived in the city.

The life of an Athenian

In the country, the Athenians were farmers. In the city, they worked as craftspeople or traders. They usually lived in modest houses. The women remained at home, in the *gynaeceum* (women's apartments). They had little freedom. The young boys went to school and then to the *gymnasium* (high school). They trained their minds as well as their bodies. Athenians participated actively in politics. They also liked banquets during which they discussed philosophy.

Athena

The Acropolis – kingdom of the gods
This hill, which dominates the city, was in the past only a fortress. In the fifth century BC, it was transformed by Pericles into an immense sanctuary.

Magnificent temples such as the *Parthenon*, built in honour of Athena, or the *Erechtheum*, overlooked the city below. Athens became the leading city in the Greek world.

Athens and Sparta – enemy cities

Sparta was the great rival of Athens. A strict government, an *oligarchy*, ruled the people. The education of young boys was especially strict because they were trained to become warriors.

Festivals
Gods such as Athena were honoured during the *Panathennea festivals*, when a procession of maidens offered her a veil. The god Dionysus was honoured during the great festivals held in open-air theatres.

Discus thrower

Sports
Every four years each city participated in the Olympic Games held in honour of Zeus. Athletes competed in various events – chariot races, wrestling, discus throwing and javelin throwing.

Chariot race

Athens, the artistic centre of Greece, was the rival of this warlike society. In 404 BC, the two cities fought the Peloponnesian War and Athens lost. It fell into the hands of the Spartan leader, Lysander.

Sea trade
The Athenians sold the products of their land (oil, wine, figs) and their workshops (vases, fabrics).

Rome and the Romans

Legend and truth

According to legend, Rome was founded in 753 BC by two abandoned twins, *Romulus* and *Remus*, who

were adopted and nursed by a she-wolf. This small town of Latium, after having fought its neighbours, in particular the Etruscans, finally conquered all of Italy.

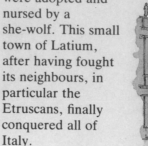

Rome had three political systems in its history. These included:

- a *royal kingdom* in the beginning (until 509 BC)
- a *republic* during the period of conquest (until the first century BC)
- an *empire* during the periods of triumph, followed by decline.

Roman forum (western section)

Rome, the capital of an empire

After having conquered Italy, Rome gradually extended its rule over a vast empire.

The Roman empire lasted almost *five centuries!*

The armed peace (called the *Pax Romana*) assured the prosperity of the empire.

The Roman language, Latin, spread with the invaders all over the Mediterranean and into northern Europe.

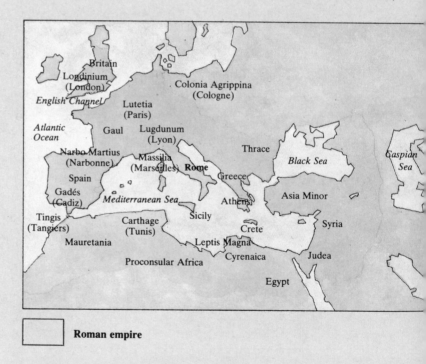

Roman empire

The great road-builders

For the security of this huge empire, the Romans organized a powerful army, the *legions*.

To ease their movements, they built a large network of roads, stretching for over 88,000km (55,000 miles). These roads improved trading between cities.

The Mediterranean Sea, centre of the empire, was an important communication link.

Like the Athenians, the Romans were very religious. They

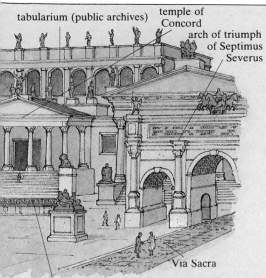

tabularium (public archives)
temple of Concord
arch of triumph of Septimus Severus
Via Sacra
rostrum (stage) for public speaking

Power and wealth

Like Athens before it, Rome was the centre of important economic, artistic and cultural development.

With its temples, theatres, public baths, circuses, schools, gymnasiums, gardens, libraries, market-places and elegant villas, it became a rich city that neighbouring towns tried to imitate.

The city of Rome was a very busy and exciting place to live. The streets were filled with people, chariots and animals being brought to market. Outdoor markets were filled with food and goods for Romans to buy.

Ideas and learning were also important in Rome. Philosophers and poets gathered there to discuss the ideas of the earlier, great Greek philosophers.

The market in a Roman city: merchants were sheltered by arcades and raised stones allowed pedestrians to cross the street while the wheels of chariots ran between the stones.

adopted Greek gods, adding them to their own gods but giving them different names. *Jupiter* (the equivalent of Greek Zeus) was the supreme god.

Emperors ruled with absolute power. Upon their death, they were considered gods. Octavius, because of his skill and political insight, became master of the Roman world after defeating his rival Antony at Actium. Under the name of Augustus Caesar, this emperor brought the power of the *Roman Peace*.

Augustus Caesar, grand-nephew and successor of Julius Caesar, shown here in the dress of the emperor.

The Byzantine Empire

Rome falls but the eastern empire survives

Over the years, the empire grew weak and it was divided into two parts – the western Roman empire and the eastern Roman empire. Invasions of the western Roman empire caused it to fall in AD 476, and it was conquered by German tribes.

After the fall of the western Roman empire, the *Byzantine* or eastern Roman empire continued for 1,000 years. The empire was located at the eastern tip of Europe, in Asia Minor, and in North Africa. The heart of the empire was the city of Byzantium, or Constantinople, known as the 'crossroads of the world'.

Reasons for the Byzantine empire's long survival were its wealth, its location where Europe and Asia meet, and the strict rule of its emperors. This empire preserved Roman law and kept alive classical civilization (Greek, Roman and Oriental). Its culture was Greek and Middle Eastern. It became the foundation of the later Russian and Balkan civilizations.

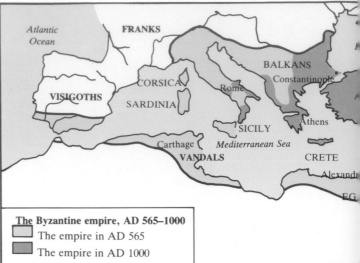

The Byzantine empire, AD 565–1000
☐ The empire in AD 565
■ The empire in AD 1000

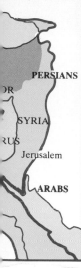

A rich trading empire

The Byzantine empire grew rich through trade and industry. Skilled workers produced silk cloth, gold and silver jewellery, perfumes, tapestries and fine glass. Merchants exported these luxuries to Italian cities and to Russia. They imported Far Eastern raw silk, spices and precious stones.

The city of Constantinople

Constantinople was a magnificent city, with paved streets, beautiful homes, churches and palaces, fine parks, museums, libraries and schools. Artists adorned building interiors with brilliant *mosaics* – pictures or designs formed by fitting together small pieces of glass, stone or tile.

Decline of the empire

For centuries, the empire battled against various invaders: Lombards in Italy, Visigoths in Spain, Arabs in Africa and Asia Minor, and Turks in the Balkans. The Byzantine empire ended when Constantinople fell to the Ottoman Turks in 1453.

Ancient India and China

Early Chinese civilization

An important civilization developed in the Yellow River (Hwang Ho) Valley between 1000 and 200 BC. Under the Chou *dynasty* (a line of kings from the same family), iron tools, written laws and metal coins were introduced (1000–256 BC). China was united for the first time under the Ch'in dynasty (256–206 BC). From 'Ch'in' came the name *China*. The Great Wall was built to keep out northern invaders. It was 3,460km (2,130 miles) long.

The rule of the Han

Under the Han rulers (206 BC–AD 220), literature, art, commerce and good government became highly developed. By 200 BC, about 30 million people were living in China. They raised rice, tea and mulberry leaves (to feed silkworms). They made porcelain and silks, discovered how to make paper and gunpowder, studied eclipses and created a modern solar calendar.

Statue of Buddha

Confucius

Chinese culture

The system of Chinese writing existed by 1500 BC. In it, each of thousands of characters (originally pictures) represents a distinct idea or sound.

The Chinese lived mainly in large, close-knit families. The oldest person was the head of the family and was always obeyed. Loyalty to the family was more important than loyalty to the nation.

For over 2,000 years, the Chinese people have followed the teaching of three wise men who lived in the sixth century BC. *Confucius* and *Lao-tzu* were Chinese philosophers. *Buddha* was a native of India. Much of ancient Chinese philosophy consisted of written works by and about Confucius.

Ancient Chinese art included decorated bronzes and ceramic vases, fine jewellery and figurines made of jade, and landscape paintings. A special Chinese structure was the pagoda – a many-storeyed, tapered temple with a series of upward-curving roofs.

The Great Wall of China

Ruins of an early fortified Indian city

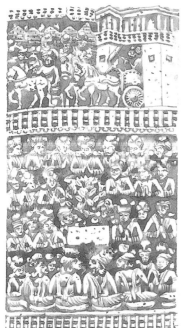
A gateway to a Buddhist shrine

Early Indian civilization

The first Indian civilization developed in the Indus Valley. Between 2500 and 1500 BC, the cities of Harappa and Mohenjo-Daro were the main centres of this civilization.

The Aryan invasion

Between 2000 and 600 BC, the Aryans crossed the northwest mountain passes from Persia and invaded India. They conquered the people of the Indus Valley. During the Aryan period of rule, the foundation of traditional Indian culture was developed. *Hinduism* and *Buddhism*, two of the world's important religions, also developed in this period. *Sanskrit* became the spoken and the literary language of India. The Aryans began a *caste system* of inferior and superior peoples.

Great Indian empires

The Maurya dynasty, which ruled between 321 and 184 BC, united much of present-day India for the first time. The emperor Asoka (273–232 BC) ruled over two-thirds of present India. As a ruler, he stressed truth, justice, charity, religious tolerance and non-violence. Asoka became a Buddhist and sent teachers to convert other people in Asia.

During the reign of the Guptas (AD 320–535), India reached its golden age. There were great achievements in literature, science, art and mathematics. Indian art included statues of humans and animals, cave-temple wall-paintings, and ornate temple architecture. The stories of the *Arabian Nights* were written. Knowledge of chemistry was applied to dyeing cloth, tanning leather, making soap and glass, and refining iron ore. Mathematics in India was advanced. It used the decimal system, the idea of zero and the symbols for numbers we use today.

The Hindu god Shiva

Four Great Religions

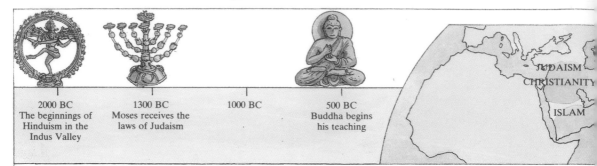

2000 BC
The beginnings of
Hinduism in the
Indus Valley

1300 BC
Moses receives the
laws of Judaism

1000 BC

500 BC
Buddha begins
his teaching

JUDAISM
CHRISTIANITY

ISLAM

Judaism

Moses descends from Mount Sinai where he received the Ten Commandments.

The rabbi reads from the Torah in a synagogue.

This religion was born in the Middle East 4,000 years ago and was revealed to the Jewish people by great prophets such as *Moses*. The Jews were the first people to worship only one God.

The teachings of Moses are found in the *Torah* (the first five books of the Bible), and contain the *Ten Commandments*.

Passover is a major Jewish holiday that celebrates the freedom of the ancient Israelites from slavery in the Egypt of the pharaohs.

Religious services are conducted by a *rabbi* (teacher) in a *synagogue* (temple).

Some Jewish people await the arrival of the *Messiah* (a messenger from God), as promised by the prophets.

Christianity

Jesus is crucified on Mount Golgotha near Jerusalem in Palestine.

The priest celebrates Mass in a church.

At the beginning of the first century, *Jesus of Galilee* was recognized by some as the Messiah promised by the Hebrew prophets. He taught his doctrine to his disciples – love of God, love of one's fellow humans, and forgiveness.

He was crucified by the Romans.

After three days, Jesus returned from the dead and appeared to his disciples, who then began to preach the word of Christ throughout the world.

The *New Testament* (second part of the Bible) includes the *Gospels*, which relate the acts and the words of Jesus.

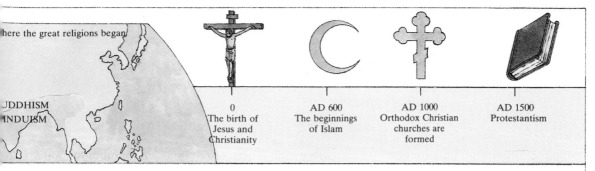

here the great religions began

BUDDHISM
HINDUISM

| 0 | AD 600 | AD 1000 | AD 1500 |
| The birth of Jesus and Christianity | The beginnings of Islam | Orthodox Christian churches are formed | Protestantism |

Islam

The angel Gabriel presents the Kaaba (sacred stone) to Abraham.

Praying Muslims turn towards Mecca.

Begun in Arabia in the seventh century, Islam follows a sacred book, the *Koran*, transmitted by *Mohammed*, who was born in *Mecca*.

Islam teaches that Mohammed is a prophet sent by God after Moses and Jesus. Its doctrine teaches the worship of a single God, *Allah*. It requires prayer, fasting, charity and a pilgrimage to Mecca. The services are conducted in *mosques*. Followers of Islam are called Muslims.

Mohammed favoured *Holy Wars*. Those killed in such wars were promised the reward of heaven.

Buddhism

Prince Gautama (Buddha) meditates to discover the way to nirvana.

A Buddhist temple is tended by monks in yellow robes.

Practised in many parts of Asia, Buddhism was founded in the sixth century BC in India by Gautama, the *Buddha*, or 'Enlightened One'. Buddha taught his disciples that people must overcome desire, the source of all pain, in order to attain *nirvana* (a state of perfect peace).

Those who do not reach nirvana are condemned to be reborn in another form, either human or animal. This is called *reincarnation*.

Buddhists believe that the way to achieve nirvana is to follow the *Middle Way*. This consists of guidelines called the *Eightfold Path*. Buddhists do not believe in a god who is separate from people or the world that they live in.

Invasions of Europe

Because of its wealth and mild climate, the Roman empire was attractive to the Germanic peoples. They crossed the northern frontier of the empire and tried to settle. From the third century, the Roman legions could no longer successfully defend the empire's frontiers. The Roman empire was about to go through a long period of invasions. The Romans called their attackers 'barbarians'.

Germanic invasions
(fifth century)

Germanic people invade the Roman empire

Shortly before AD 400, the *Visigoths* entered the Roman empire and settled there. In the 400s, other Germanic peoples invaded the empire: the *Franks*, the *Burgundians* and the *Vandals*.

As the Vandals crossed Rome, they plundered it. The *Angles* and the *Saxons* invaded what is today Britain.

Skilled craftspeople
Germanic people knew how to make weapons and jewellery of high quality. Here is a masterpiece by a goldsmith. This jewellery box is made of gold, encrusted with precious stones and decorated with enamel.

The Roman empire came to an end in AD 476, and Germanic kingdoms were set up in Europe.

Invasion of the Huns (fifth century), nomadic tribes who came from the steppes (plains) of Central Asia.

The Huns spread terror

In AD 451, the *Huns*, led by Attila, invaded the empire and terrorized its inhabitants. Roman armies and Germanic people joined to fight them. Finally beaten, the Huns retreated.

According to a Hunnic legend, a shepherd dug up a magnificent sword. He went to Attila's camp and presented it to him. The king of the Huns declared this mysterious weapon a sign from the sky entrusting him with the mission to conquer the world. This is the origin of his nickname, 'Wrath of God'!

Arab invasions (eighth century)

The Muslim empire extended from Arabia to Spain.

The Arabs wage a 'holy war'

In the eighth century, the Arabs entered Europe. They tried to spread a new religion, *Islam*, preached by the prophet Mohammed. The Muslim invasion was halted by Charles Martel of France in AD 732.

The Vikings raid and terrorize Europe

During the ninth and tenth centuries, Vikings invaded Europe. They sailed up the major rivers with fast boats, called *drakkars*. They raided towns and villages throughout Europe and killed their inhabitants. To stop these massacres in France, the king gave them a territory in AD 911, which was called *Normandy*.

A few years later, in 1066, the Normans (the Vikings who settled in Normandy) began the conquest of England. The conquest was led by William the Conqueror. He and his Norman forces defeated the Saxons at the Battle of Hastings. William killed the English king and was crowned King William I of England.

The drakkar was about 24.5m (80ft) long and 5m (16ft) wide. It held 35 rowers and as many passengers. It could reach a speed of 10 knots (about 17.5kph or 11mph) and was able to navigate in high seas because it had a keel. It is thought that Viking drakkars reached North America.

GREENLAND NORWAY

NORTH AMERICA ICELAND

Viking invasions (ninth century)

The Dark Ages

Europe after the Romans

The period from the breakup of the Roman empire to the rise of modern European nations is called the *Middle Ages* or the *medieval period*. The first half of the Middle Ages is often called the *Dark Ages* (AD 500–1000). Culture and learning almost disappeared in Europe as a result of the confusion and lack of organized government following the barbarian invasions. However, the medieval Church, the Byzantine empire and the Emperor Charlemagne all promoted learning and strong government.

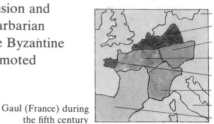

Gaul (France) during the fifth century

Saxons
Franks
Alamanni
kingdom of Syagrius
Celts
Burgundians
Ostrogoths
Visigoths

The baptism of Clovis in 496

Clovis

The Franks were the first Germanic tribe to create a powerful and lasting kingdom during the Middle Ages. Clovis was only 16 when he became king of the Franks (481–511). A capable military ruler, he conquered the other Germanic tribes in Gaul (France). When he converted the Franks to Catholicism, he gained the support of the Pope and of Gaul's large Christian population. His conversion was due to his wife's influence.

Charlemagne (Charles the Great)

Charlemagne (768–814) was the most important figure in the early medieval period. His grandfather, Charles Martel (the Hammer), led the Frankish army that stopped the Muslim invasion of Christian Europe. His father, Pepin, drove the Lombards out of Italy, and gave their lands to the Pope. That area, called the Papal States, was then ruled by the Church for 1,000 years. By conquest, Charlemagne expanded the Frankish kingdom, which had started as a small area around Belgium, into an empire covering most of western Europe.

A great empire

In the year 800, Charlemagne was the ruler of a vast territory. On Christmas Day in Rome, the Pope crowned him emperor of the Holy Roman Empire. He divided his empire into provinces, each headed by a noble responsible to him. To keep control over them, he sent royal agents to report on each noble's loyalty and ability.

Charlemagne believed in education. The age of Charlemagne has been called 'a light in the Dark Ages'.

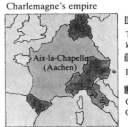

Charlemagne's empire

The Frankish kingdom in 768

Papal States

Conquests by Charlemagne

Charlemagne, here wearing the imperial crown (closed at the top), took an interest in education and set up schools. Teaching was usually done by monks.

England before the Norman conquest

The Romans left England and Wales in AD 407. The Dark Ages that followed were far from peaceful. England was invaded by Picts from Scotland, Angles and Saxons from Germany, and Jutes from Denmark. Most of England came under Anglo-Saxon rule, but by 850 Vikings from Denmark had begun to settle in northern England. These must have been difficult times for the people of Britain.

Peace was restored for a while when King Alfred ruled the south and west of England (871–899). He made a treaty with the Danes, allowing them to rule the north and east of England, which was known as *Danelaw*. In under 100 years, the Danes were driven out of England and the country was united under one king, but Vikings continued to attack from time to time.

When King Edward the Confessor died in 1066, he left no children. William of Normandy, himself descended from Viking raiders, claimed the throne. After defeating his rival, Harold, at the Battle of Hastings, he became William I of England.

The Feudal System

The strong protect the weak

Under the feudal system, powerful lords provided protection to the less powerful nobles, their *vassals*. In exchange, each vassal pledged allegiance to his lord. He owed him obedience and his main duty was to help in warfare.

The lords go to war

War was the main occupation of the powerful lords. When they were not fighting, the knights organized violent games, called *tournaments*, or went hunting on their land.

The rules of a tournament

At a given signal, two knights on horseback rushed against each other, lance in hand. Each tried to unseat the other.

Many were wounded; some died. The winner received from the loser his armour and his horse.

Fortified castles

Castles provided good protection for the lords and inhabitants of the land. However, since the buildings were poorly lit and badly heated, they were not very comfortable places to live.

Peasants do all the work

Poor people without land of their own (peasants) were the largest group of people. They farmed the lord's land and led a hard life.

Some of them, the *serfs*, did not have the right to leave the land of their master.

Serfs lived in poor huts and often fell victim to famine and disease.

The corvée (a labour tax)
Peasants had a duty to work without pay for the lord at certain times. The life of peasants slowly improved because of technical progress in agriculture.

The monks pray and study

After the year AD 1000, numerous churches were built in Europe. Religious faith was very important.

Bishops lived as lords. The *priests* in the villages taught the basic religious ideas to the faithful. *Monks* lived in monasteries and were the best educated people at that time. They divided their time between prayer, studies, and manual labour. Some monks copied manuscripts.

A manuscript
This is a book written by hand. At that time, parchment made from tanned and rubbed sheep's hides was used. These manuscripts are richly decorated.

The Creation of Nation States

The decline of feudalism

There were many reasons for the decline of feudalism. Many nobles were killed in the frequent wars. The growth of towns and trade, starting in the year AD 1000, resulted in the rise of a middle class that sided with the kings against the nobles. Increased trade brought new products, methods and ideas to Europe.

Serfdom declined as many serfs fled from the manors to the towns.

Nation states in the Middle Ages

As feudalism declined and the power of the nobles lessened, kings began to increase their power.

By the 1300s, after long struggles with the nobility, kings began to regain power, to establish strong central governments, and to win the allegiance of their people. They created *nation states* out of feudal kingdoms. Loyalty was shifted from the nobles to the kings. To rule such large areas without giving power to nobles, kings and queens needed strong armies and good systems of laws. They also developed taxes so that they would have enough money to run the armies and pay government officials.

England was one of the first countries to develop a national government. After the Norman conquest in 1066, *William the Conqueror* (1066–1087) ended Anglo-Saxon rule and forced the nobles to swear allegiance to him. He set up a strong central government. *King Henry II* (1154–1189) started a jury system and improved the courts.

In France, starting with *Hugh Capet* (987–996), capable French rulers took over the lands of the nobility, established royal courts, created a standing army, and centralized the government.

EUROPE ABOUT 1500
— Boundary of the Holy Roman Empire

A section of the Bayeux tapestry showing the Norman invasion of England

Most of central Europe was joined in a loose union, known as the Holy Roman Empire, that included the lands that later became Germany, Austria and northern Italy. Prussia, one of the largest states, expanded its boundaries by conquest, purchase or inheritance, and tried to control this union of states.

Louis XIV

Absolute monarchs in Europe

During the 1500s and 1600s, European kings and queens gained great power. They developed strong armies that took the place of the private armies of the nobles. They took over more territory. Kings and queens created strong royal governments that began to have strict control over the lives of the people. They were known as *absolute monarchs*, that is, rulers who had complete authority over the government and the people.

In England, the popular and able Tudor monarchs promoted trade and prosperity. *Henry VIII* (1509–1547), and his daughter *Elizabeth I* ((1558 1603) also encouraged learning.

France became an absolute monarchy under the Bourbon kings (1598–1792). Under *Louis XIV* (1643–1715), France became the leading power in Europe. The palace at Versailles became a cultural centre for outstanding writers, artists and scientists.

Henry VIII

In Spain, the marriage of *Ferdinand of Aragon* to *Isabella of Castile* united that nation under their control. In the 1500s, Spain gained a vast empire in the New World from Mexico and the Caribbean islands to Argentina. Spain became rich and powerful.

In eastern Europe, Prussia and Austria became powerful national states. Rulers like *Peter the Great* of Russia (1682–1725), *Frederick the Great* of Prussia (1740–1786), and *Maria Theresa* of Austria (1740–1780) enlarged the size and power of their countries and brought the nobles under royal control.

Elizabeth I

The Crusades

Reasons for the Crusades

The Crusades were a series of religious wars fought between 1095 and 1270. Their aim was to free the Holy Land, Palestine, from the Muslim Turks. In the 11th century, the Seljuk Turks took Jerusalem and prevented Christian pilgrims from visiting holy places in Palestine. When the Turks threatened to invade Constantinople, the Byzantine emperor appealed to the Pope (head of the Roman Catholic Church) for soldiers to defend his city and reclaim the Holy Land.

Pope Urban II called on the nobles and all Christians to join in a war to win back the Holy Land. The Crusaders felt they were doing God's will. If killed, they were promised they would go to heaven. Some feudal nobles fought in the hope of conquest, wealth and adventure. Many serfs went along with their lords because they were promised freedom on their return.

The major Crusades

The *First Crusade*, from 1096 to 1099, was the only successful one. It is known as the 'Peasants' Crusade' because many peasants, or poor farmers, took part. Many joined this Crusade because they hoped to see something of the world and improve their harsh lives. Most of them were killed. French and Norman nobles led the army in the Crusade, which captured the city of Jerusalem.

The *Second Crusade* began in 1147 after the Muslims took back the city of Edessa, which was won in the First Crusade. The Second Crusade was led by King Louis VII of France and the Holy Roman Emperor Conrad III. It was a failure and the defeated armies returned to Europe.

Crusaders were rowed across the Mediterranean in ships called galleys.

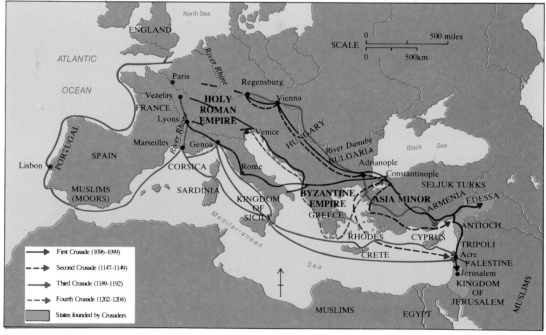

Routes of the Crusades

Crusaders kill the Muslim defenders of the city of Jerusalem.

The *Third Crusade* was fought from 1189 to 1192 to take back Jerusalem, which had been recaptured by the Muslims. It involved many famous rulers, including King Richard the Lion Heart of England, and Saladin, the able Muslim leader.

The *Fourth Crusade* (1202–1204) was organized by the merchants of Venice. They were not interested in defeating the Muslims, but wanted to destroy the competition for trade from Byzantine ships in the Mediterranean. This Crusade ended when the Crusaders invaded Constantinople in 1204 and set up their own kingdom. It took the Byzantines 50 years to win back Constantinople.

Results of the Crusades

The Crusades had important short-term results. Although the Christians took back the Holy Land for a short time, they failed to regain it permanently. The Byzantine empire was weakened by the attacks of the Crusaders, who looted Constantinople on their way to the Holy Land. Italian city-states such as Venice and Genoa grew rich by trading with the Crusaders and transporting them by ship to the Holy Land.

There were also important long-lasting results. Feudalism in Europe was weakened and never recovered. Kings increased their power. Many nobles were away from their land, and many lords died in the Crusades. Serfs left the lord's manor for the Crusades or to live in towns because 'town air is free air'. Cities grew as trade and manufacturing increased. Finally, Europeans came into contact with new ideas and products from the more advanced Muslim and Byzantine civilizations.

These are the ruins of a castle built by Crusaders in the Holy Land. The castle of Belvoir was on a cliff overlooking the Sea of Galilee.

Medieval Towns

Beginning in the 11th century, greater security on the roads allowed trade in Europe to start again, and towns began to develop.

Towns became free

After having been ruled by lords, the towns became free.

Master potter and his family

Cabinet-maker

Master tailor

Each guild had apprentices (beginners), workers and masters.

Towns were small and often surrounded by walls. Merchants and craftspeople had their shops in narrow streets that were often dirty but very lively. Since most of the inhabitants could not read, shop signs had symbols that identified the various trades. Most houses were built of wood and fires were common. The towns usually had a small population of no more than 10,000. Paris, at that time one of the largest cities in Europe, had only 100,000 inhabitants.

Burghers (inhabitants of towns) elected a *mayor* and a *council of municipal magistrates* to run the town.

Craftspeople and merchants

All those who practised the same trade belonged to organizations called *guilds:* blacksmiths, tailors and so forth. Each guild had a set of regulations that defined working conditions and set prices and wages.

The age of cathedrals

During the 12th century, magnificent churches were built in the large cities of Europe. These were called *cathedrals*.

These churches were tall, bright and delicately sculptured.

Their construction took a long time. It took 75 years (1160–1235) to construct Notre Dame in Paris.

Chartres cathedral

A centre of community life

At that time, a cathedral was not only a place of worship but also the site of meetings, a place to hide in case of danger, and even a shelter for merchants in case of rain. Plays with religious themes were performed in the courtyard in front of the cathedral. These were called *mystery plays.* Jugglers and acrobats also performed there.

The Age of Great Discoveries

Beginning in the 15th century, great inventions (printing and paper manufacturing, to name two) and discoveries (the route to India, the existence of America) changed people's lives.

Manuscripts for the rich

Two hundred sheep for a manuscript! That was the price paid by the Countess of Anjou. It is said that King Charles V of France tied his books to his desk with a chain for fear of thieves!

Until the 15th century, books were rare and very expensive because months and sometimes years were needed to copy a manuscript.

Printing shop at the time of Gutenberg

The invention of printing

A remarkable new invention, printing, was introduced in the 1400s. At first, books were printed from carved wooden blocks that were inked and pressed on paper. By the 1440s, movable type had been invented in Germany. Movable type consisted of small pieces of metal each engraved with a letter that could be combined to form words and sentences. They could be used again and again. In 1450 Johann Gutenberg of Germany invented a printing press that used movable type. He was the first to print a book in Europe. Printing spread rapidly.

Invention of paper

The Chinese invented paper in the second century AD. At first, writing was done on papyrus, a paper made from the stems of a kind of reed. Later it was done on parchments (animal skins). After the 10th century, rags were used to manufacture paper. Today, wood pulp is used.

Cannon powder and firearms

The invention of *gunpowder* (probably in China) led to the use of the first cannons and the manufacture of the first individual firearms.

Adventurers and caravels

By using the *compass*, borrowed from the Chinese and the Arabs, navigators sailed the oceans in powerful ships called *caravels*. They searched for new routes to reach the lands that were rich in spices and gold.

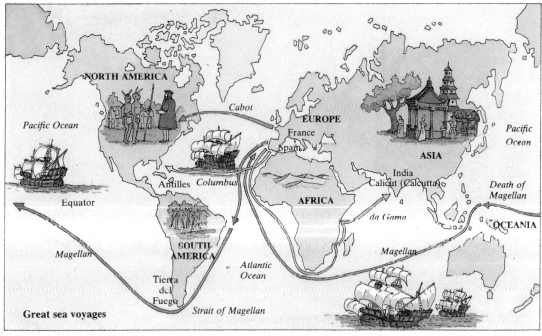

Great sea voyages

1492

Christopher Columbus, searching for the western route to India, reached the Bahamas off the coast of America.

1498

The Portuguese *Vasco da Gama* discovered the most direct route to India. He sailed around the southern tip of Africa.

1519–1522

The expedition of the Portuguese *Ferdinand Magellan* sailed around the world. Out of the five sailing ships and 234 sailors that left Spain, only one ship and 18 survivors returned. Magellan himself died along the way. This expedition proved that the Earth is round.

1497

The Italian *John Cabot*, on behalf of England, reached Canada.

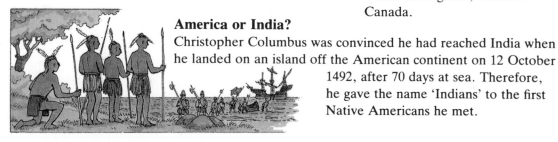

America or India?

Christopher Columbus was convinced he had reached India when he landed on an island off the American continent on 12 October 1492, after 70 days at sea. Therefore, he gave the name 'Indians' to the first Native Americans he met.

The Renaissance

The Renaissance starts in Italy

The word *Renaissance* is French for rebirth. The period from the 14th to the 16th centuries was a time of the cultural rebirth of Europe, and the beginnings of modern times.

The Renaissance began in Italy as Italian writers and artists began to show a new curiosity about human beings and the world in which they lived. Why did it begin there? Starting with the Crusades, trade and commerce grew in the area around the Mediterranean Sea. The large Italian cities such as Rome, Florence, Venice and Genoa grew very rich. Wealthy merchants became the patrons, or supporters, of painters, architects, sculptors and writers. These artists and writers studied the works of ancient Greece and Rome and drew upon them for inspiration. Their creative genius caused the rebirth of a brilliant civilization. Later, the Renaissance spread to northern and western Europe.

Great artists

The greatest artist of northern Europe was *Rembrandt van Rijn*, a Dutch painter.

Artists such as *Raphael, Michelangelo* and *Leonardo da Vinci* were the creative geniuses of the Italian Renaissance.

Leonardo da Vinci (1452–1519) excelled in many fields, as a painter, musician, sculptor, poet and scientist. As an inventor, he drew up plans for aeroplanes, submarines and military weapons.

Michelangelo (1475–1564) was another many-talented Renaissance genius. He worked in Florence and Rome, and was a fine painter, sculptor, poet and architect. He painted scenes from the Bible on the ceiling of the Sistine Chapel in the Vatican. He sculpted the *Pietà*, showing Mary with Jesus, and carved huge, lifelike statues of Moses and David. Michelangelo designed the vast dome of St Peter's Cathedral in Rome.

Renaissance literature

During the Renaissance, writers began to use their own spoken languages instead of writing in Latin.

Dante Alighieri wrote *The Divine Comedy* in Italian verse.

Miguel de Cervantes wrote his novel, *Don Quixote*, in Spanish.

François Rabelais wrote his satires in French.

Desiderius Erasmus criticized the Church in Dutch.

William Shakespeare wrote all his world-famous plays in English.

The scientific Renaissance

A scientific revolution came along with the Renaissance. The way in which people viewed themselves and the world changed a great deal.

Renaissance scientists emphasized direct observation of nature and experimentation.

Copernicus, a Polish astronomer, came to believe that the Sun, rather than the Earth, is the centre of the solar system.

The Flemish *Vesalius* advanced knowledge of human anatomy.

William Harvey, in England, discovered the circulation of the blood.

Isaac Newton, also English, showed the law of gravity as a mathematical formula.

These findings were important discoveries in the scientific revolution.

Changes brought by the Renaissance

An emphasis on reason, a questioning attitude and scientific experimentation began to replace the medieval concern with faith, authority and tradition.

A spirit of freedom, enquiry, and interest in the pleasures of *this* world replaced the earlier emphasis on preparing oneself for salvation and the *next* world.

By the end of the 1500s, countries on the Atlantic Ocean became cultural centres of the Renaissance. England, France and Spain also spread their literature and learning to their empires overseas.

The Renaissance signalled an end of the medieval world in Europe and the beginning of the modern era.

America is Colonized

Why England established colonies

- English merchants wished to make profits from trading with colonies in the New World. They imported raw materials – cotton, tobacco and timber – and sold manufactured goods.
- Overseas colonies were an outlet for the growing English population, and a place to settle dissatisfied religious groups.
- English rulers wanted to increase England's power and prestige.

The English colonies in America

By the 18th century, England had established 13 colonies along the Atlantic seaboard of North America. Several more were established in the West Indies (Bahamas, Barbados, Jamaica). By 1763,

The Pilgrims gather for church services.

there were two million people living in the English colonies in America. More than one-third of the population was non-English, including Scotch-Irish, German, French, Swiss, Dutch, and African slaves.

Jamestown, 1607

The first permanent English colony in the Americas was settled at Jamestown, Virginia, in 1607. By 1619, after a shaky beginning, Virginia was a successful colony with a thriving tobacco trade. It had also established the first representative assembly, or law-making group (the Virginia House of Burgesses). In 1619, the first group of English women arrived, as did the first group of Africans. The Africans were later made slaves.

Plymouth, 1620

The Pilgrims landed at Cape Cod, Massachusetts, and stepped on to Plymouth Rock. They left England because they wanted religious freedom. They wished to separate completely from the Church of England (Anglican Church) and have their own church. Before landing, the leaders of the 41 families aboard signed the *Mayflower Compact*. This was an agreement to make 'just and equal laws' that they all promised to obey. This compact is the first example of self-government in the New World.

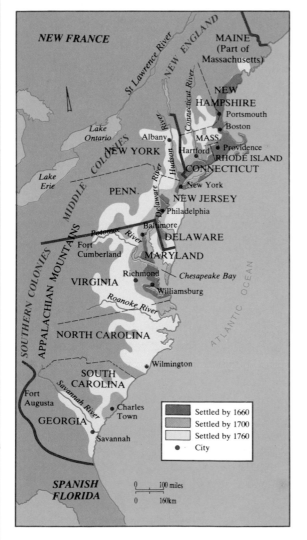

NEW FRANCE

St Lawrence River

NEW ENGLAND

MAINE
(Part of Massachusetts)

NEW HAMPSHIRE
- Portsmouth
- Boston

Lake Ontario

Albany
NEW YORK
MASS.
Hartford
Providence
RHODE ISLAND
CONNECTICUT

Lake Erie

MIDDLE COLONIES

PENN.

New York

NEW JERSEY
- Philadelphia

Hudson River

Delaware River

Baltimore

Potomac River

Fort Cumberland

DELAWARE

MARYLAND

Richmond
Chesapeake Bay

VIRGINIA
- Williamsburg

Roanoke River

APPALACHIAN MOUNTAINS

SOUTHERN COLONIES

NORTH CAROLINA

- Wilmington

SOUTH CAROLINA

Fort Augusta

Savannah River

Charles Town

GEORGIA
- Savannah

ATLANTIC OCEAN

Settled by 1660
Settled by 1700
Settled by 1760
- City

SPANISH FLORIDA

0   100 miles
0   160km

The Puritans, 1630

The Massachusetts Bay Colony was founded in and near Boston in 1630. The *Puritans* who settled this colony wanted religious freedom. They did not wish to separate from the Anglican Church. Instead, they wished to purify it, and so were called Puritans. Their colony grew quickly and was a great success.

The colony of Jamestown

Other English colonies

In 1623, the colonies of New Hampshire and Maine were begun. Massachusetts took over Maine and the southern towns of New Hampshire.

William Penn

In 1624, the Dutch founded the colony of New Amsterdam, which included New York and New Jersey. England took over both colonies in 1664. New Jersey became a separate colony in 1738.

Maryland began in 1634 as a colony where Catholics were free to practise their religion.

In 1636, Roger Williams left Massachusetts to start Rhode Island. This was the first colony to grant religious freedom to all religions and even to non-believers. Connecticut was founded in the same year.

In 1638, people from Sweden settled in Delaware. That colony was conquered by England in 1664.

Individual English proprietors, or owners, who were granted land by the English king, founded the other four colonies:

1665: North and South Carolina. They became separate colonies in 1711.

1683: Pennsylvania. William Penn began a Quaker settlement at Philadelphia.

1733: Georgia. This became a buffer between Spanish Florida and the Carolinas.

William Penn signs a treaty with the Indians

A colonial plantation in South Carolina

The American and French Revolutions

American colonists demand independence

Britain's American colonies along the Atlantic seaboard were separated from the mother country by 4,800km (3,000 miles) of ocean, which proved to be a barrier to understanding. After the British drove the French out of the Ohio Valley in the *French and Indian War* (1754–1763), the British government wanted the colonists to help pay the cost of that war and they began to tax the colonists. In time, Britain's new policy towards the colonies and new taxes caused the colonists to revolt.

In 1773, American colonists disguised as Indians threw overboard the cargo of tea off a British ship anchored at Boston. They were protesting about British imports and taxes. The Boston Tea Party, as it was called, was one of the events leading up to the American Revolution.

Causes of the American Revolution

- Colonial manufacturers and merchants rejected the idea that the colonies existed to make the parent country rich.
- The colonists felt the taxes voted by the British Parliament (law-making body) were unfair. They claimed that since they did not send representatives to Parliament, it was 'taxation without representation'.
- After living in the New World, many colonists considered themselves Americans, not British subjects. Non-English colonists (Dutch, French, Irish) came from nations hostile to Britain.

The ideas of philosophers like *John Locke* of England, and later *Jean-Jacques Rousseau* of France, influenced colonial leaders. These philosophers wrote that the purpose of government was to protect rights to life, liberty, and property. They said that when the government failed to live up to its purpose, the people had the right to change or end that government, even by force.

After several years of conflict with Britain, compromise proved impossible.

In 1776, the Second Continental Congress, representing the various colonies, adopted the Declaration of Independence. The colonies had to fight the British to win their independence. The American Revolution came to an end in 1781 with an American victory. A new nation, the United States of America, was created.

Effects of the American Revolution

- The *Constitution* of the United States (1789) created the basis for a democratic government that continues today.
- The American Revolution encouraged the colonies of Spain and Portugal in Central and South America to revolt in the early 1800s and win independence. In Europe, it encouraged Greece and Belgium to gain their independence by 1830.
- Britain had to change its policy towards its colonies. Gradually over the next 150 years, most British colonies gained their

George Washington led the colonists to victory and became the first President of the United States.

On 14 July 1789, a Paris mob stormed and captured the Bastille, the hated royal prison. In France, every 14 July is celebrated as Bastille Day, or the beginning of French independence. It is a national holiday, similar to Independence Day (4 July) in the United States.

independence.

- In France, the American example encouraged the French people to replace their absolute monarchy in the French Revolution of 1789.

Causes of the French Revolution

The French Revolution was an attack upon the unlimited power of the king and nobles in the 1700s. Like most other European kings of that time, *King Louis XVI* ruled as an absolute monarch. The nobility had all the privileges and received the high government positions, but they paid few taxes. The middle class merchants, the poor workers, and the peasants (small farmers) made up over 90% of the population. They did all the hard work and paid most of the taxes, but had no voice in the government.

When the French treasury became bankrupt in 1789, representatives of *all* classes in France formed a National Assembly, which made far-reaching reforms:

- All remaining feudal privileges (of the nobles and Church leaders) were ended.
- The new Constitution of 1791 (France's first) limited the powers of the king.
- The power to make and enforce laws was put into the hands of a Legislative Assembly. Its members were to be elected.

The 'Reign of Terror'

In 1791, the French Revolution turned violent and the so-called 'Reign of Terror' began. Radical, or extreme, leaders who did not want a king came to power. The king and queen and many nobles were put to death. Order was restored when *Napoleon Bonaparte* gained control of the French government. His wars made him the master of Europe for a time and he carried the reforms of the French Revolution to other parts of Europe.

The American Revolution involved hard fighting and terrible conditions for soldiers on both sides.

The United States Constitution

Washington presides over the Constitutional Convention.

The Constitutional Convention

The American Constitution was written in Philadelphia in the spring and summer of 1787. It was an agreement about how the United States should be governed. The 55 delegates at the Constitutional Convention came from every state except Rhode Island. They included some of the nation's most able leaders, such as *George Washington* and *Benjamin Franklin*, the oldest delegate. The Founders made compromises on important points in order to form a government that all could agree to. The Constitution they wrote has been the basis of government in the United States for over 200 years.

Important ideas in the United States Constitution

- The central, or national, government was given certain powers (to coin money, to make war), while the state governments kept other powers (to regulate marriage and education). This division of powers between the national government and the state governments is called a *federal system*.
- The three branches of the national

government are separated, so that none of them can gain too much power: the *legislature,* Congress, makes the laws for the whole country; the *executive branch,* president and advisers, enforces or executes the laws; the *judicial branch,* Supreme Court and other federal (national) courts, sees that the laws are carried out. The courts interpret, or say, what the laws mean.

- Each branch has certain checks on the actions of the other two branches in order to prevent any abuse of power and to prevent any one branch from becoming too powerful. For example, the Supreme Court can declare a law passed by Congress or an executive act to be unconstitutional. That stops it.
- A major compromise at the Constitutional Convention was to form a Congress made up of two houses. In the *Senate*, each state is equally represented and has two senators. In the *House of Representatives*, the number of each state's representatives is determined by the size of that state's population. All laws must be passed by both houses of

George Washington is inaugurated as the nation's first president.

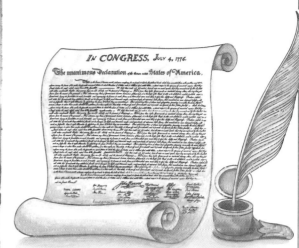

The Declaration of Independence was written by Thomas Jefferson. Its ideas of human rights have inspired people all over the world for more than 200 years.

Congress and approved by the president.

- The *Bill of Rights* is included in the first ten amendments (or additions) to the Constitution. The Bill of Rights was added to spell out clearly the rights of citizens. It prevents the government from interfering with such basic liberties as freedom of religion, freedom of the press,

freedom from unlawful imprisonment and trial by jury

Important American leaders

Thomas Jefferson, author of the Declaration of Independence in 1776, was not present at the Constitutional Convention. At the time he was serving as the American minister to France. He approved the Constitution, but only with a Bill of Rights included.

James Madison is considered the 'Father of the Constitution'. He kept a careful record of the secret discussions at the Constitutional Convention. He also helped to write the *Federalist Papers*, a series of essays, to answer the objections people had to the new Constitution.

George Washington, military hero of the American Revolution, was the chairman of the Convention, and was elected the first president of the United States. He was 'first in war, first in peace, and first in the hearts of his countrymen'.

Ben Franklin, over 80, was the oldest delegate. Weak and in pain, he often had to be carried to meetings.

Thomas Jefferson could not attend the Convention because he was in France, but many of his ideas may be found in the document.

The Industrial Revolution

Numerous inventions revolutionized human life during the 18th and 19th centuries. These changes, which began in Great Britain, marked the beginning of the modern world in the United States and Europe. They caused such important changes that they are called the *Industrial Revolution*.

A new force – steam

The leading principle is that water in a boiler produces steam. The controlled escape of steam provides a usable force. In the 18th century steam engines were invented. They were perfected and their use became widespread. At the end of the 19th century, their number reached more than 73,000!

From stagecoach to railway

The British and Americans constructed the first steam locomotives capable of pulling carriages on rails.

The *railway* was certainly the most popular invention of the century. By 1850, travelling was faster (51kph, almost 32mph) and more comfortable. Large amounts of goods were also transported. Starting in 1825, railways were built to connect major cities.

Ships without sails and oars

Starting in 1819, steamships began to cross the Atlantic. They brought the continents closer together and encouraged trade. The crossing lasted about 15 days, whereas a sailing ship took between 30 and 40 days.

The first factories

Agriculture also used the power of engines, which made farming easier. However, technical progress took place mostly in industry. In countries rich in the coal necessary to run the engines, the first *factories* were built and attracted many workers.

Hundreds of poor farmers left their

The first factories
They replaced small workshops and represented industrial development. Their number increased rapidly.

Steam thresher
Steam moved the engines of threshers. Work became easier and faster.

Aeroplanes
At the beginning of the
20th century, humans went
up in the sky in strange
machines.

Ships
The pressure of huge
steam-propelled paddle
wheels moved ships.

nboat, around 1850

The Rocket, 1830

Cars
Their performance became incredible. In 1894,
they could travel at a speed of 21kph (13mph).
In 1903, they reached speeds of 104kph (65mph)!

villages for the cities to become workers, but
living conditions were miserable. They
worked 12 to 14 hours a day for low salaries.
Even seven-year-old children were
employed. Living conditions improved only
at the end of the 19th century.

The first cars

Just before 1900, the first petrol-powered
cars appeared. Coughing and backfiring,
they frightened people and their horses.
However, motor cars soon became a way of
life for almost everyone. The car industry
kept developing better vehicles.

A mysterious force – electricity

Electrical energy was first used in the middle
of the 19th century and progress in
developing electricity was rapid. By the end
of the century, many machines were
powered by electricity. The lighting of cities
by gas was gradually replaced by electricity.

Other discoveries of the 19th century

1807	*Fulton* built the first successful *steamboat*.
1825	*Niépce* invented *photography*.
	Stephenson built the first successful *steam locomotive*.
1834	*McCormick* patented the *reaper* for farming.
1837	*Morse* invented the *telegraph*.
1846	*Howe* made the first successful *sewing machine*.
1855	*Bessemer* manufactured *steel* from cast-iron.
1859	*Drake* drilled the first successful *oil well*.
1865	*Lister* used *antiseptic* methods in surgery.
1869	*Gramme* invented a machine to produce *electricity*.
1869	*Berguès* produced electrical current by means of a waterfall (*hydroelectric power*).
1876	*Bell* invented the *telephone*.
1879	*Edison* made the first *electric light bulb*.
1880	*Edison* invented the *gramophone*.
1885	*Daimler* and *Benz* produced a *petrol-powered car*.
1888	*Pasteur* produced a vaccine against *rabies*.
1896	*Marconi* invented *wireless telegraphy*.
1890s	*Röntgen* discovered *X-rays*.
1896	*Henry Ford* produced his first successful *car*.
1897	*Ader* constructed an engine-driven flying machine: the *aeroplane*.

America in the 1800s

Westward expansion

Americans began to move west from the time of the first settlements. Most were attracted by cheap, fertile land and the chance to improve their lives. After the Revolution, some pioneers settled in the western areas of New England, New York and Pennsylvania. Others pushed across the mountains and down the Ohio Valley into Ohio, southern Indiana and Illinois. Western settlement soon brought statehood to Vermont, Kentucky, Tennessee, Ohio and Louisiana.

Between 1812 and 1861, eastern settlers westward into Tennessee and Kentucky.

In New York, the *Erie Canal* (1825) joined the Hudson River at Albany to Lake Erie at Buffalo. This opened eastern markets to farm products from the Midwest and helped immigrants to settle there.

Railways built between 1830 and 1860 linked the cities along the Atlantic coast with the cities of the upper Midwest.

Frontier life

Life on the frontier was primitive, hard and lonely. Most pioneers were poor farmers who struggled to support their families.

Settlers travelling west stop at an inn along the National Road.

and European immigrants settled east of the Mississippi River. They also crossed into Iowa, Minnesota, the Dakotas, the Oregon Territory and California. During those years, 17 new states entered the Union.

Internal improvements

In the early 1800s, poor roads made travel difficult. This need for improved transport led the government and private companies to build roads and canals. The *National* or *Cumberland Road* went from Cumberland, Maryland, across the Appalachians to Wheeling (now West Virginia) by 1818. It was later extended to Vandalia, Illinois. Further south, the *Wilderness Road* ran

They lived in crude log cabins (or turf houses in the Dakotas), made their own clothing, furniture and utensils, and had few neighbours, schools or churches.

The sections

In the 1800s, the three sections, the North-east, South and West, developed in different ways. By the 1840s the *North-east*, the nation's chief manufacturing region, produced textiles, leather goods, iron tools, utensils and machinery. The South and West were a growing market for its goods.

The *South* had many small-scale farmers, but was dominated by a small number of wealthy and influential plantation owners.

A slave auction

On their land, black slaves raised cash crops – cotton, tobacco, sugar cane and rice – for the market.

After *Eli Whitney*'s invention in 1793 of the cotton gin, which separated the cotton fibre from the seeds, cotton became king. American cotton production grew from over 900,000kg (two million lb) a year in the 1790s to 150 million kg (330 million lb) by 1826.

The *West* consisted of small, family-sized farms in the North Central states. Farmers sold their surpluses of wheat, rye, corn and meat to cities in the North.

By the mid-1820s, the three sections held differing viewpoints on various (economic) issues.

Abraham Lincoln

Sectional loyalty began to replace loyalty to the nation.

The Civil War

The biggest conflict between the sections developed over the issue of the *extension of slavery* into new territories and states. The Southern planters insisted upon it. Northern workers and farmers opposed it. After the *Mexican War* (1846–1848), the United States gained a vast amount of new territory. This opened new areas to the possibility of slavery and caused conflict between the North and South. Great bitterness developed. Many Northerners were opposed to slavery on moral grounds. In 1854 the Republican Party was formed, pledged to prevent the further expansion of slavery.

The election of a Republican, *Abraham Lincoln*, as president in 1860, caused seven Southern states to *secede* from, or leave, the Union (the United States). They formed the *Confederate States of America*. The North and South fought each other in the *Civil War*. The war began with a Confederate attack upon a Union fort – Fort Sumter in the harbour of Charleston. This was the most destructive in American history, and ended both slavery and the previous Southern way of life.

The Battle of Antietam (1862)

Colonialism

The race for colonies

Colonization is the takeover and control of other lands by a given country. It started in the 16th century and increased so much during the 19th century that some countries established vast empires.

Europeans took possession of a large portion of the world in the late 1800s, especially in Africa and Asia.

By 1914, Great Britain ruled an empire containing a quarter of the world's population. France then governed an area 28 times its own size.

The map below indicates the extent of British and French colonialism in 1914, just before World War I.

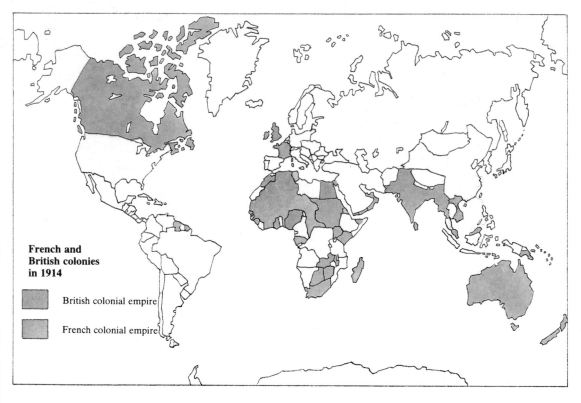

French and British colonies in 1914

British colonial empire

French colonial empire

Why the need for colonies?

Colonies gave countries the opportunity to assert authority, to exploit the riches of the conquered lands, to find outlets for industry and trade, and to 'civilize' other people by spreading the ruling country's language, beliefs and techniques.

Europeans settled many colonies in Africa and in Asia. The United States had colonies in the Pacific.

Gathering rubber

Ruins of Angkor Wat in Cambodia

A missionary in an African village

violent (Algeria, Indo-China). Some of them led to *genocide* (extermination of native populations).

The partition of Africa

During the 19th century, the African continent was the site of European colonial expansion. In 1914, seven European countries had African colonies.

Missionaries and explorers

These people often started the conquests. They explored poorly known parts of the world and tried to convince the native people to put themselves under the protection of their countries.

These conquests were sometimes peaceful, but more often they were

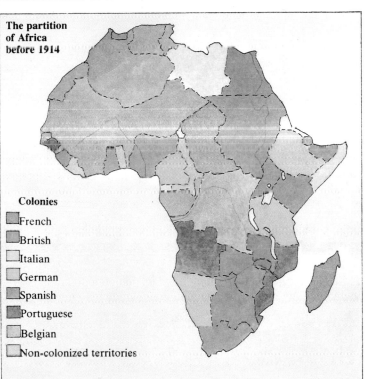

The partition of Africa before 1914

Colonies
- French
- British
- Italian
- German
- Spanish
- Portuguese
- Belgian
- Non-colonized territories

Rafting logs in equatorial Africa

India and Canada

France and Britain were rivals for colonies in the 18th century. By 1763, Britain had gained control and driven the French out of India, Canada and the Ohio Valley.

India was the 'jewel' of the British empire. Queen Victoria of Great Britain was proclaimed Empress of India. In 1867, Canada became the first self-governing territory, or *dominion*, in the British empire.

American colonization

In the late 1800s, the United States acquired the Midway Islands in the Pacific (1867) and annexed Hawaii (1898). After the American victory in the Spanish-American War of 1898, Spain turned over to the United States its colonies of Puerto Rico, Guam and the Philippines. The United States then had a colonial empire, and had become an important world power.

1914–1918: World War I

A shooting starts the war

The event that led to World War I took place in Austria-Hungary, located in south-eastern Europe. A group of people called *Serbs* lived there but did not like Austrian rule. They wanted to become part of the nation of Serbia. On 28 June 1914, in the city of Sarajevo, a Serb shot and killed *Archduke Franz Ferdinand,* who was to become the next emperor of Austria-Hungary. Four weeks later, on 28 July 1914, Austria-Hungary declared war against Serbia. One by one, most of the nations of Europe entered the war.

The assassination of Archduke Franz Ferdinand

What caused the war?

Two alliances of powerful European nations opposed each other and quarrelled for economic and political reasons. On one side were France, Russia and Britain; on the other side, Germany, Austria-Hungary and Italy. When Germany declared war on Russia, all the allies entered the war.

August 1914

Germany declared war on France and invaded. Shortly afterwards, Great Britain came into the war. British and French troops stopped the advancing German army at the Marne River, near Paris, France.

The underground armies

From 1914 to 1917, soldiers lived in mud, cold and terror at the bottom of the *trenches*, which they left only for attacks. The opposing armies' trenches were separated by an area called *No Man's Land,* where the fighting took place.

Losses of human lives were enormous.

Soldiers are shown here leaving a trench and crossing barbed wire under enemy fire of shells, grenades and machine-gun bullets.

700,000 dead in 5 months!
This was the death toll of a terrible battle between French and German soldiers at *Verdun* in 1916.

With neither side able to win decisively, German troops and French and British troops remained in their facing lines of trenches.

American reinforcements
The *United States* joined the war in 1917. They joined the allied troops under the French general *Foch*. The Germans were finally defeated in 1918.

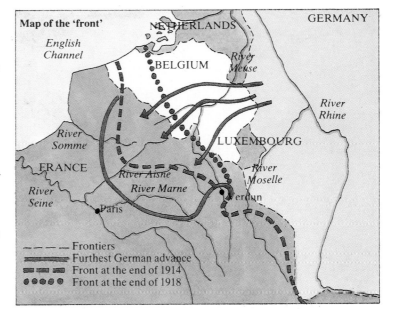

Map of the 'front'

- – – – Frontiers
- ━━━━ Furthest German advance
- ▦▦▦ Front at the end of 1914
- ●●●● Front at the end of 1918

Signing the armistice on 11 November 1918
Allied leaders (seated at the table) met the German officers who came to surrender in a railway coach at Rethondes in France.

11 November 1918
This was the end of the war. Germany signed the *armistice*. The following year, at the *Treaty of Versailles*, Germany had to give up territory and colonies, and agreed to pay war damages.

The price of war
In four years, at least 10 million soldiers died in the war and one million were wounded. Millions of people in the home front were also killed and there was tremendous property damage.

Why did Russia leave the war in 1917?

While there was a stalemate in the warfare on the western front, the Germans invaded Russia on the eastern front. Suffering from problems caused by their government (which was an absolute monarchy), poverty, and military defeat, the Russians overthrew their emperor (the Tsar) in 1917, and made a separate peace with Germany.

1939–1945: World War II

Adolf Hitler (1889–1945), called the *Führer* (leader), became ruler of Germany in 1933. He was eager for revenge and conquest.

prices enabled Hitler to play on the hopes, fears and hatreds of the German people, who felt unjustly blamed and punished for causing World War I. He seized power in 1933 during a world-wide depression.

Dictatorships in Europe

After World War I, dictatorships were established in Russia, Italy and Germany. In Russia, the *Communists* seized power in 1917. In Italy, *Benito Mussolini* set up a *Fascist* government in 1922. In Germany, *Adolf Hitler* led the *National Socialist* or *Nazi* party. Too few jobs and sky-high

Nazi aggression

Hitler rebuilt the German army and announced his intention of taking over the countries bordering Germany. In 1938, Hitler joined Austria to Germany. In 1939, he took over Czechoslovakia.

Blitzkrieg

In 1939, Hitler invaded Poland. Great Britain and France declared war on Germany.

Suddenly, in April 1940, Germany struck and defeated Norway and Denmark. Then, on 10 May 1940, the Germans invaded

Europe before 11 November 1942

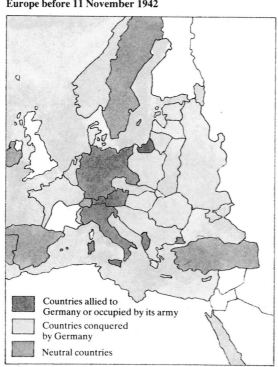

Countries allied to Germany or occupied by its army

Countries conquered by Germany

Neutral countries

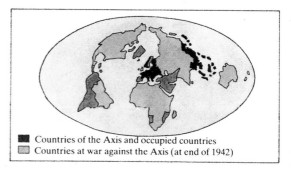

Countries of the Axis and occupied countries
Countries at war against the Axis (at end of 1942)

France, Belgium, the Netherlands and Luxembourg. In less than 40 days, France was defeated. Only Great Britain remained to oppose Germany.

In the spring of 1941, Hitler invaded the Soviet Union. Germany was now fighting Great Britain and the Soviet Union.

The Japanese attack Pearl Harbour.

The United States enters the war

On 7 December 1941, Japan, an ally of Germany, attacked the United States. It bombed the American naval base at Pearl Harbour, Hawaii. This attack completely stunned the nation and caused tremendous casualties in lives, property and aeroplanes. The next day, the United States declared war on Japan. Germany and Italy then declared war on the United States, which had been providing the British with supplies to help in their fight against Hitler.

Concentration camps

Hitler's police, the *Gestapo* and the *SS*, arrested, tortured and imprisoned in concentration camps millions of men, women and children, especially Jews, whom the Nazis wanted to kill for racial reasons.

Ten million people died, among them six million Jews. As a result of this horrible massacre of innocent people, known as *the Holocaust*, the major Nazi leaders were sentenced to death as 'war criminals' after the war.

Germany defeated

In 1941, the war spread throughout the world. The United States and the Soviet Union fought against Germany and its allies, Italy and Japan. On 6 June 1944, 'D-Day', the British and Americans landed on the coast of Normandy to fight the Germans. It was the beginning of the liberation of occupied Europe.

Hitler committed suicide on 30 April 1945 and Germany surrendered on 7 May.

The war ended three months later when the United States dropped the *atomic bomb* on Hiroshima and Nagasaki in Japan.

World War II had caused almost 50 million deaths and tremendous suffering and destruction.

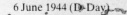

6 June 1944 (D-Day)

East–West: the Two Blocs

Occupied Germany

In February 1945, a conference was held at Yalta in the Soviet Union by the

Churchill, Roosevelt, Stalin

British, the Americans and the Soviets to decide upon the occupation of Germany. The German territory was divided into two parts:
– in the east, a zone to be occupied by the Soviet army;
– in the west, a zone to be occupied by American, British and French armies.

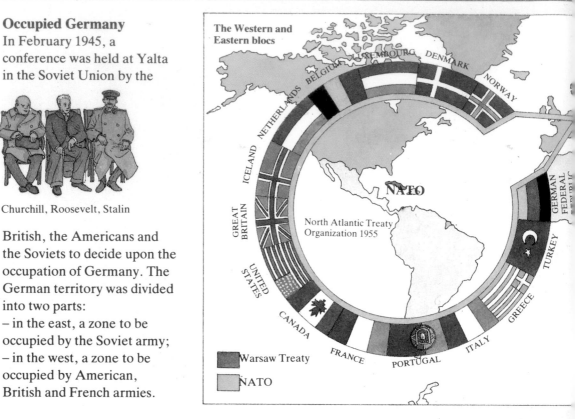

The Western and Eastern blocs

NATO
North Atlantic Treaty Organization 1955

ICELAND · NETHERLANDS · BELGIUM · LUXEMBOURG · DENMARK · NORWAY · GERMAN FEDERAL REPUBLIC · TURKEY · GREECE · ITALY · PORTUGAL · FRANCE · CANADA · UNITED STATES · GREAT BRITAIN

■ Warsaw Treaty
□ NATO

The four occupied zones in Germany and Austria after their surrender

USSR
UNITED STATES
GREAT BRITAIN
FRANCE
Berlin
Vienna

The victors are divided

The Soviet Union, the centre of Communism, extended its influence over a large part of eastern Europe. The dividing line between eastern and western Europe was called the *Iron Curtain*.

The United States, to prevent further Communist expansion, gave financial help to the countries of western Europe to help them recover from the war.

From then on, two blocs, the Soviet and the Western bloc, opposed each other, and the danger of a new war threatened the world.

The United Nations

The United Nations (UN) was founded on 26 July 1945 to avoid new wars and to encourage international co-operation. Its headquarters are in New York. Today, 159 countries are members of the UN. It can send troops, supplied by member nations, to troubled areas to restore order.

A UN health agency, WHO, has helped wipe out smallpox. UNICEF, the UN Children's Fund, has helped millions of underprivileged children.

What was the 'Cold War'?

The Cold War was the name of the political and economic rivalry that began after World War II between the two superpowers, the Soviet Union and the United States. Today, the two nations have begun to work together and have signed a treaty to limit some weapons.

In 1949, 12 countries of the Western bloc signed a military defence treaty. Others joined later. This grouping is known as NATO.

Similarly, in 1955, seven eastern European countries, including Poland, Hungary, East Germany, Romania and Bulgaria, signed a treaty of

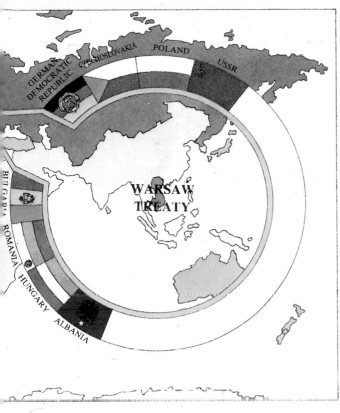

The Berlin wall

Constructed in 1961 by the authorities of East Germany, this wall divided Berlin in two, preventing the people of East Berlin from going to the West. The wall came to symbolize the opposition between the two blocs.

In the same way, the wall came to symbolize a new feeling of freedom in Europe when it was pulled down in 1989. This event, which led to great celebrations in Berlin itself, was one stage in a process that led to the re-uniting of East and West Germany in 1990.

military alliance with the Soviet Union. This was known as the Warsaw Treaty or Pact.

The blocs never fought directly. However, they have supported opposing sides in wars in the Third World of developing nations.

The changing face of Europe

In recent years, the Soviet Union has been undergoing great changes as it begins to move away from Communist government and towards the kind of economy that Western-bloc countries operate. At the same time, the military and trade agreements between Eastern bloc countries have loosened, so that more and more Warsaw Pact countries are turning away from the USSR and towards Western Europe. Such large-scale changes are not easy. In some countries fighting has broken out as the people try to decide for themselves how they will be governed in future. In the meantime, such organizations as the European Community (EC) have become stronger and are trying to help bring about peaceful change in Europe.

Major Changes in the Post-War World

The end of Western colonialism

After World War II, the colonial peoples of Asia and Africa demanded and obtained freedom from European rule. From 1950 to 1970, more than 35 newly independent nations emerged in Africa. Today, only at the southern tip of Africa in the Republic of South Africa has this process still to be completed.

The Vietnam War

In Vietnam, which is located in south-east Asia, first France (1946–1954), then the United States (1954–1973) opposed a Communist-led independence movement. The result was a long and costly war which the United States was not able to win. In the Vietnam War 46,000 Americans were killed and 300,000 wounded. About 140,000 million dollars was spent on this war, which severely divided the American people. It caused terrible hardship and thousands of deaths in Vietnam, Laos and Cambodia (formerly French Indo-China).

The Marshall Plan (1948–1952)

Undamaged by World War II, the United States developed a programme of economic aid to help the European nations (including its former enemies, Germany and Italy) recover from wartime destruction. This programme, the *Marshall Plan*, sought to improve living standards and re-establish European trade with America. Meanwhile, co-operation between the European nations helped to build the trust needed to form the European Economic Community or Common Market, now known as the EC.

Abuse of the environment

The *greenhouse effect* is a general warming of the temperatures on Earth, along with drier conditions. It is the result of damage to the ozone layer over the Earth. This thinning of

Europe lay in ruins after the war.

An atomic explosion

ozone is caused by burning fossil fuels like coal and oil products, fluorocarbons used in aerosols and air conditioners, and by rapid cutting down of forests. If allowed to continue, it may cut down the world's food supply and lead to floods along our low-lying coastlines.

Rain forests such as those in Brazil and south-east Asia, contain two-thirds of the known species of plants and animals on Earth. Every year, huge areas of the Amazon rain forest are purposely burned. This rapid loss of the rain forests is a serious problem. Cutting down the trees means less oxygen in the environment. Also, some of the plants there may be the key to our future survival. Once a plant becomes extinct, its possible value to mankind can never be known.

The first person walks on the Moon.

Refugees

Wars and natural disasters have made millions of persons *refugees* – individuals who have lost their homes and who need help to rebuild their shattered lives. Recent wars in Afghanistan, south-east Asia and the Middle East have created countless refugees. In Indo-China, since 1975, more than one million Vietnamese, Cambodians and ethnic Chinese have had to flee for their lives.

Spread of nuclear weapons

In the 1950s, only the United States and the Soviet Union had atomic bombs. In 1968 those two nations agreed on a treaty limiting the spread of nuclear weapons.

Unfortunately, the arms race between America and the Soviet Union continued. Moreover, other nations obtained nuclear weapons and Third World nations paid industrial powers to provide them with nuclear plants, fuel and technology. Some succeeded in building nuclear bombs.

In many countries, organizations such as the Campaign for Nuclear Disarmament (CND) campaigned against nuclear weapons. They feared that the use of such weapons could destroy the world as we know it. Other people believed that because they were so frightening, the weapons acted as a *deterrent*. In other words, the threat of such weapons being used stopped wars from starting.

The easing of tension between the Eastern and Western blocs in recent years has meant that fears of a nuclear war have lessened and attempts have been made to reduce the numbers of nuclear weapons.

Changes in society

Traditional patterns of living and working are changing all over the world. In developing countries, millions of people have been forced by poverty or natural disasters to move from the countryside to the cities, where they hope that their lives will be better. In fact, there is often very little work available and not enough housing, so their lives do not improve.

In developed countries, an important change has been that many women have taken up jobs and careers outside their homes.

Terrorism

Extremist groups have used modern technology as well as crude weapons in terrorist attacks – deliberate violence against innocent civilians – to further their political goals.

Emerging World Powers

After 1945, there began great economic growth everywhere in the world. New world powers developed to challenge the economic and commercial might of the United States, the Soviet Union and Europe.

The Japanese miracle

Defeated and ruined in 1945, Japan began an extraordinary industrial growth and 20 years later became the third economic power in the world!

Because of its population – about 120 million inhabitants – Japan has a vast market and a large pool of skilled workers. Its production of machinery and electronics is exported in great quantity.

Hitachi, Toyota, Mitsubishi, Honda – these brand names have become familiar to the Western world since the Japanese started to produce television sets, video recorders, stereo equipment, motorcycles and cars.

However, Japan is confined to a very small living space of 377,815 sq km (145,874 sq miles), and must fight continuously against pollution caused by its vast industries. Korea, Japan's neighbour, is becoming another industrial power in Asia.

A robot in action – one of the marvels of Japanese electronics. A camera reads the screen and transmits orders to mechanical hands which press the keys of the keyboard.

NORTH AMERICA

SOUTH AMERICA

Brazil: its power and its weakness

Once a Portuguese colony, this country, almost as large in area as the United States, is populated by 125 million inhabitants. It witnessed fast changes after 1965. Cities developed following the American model and large industries were created.

Agriculture and cattle raising occupy immense newly-cleared lands.

However, profits of this extraordinary economic growth are poorly distributed and 4 out of 10 Brazilians go hungry.

Ever since 1980, Brazil has known a severe crisis. Today it is one of the countries with the highest foreign debt in the world. Its economy is in urgent need of reorganization: 50% of all lands that could be used for agriculture are still unused; they represent the greatest reserve in the world. However, burning

Land of contrast – these hovels (called *favelas*) are next to modern buildings in the rich section of the city.

areas of the Amazon jungle to clear the land has destroyed plant species, animal habitats and the ozone in the atmosphere.

More than 1,000 million people marching towards progress!

The birth of a giant: China

China with 1,000 million inhabitants is a huge nation, gradually becoming modernized. Until 1949, constant warfare held back its development and caused it to fall behind other industrial countries. After 1949, China, led by Mao Tse-tung, became a Communist nation. In 1958, it broke off relations with the Soviet Union and followed its own ideas. However, progress did not come overnight because, besides some modern industrial techniques, China still kept many traditional ones. Furthermore, China counted only upon its own power to exploit its important natural riches.

After the death of Mao, China adopted a more open policy towards the world and increased its commercial ties with other countries.

ASIA

UROPE

AFRICA

India: the will to succeed

This very heavily populated land of 775 million inhabitants – 1,000 million is forecast for the year 2000 – has changed very slowly.

Although agricultural methods have become increasingly modern, India is still part of the Third World and suffers great hunger and poverty. Over-population and the export of most of its farm products are the principal causes of these problems. Efforts are being made to overcome these difficulties. Being careful to keep its neutrality, India has nevertheless accepted help from the great industrial powers.

Hindi is the official language, but English and sixteen regional languages are recognized by the Indian Constitution. Some 4,000 languages and unofficial dialects are also spoken in India.

India is a country of contrasts too. It has very modern factories and cities but in the countryside many people are very poor and have hard lives.

Who was Gandhi?

Called the *Mahatma*, 'the Great Soul', he led the fight against the British for independence and preached *non-violence*. He was murdered in 1948. He inspired the non-violent US civil rights movement in the 1960s.

69

Technological Revolution

Since 1945, many discoveries and important technological advances have revolutionized human life.

Life span has been lengthened

Medicine has made great breakthroughs. *Vaccines* have been discovered to eliminate and prevent dangerous diseases, such as tuberculosis, tetanus and polio. New medicines, such as *antibiotics,* bring relief to many sick people. The first *organ transplants* (heart, kidneys, lungs) were tried and succeeded.

A CAT scan
This is a device for examining human tissue for exact information about its functioning.

Machines replace humans

Thanks to *automation,* work has become easier. Agriculture and industry have been modernized. The first *robots* have appeared.
  Computers, capable of solving very complicated problems in a few seconds, represent a new stage in this development.

Automated assembly line
This robot alone solders pieces together.

Peaceful atoms

Atomic power is not only used for destruction. Today, great *nuclear plants* use atomic energy to produce electricity.

Rocket Ariane (over 40,000kph, nearly 25,000mph) launches European satellites. It puts in orbit satellites that are heavier than 2 tonnes.

The space shuttle is used for orbiting, for launching and for recovery of satellites. A reusable rocket during launching and a plane when landing, it is equipped with three engines, each with a thrust of 208 tonnes.

Nuclear plant
Atomic energy plants have helped replace the burning of fossil fuels (coal and oil), which pollute the atmosphere.

Telecommunications satellite
Its solar panels capture the energy necessary for its operation.

However, many people are afraid of atomic power and opposed to nuclear energy programmes. They fear exposure to radiation from atomic fuel and atomic waste.

Communication by waves

Radio, telephone and television have greatly improved the spread of information and of world understanding, and have brought human beings together. They have helped shrink the globe to a *world village*.

The speed of travel

Long distances can be covered with increasing speed by several means of transport. Motorways span the continents of Europe and North America.

At more than 1,930kph (1,200mph) the supersonic *Concorde* aeroplane crosses the Atlantic in three and a half hours.

The world's fastest trains are being built in Japan and West Germany. They run by magnetic levitation, *Maglev* for short, and will travel at 480kph (300mph) or more in a shallow trough or along a magnetized guideway.

Concorde
Built in France and Great Britain, it is capable of transporting 130 passengers at a speed of over 1,930kph (1,200mph).

The conquest of space

In 1957, the Soviets launched the first Earth-orbiting satellite – Sputnik I.

In 1969, the Americans *Neil Armstrong* and *Edwin Aldrin* walked on the Moon for the first time.

In 1981, the space shuttle *Columbia* made its first flight.

Today, numerous satellites revolve around the Earth. Some are used for telecommunications (radio, television), others for meteorology (weather forecasts), still others for military observation. With the American space shuttle, some non-working satellites can be brought back to Earth to be repaired.

TGV
This very fast train was developed in France.

Combine
Straw and grain are automatically separated.

Nuclear-powered submarine
It can remain completely submerged for several days.

Human Rights

In 1948, the General Assembly of the United Nations adopted the *Universal Declaration of Human Rights*. It was inspired by the American *Bill of Rights* and the French *Declaration of the Rights of Man*.

Although the ideals expressed will not soon be realized throughout the world, they provide a 'standard of achievement for all peoples and all nations', including the 159 member nations of the UN.

The flag of the UN symbolizes peace in the world.

The Declaration states that all human beings are born free and equal, and are entitled to:

- *civil rights*: life, liberty, freedom of religion, speech and assembly; and a voice in their government;
- *legal rights*: freedom from arrest without cause, and the right to a fair trial;

- *economic rights*: a job, enough to live on, private property, and leisure time;
- *social rights*: an education and a cultural life.

Distinction between races

The idea of a superior race is a violation of article two of the Declaration. *Racism* is an attitude of hostility or persecution towards individuals of different races. In the name of that difference, Nazis killed millions of human beings during World War II.

Today, in the Republic of South Africa, a white government rules over the black majority of the country with a policy of *apartheid,* that is of 'separate development'. Many organizations and individuals are working to change this situation.

Imprisoned because of their opinions

The Declaration of Human Rights says in article two that freedom of political opinion and religion must be respected.

However, in some countries, especially those ruled by dictators, these freedoms are not recognized. Those opposed to the government are hunted down and imprisoned. Sometimes they are killed.

Many people are forced to flee their own country for political and economic reasons.

Amnesty International

Founded in 1961 by an English lawyer, *Peter Benenson,* this independent organization works closely with governments and tries to arouse international opinion in its fight against the death penalty and all forms of torture. It brings help and assistance to victims imprisoned because of their ideas, their beliefs, or their origin.

Since its founding, more than 7,000 prisoners have been set free because of the intervention of Amnesty International.

Every year, it publishes a report denouncing governments that do not respect human rights.

The Red Cross

This humanitarian organization was founded in 1863 by the Swiss *Henri Dunant* to help war casualties regardless of nationality. The Red Cross intervenes today in many fields – catastrophes, helping the elderly, the handicapped, and refugees (International Committee of the Red Cross).

amnesty international

This poster symbolizes hope for freedom.

Torture

Even today, bodily violence is used against certain prisoners to punish them or to pressure them to admit to, denounce, or give up their ideas and beliefs.

These barbaric practices are condemned by most large states.

UNESCO

UNESCO's full name is the United Nations Educational, Scientific and Cultural Organization. It is one of the many agencies of the UN. It works to maintain peace by encouraging co-operation between nations in education, science and culture. To carry out that purpose, it developed a worldwide programme to teach reading and writing, thus responding to article 26 of the Universal Declaration of Human Rights: 'Everyone has the right to an education.'

The permanent headquarters of UNESCO are based in Paris.

Racism in democratic nations
Every democracy must be careful to see that racism does not develop among its own population. Human rights are very fragile and always in danger of being jeopardized.

Children learn reading and writing in an African village.

Planet Earth

The lines of the Earth

Imaginary lines help to locate where we are on the Earth.

The *Equator* divides our globe into two hemispheres – the northern hemisphere and the southern hemisphere.

Imaginary lines running parallel to the Equator are called *parallels of latitude*.

Imaginary lines joining the *North* and *South Poles* are called *meridians of longitude*.

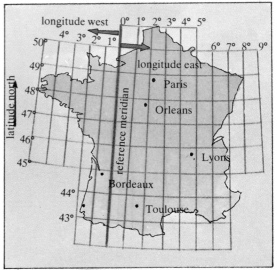

Important facts

Only a small blue dot in the universe, the Earth was born about 4,600 million years ago.

Shaped like a ball that is slightly flattened at the poles, its circumference (width around)

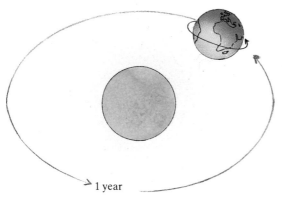

1 year

at the Equator is about 40,000km (25,000 miles).

It weighs about 6,000 million million million tonnes. Its surface is 510,066,000 sq km (196,950,000 sq miles).

The Earth turns on its axis from west to east in 23 hours, 56 minutes and 4 seconds.

At the same time, it orbits (circles) the sun in 365 days and 6 hours, thus travelling 935.23 million km (581.25 million miles) at a speed of almost 108,000kph (67,000mph) – over 29km or 18.6 miles per second!

Distinctive feature: life exists on Earth. Our planet contains 5,000 million inhabitants (world census of 8 July 1986).

The grid formed by the intersection of lines of latitude and longitude provides the precise location of a particular place.

The *latitude* of a place is the distance between the parallel on which its particular measurement is taken and the Equator.

The *longitude* of a place is the distance between the meridian on which its particular measurement is taken and some reference meridian such as that of Greenwich, or meridian 0°.

Latitude and longitude are measured in degrees.

Any place on Earth can be located exactly by its latitude and longitude. These are the *geographical co-ordinates.*

Geographical co-ordinates of Paris:
48° 50 latitude north.
2° 20 longitude east.

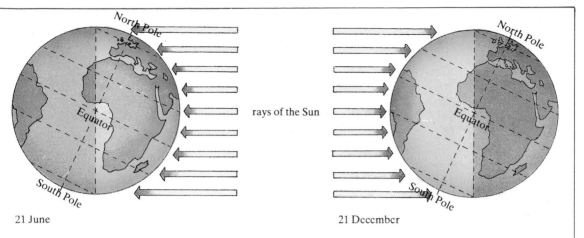

21 June   rays of the Sun   21 December

Day and night

The rotation of the Earth on its axis (once every 24 hours) and its revolution around the Sun gives us day and night.

All through the year their length varies. In the northern hemisphere, the longest day is on 21 June and the shortest day is on 21 December. In the southern hemisphere it is the other way around.

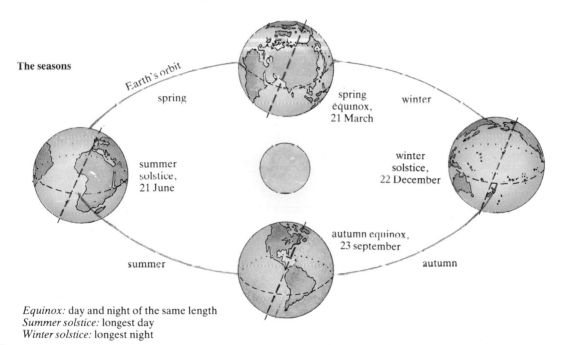

The seasons

Earth's orbit

spring

spring equinox, 21 March

winter

summer solstice, 21 June

winter solstice, 22 December

autumn equinox, 23 september

summer

autumn

Equinox: day and night of the same length
Summer solstice: longest day
Winter solstice: longest night

From one season to another

Because of its revolution around the Sun the amount of the Sun's rays that the Earth receives changes according to its position. This explains the change in seasons. The shorter the distance crossed by the Sun's rays in the atmosphere, the warmer the climate and vice versa.

Since the Earth turns on a tilted axis, it is alternately the northern and then the southern hemisphere that is tilted towards the Sun and receives most of the heat.

Time around the World

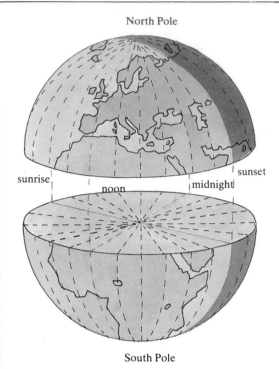

North Pole

sunrise | noon | midnight | sunset

South Pole

Time zones
The world is divided into 24 basic *time zones*. The illustration shows these time zones. Each zone is one hour earlier or one hour later than the one next to it.

Meridians of longitude

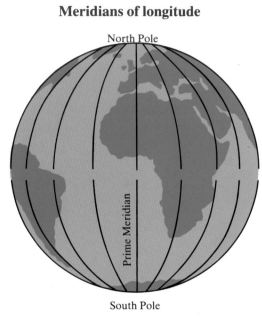

North Pole

Prime Meridian

South Pole

What is solar time?
Each position of the Sun in the sky corresponds to a precise time – solar time – which is the same for all places located on the same half-circle passing through the poles, the *meridian*.

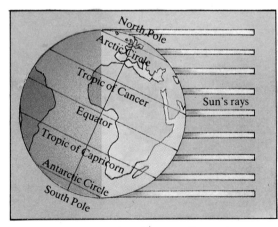

Sun's rays at the beginning of summer (21 June)

Same time all over the Earth?
Impossible! Because of the rotation of the Earth, the Sun does not rise at the same time at all points on the globe.

Since the day contains 24 hours, the Earth's sphere of 360° is divided into 24 parts. The rotation of the Earth pushes it through 15° of longitude each hour. The Prime Meridian (0°) was chosen to be the starting position in the 24-hour day. Thus when it is noon at 0° longitude, it is 1 p.m. at 15° east, 2 p.m. at 30° east and so forth. It is one hour earlier at 15° west and so on. When it is 4 a.m. in Los Angeles, it is 5 p.m. in Bombay, India.

Time in different parts of the world is measured from the Prime Meridian or Greenwich Meridian, located near London. The time there is called GMT (Greenwich Mean Time).

Each time zone is bounded by two meridians. The territories belonging to the same time zone have the same time – *standard time*. Time zones generally follow national boundaries.

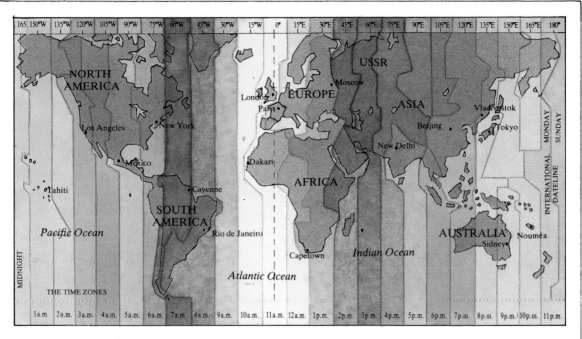

The time zones

Clock and sundial on the front of an old house. The sundial indicates solar time

Planes and time changes

Examples of flights of *Concorde:*

1 Paris–New York (the plane flies westward)
   Departure from Paris: 11.00 a.m. Arrival
   New York: 8.45 a.m.

2 New York–Paris (the plane flies eastward)
   Departure from New York: 1.00 p.m.
   Arrival Paris: 10.45 p.m.

What is a sundial?
Invented by an ancient Greek scholar around the 6th century BC, the sundial consists of a fixed rod and a flat surface that is divided into 24 parts. Each part corresponds to an hour and there are 15° triangles, each one representing the 24th portion of the circumference (360°). The shadow cast by the Sun indicates time.

Is it true that certain countries have several time zones?
Yes, it is true for large countries. The United States has seven time zones, and the USSR has 11 time zones.

Always be on time!

When changing from one time zone to another, the time on one's watch has to be changed as follows:

- It is set *back* by one hour when moving west (against the rotation of the Earth).
- It is set *ahead* by one hour when moving east (with the rotation of the Earth).

Further complications!
For economic reasons (in particular to save electricity) certain countries do not use the actual time of their time zone. The United States, for instance, sets its standard time ahead by one hour from May to October and observes *daylight savings time.*
   Sundials indicate solar time, that is true local time.
   Watches indicate standard time.

Land and Sea

Waters of the world

More than two-thirds of the Earth's surface is covered by water.

This huge amount of water consists of four great oceans that are interconnected:
- the Atlantic Ocean
- the Pacific Ocean
- the Indian Ocean
- the Arctic Ocean

and numerous other seas that are smaller and shallower, and flow into the oceans such as:

- the Caribbean Sea
- the Mediterranean Sea
- the North Sea
- the Red Sea

or totally enclosed:
- the Caspian Sea
- the Aral Sea.

The Earth's land surface

About a quarter of the Earth's surface is land. The land is in large areas called *continents*. They are:

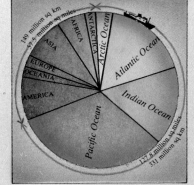

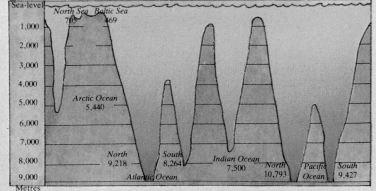

- *Europe* and *Asia*, which make up *Eurasia*
- *Africa*
- *North America* and *South America*, which make up the *American* continent
- *Antarctica*
- *Oceania* which includes Australia and the islands of the Pacific.

A tenth of all the Earth's land above water is covered by ice.

High mountains and great depths

The surface of the Earth above and below the water displays many similarities – deep valleys, mountain chains, plains and plateaux.

Islands are emerged summits of gigantic underwater mountains.

The greatest difference of relief occurs in the ocean depth (Marianna Trench: nearly 11km or 36,000ft below sea-level), surpassing the record of the 'top of the world' (Mount Everest: 8.85km, or 29,028ft, or 5.5 miles above sea-level), in the Himalayas.

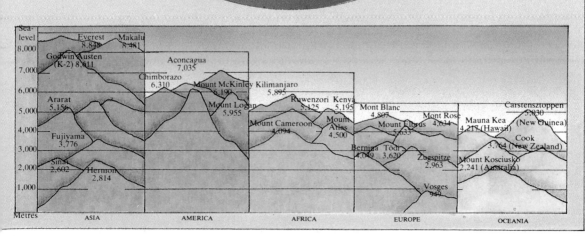

The Climates of the Earth

Variable heat of the Sun

The movements of the Earth, its spherical shape, and the tilt of its axis, all cause uneven distribution of heat by the Sun's rays.

Heat is greater where the Sun's rays strike the surface of the Earth vertically, and less where they are slanted:

Hence, three major climate zones exist:

- the tropical zone, the hottest
- the polar zone, the coldest
- the temperate zone, intermediate.

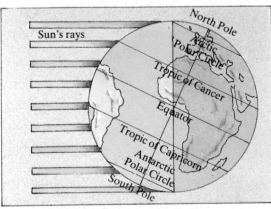

Sun's rays at the beginning of summer (21 June)

Sun's rays at the beginning of winter (21 December)

World climates

NORTH AMERICA

Atlantic Ocean

Pacific Ocean

SOUTH AMERICA

- Polar climate (permanently very cold)
- Continental climate (cold winter)
- Oceanic climate (humid with cool summer)
- Mediterranean climate (dry summer, mild winter)
- Dry climate (cold winter)
- Dry climate (permanently hot)
- Tropical climate (hot with dry summer)
- Equatorial climate (hot and always humid)

Varied climates

Inside the same climate zone, temperatures and the distribution of rain and wind are sometimes uneven.

Thus, the tropical zone consists of:

- an equatorial climate, hot and humid all year round
- a tropical climate with only one dry season.

Similarly, the temperate zone has:

- an oceanic climate, mild and humid
- a Mediterranean climate, warm and dry in summer, mild and humid in winter
- a continental climate, very warm in summer, very cold in winter.

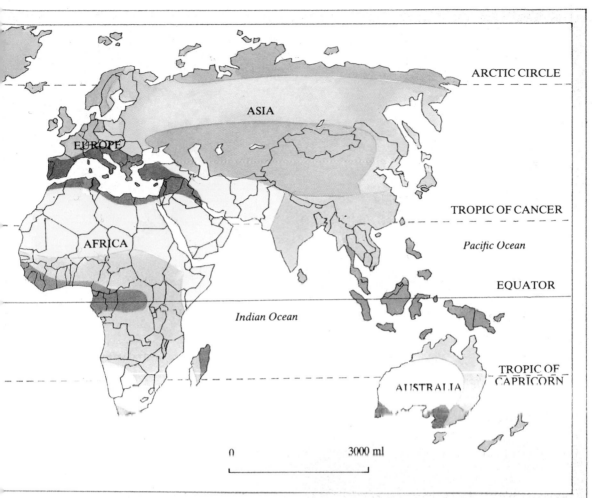

Adapting to the environment

In order to survive, human beings have to adapt to a great variety of geographical environments, some quite unfriendly. Differences in the economy, habitat, food and clothing characterize the many different life styles in the world. However, as a result of technological progress and improved communication, certain limitations of the natural environment have been gradually lessened (opening of permanent bases at the poles, digging of wells in desert areas, irrigation). But difficulties still remain and adaptation is not always possible. For instance, today, African populations flee the advancing desert. This is the drama of the Sahel (area south of the Sahara).

Climate zones in the United States

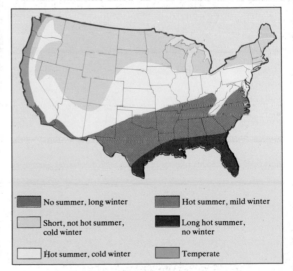

No summer, long winter	Hot summer, mild winter
Short, not hot summer, cold winter	Long hot summer, no winter
Hot summer, cold winter	Temperate

In a country as large as the United States, there is a wide variety of climate. The map shows the main variations, but there will be local differences from these.

The Moving Earth

The effects of an earthquake in a village: the ground opens, causing houses to collapse since they no longer rest on stable foundations.

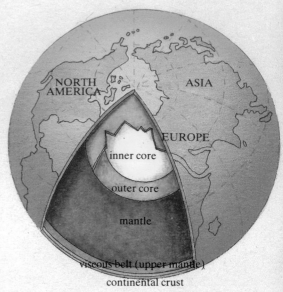

The face of the Earth changes

Volcanic eruptions and earthquakes regularly change the surface of the Earth (faults, fractures), sometimes causing great catastrophes. These movements are difficult to forecast and can be explained by the composition of the interior of our planet.

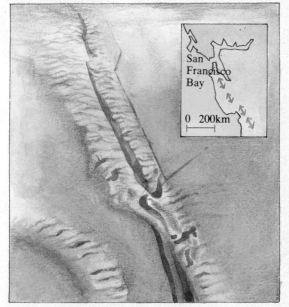

The San Andreas Fault in California (aerial view). About 967 km (595 miles) long, it runs from north of San Francisco to southern California!

What is inside the Earth?

The Earth is made up of a succession of superimposed layers (placed one above another):

- the Earth's crust (continental and oceanic plates)
- the mantle
- the core (inner and outer).

The Earth's crust consists of rigid crystal rocks (granite), and its thickness varies from 5 to 90km (3 to 56 miles). The ocean crust (basalt) is much thinner.

- The mantle is about 2,900km (1,800 miles) thick.
- The core, a huge mass in fusion at a temperature of about 5,500°C (10,000°F) forms the centre of the Earth.

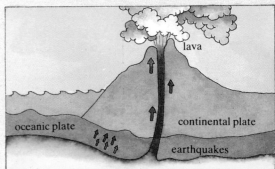

Volcanic eruption

Like drifting rafts

The Earth's crust consists of moving plates on which the continents stand and which glide continuously over the mantle. This slight

Moving plates and direction of movement

movement of the continents is called
continental drift. When the plates collide,
they cause earthquakes and volcanic
eruptions.

180 million years ago . . .

The surface of our planet was completely
different. One huge land mass
(supercontinent) took the place of the

Proof – the fitting together of Africa and America

AFRICA

SOUTH AMERICA

Rocks 200 million years old

Rocks 600 million years old

The supercontinent broke up and separated into individual continents.

Each continent drifted in its own direction.

Present-day shape and position of continents. Plates continue to move.

It is possible to measure the intensity of
earthquakes by using instruments called
seismographs. Scales
consisting of different
degrees indicate the
intensity of the
tremors (shaking).
The *Richter Scale*
consists of 9 degrees.
Above degree 6,
buildings can
collapse.

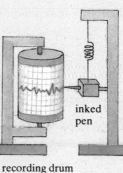

inked pen

recording drum

separated continents we know today. Over
millions of years the present shape of the
continents gradually evolved.

In 1906 the San Francisco earthquake
caused 2,000 deaths, injured 15,000, and
destroyed the fifth largest city in the United
States. This could happen again.

Coming Soon – 6,000 Million People

More and more inhabitants

The population of the Earth is continuously growing.

- 2,000 years ago: 250 million inhabitants.
- In the year AD 1000: 450 million inhabitants.
- In 1800: 1,000 million inhabitants.
- In 1900: 1,650 million inhabitants.

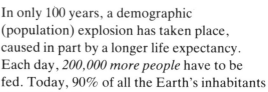

World population in 1,000 millions of inhabitants

ASIA

EUROPE
AMERICA
AFRICA–OCEANIA

| 1650 | 1700 | 1750 | 1800 | 1850 | 1900 | 1930 | 1950 | 1980 |

Today we have reached a world population of 5,000 million.

At the end of the century, there will be about *6,500 million* inhabitants on Earth!

In only 100 years, a demographic (population) explosion has taken place, caused in part by a longer life expectancy. Each day, *200,000 more people* have to be fed. Today, 90% of all the Earth's inhabitants live on only 20% of its land One inhabitant out of 10 lives in the southern hemisphere.

Unequal resources, unequal development

The various countries that share our planet do not all have the same opportunities for development. These depend mainly on relatively

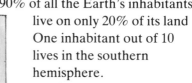

Distribution of world population

NORTH AMERICA · USSR · EUROPE · ASIA · Atlantic Ocean · Pacific Ocean · AFRICA · Indian Ocean · SOUTH AMERICA · Pacific Ocean · AUSTRALIA

◼ Populated areas ◻ Very thinly populated areas

One dot represents about two million inhabitants.

An unevenly distributed population

Mainly because of climate, extensive regions of the world are under-populated:

- cold regions (Siberia, Canadian Northern Territories)
- dry regions (Sahara, Sahel, Asian steppes).

On the other hand, there are areas of heavy population:

- East Asia, India, Europe, Indonesia.

The ten most populated countries in the world

(in millions of inhabitants, 1984 census)

1	China	1,023
2	India	730
3	USSR	272
4	United States	234
5	Indonesia	156
6	Brazil	131
7	Japan	119
8	Bangladesh	96.5
9	Pakistan	95.7
10	Nigeria	84.2

Farmers of the Third World use primitive tools and methods to cultivate the soil. Bringing new technology to their farms sometimes creates more problems, as the environment is changed too rapidly by large machines.

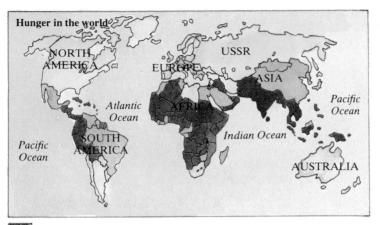

Hunger in the world

NORTH AMERICA · USSR · EUROPE · ASIA · Pacific Ocean · Atlantic Ocean · AFRICA · Indian Ocean · SOUTH AMERICA · Pacific Ocean · AUSTRALIA

▪ Insufficient daily food supply

▫ Barely sufficient daily food supply

▫ Normal or plentiful daily food supply

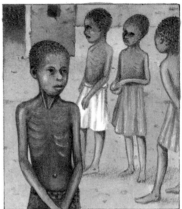

Because of undernourishment, many children are weak and have low resistance to diseases. The number who die before one year of age is twenty times higher in the Third World than in developed countries.

favourable climate conditions, soil fertility, richness of mineral resources, and surface features like rivers and harbours. Many countries are dependent on others.

A serious problem – hunger

This unequal development often has dramatic consequences.

More than two-thirds of the human beings in the *Third World* (under-developed countries) suffer from lack of food.

Through international organizations such as UNICEF and UNESCO, these countries receive help from the richer ones. However, it is believed that only a policy of self-development by these countries will enable them to solve their difficulties. Control of the population growth by means of education and family planning is important too.

Working children!

Hunger and poor living conditions force many young children to work for miserably low pay. Today, more than 50 million children work all over the world. Most of them do not attend school.

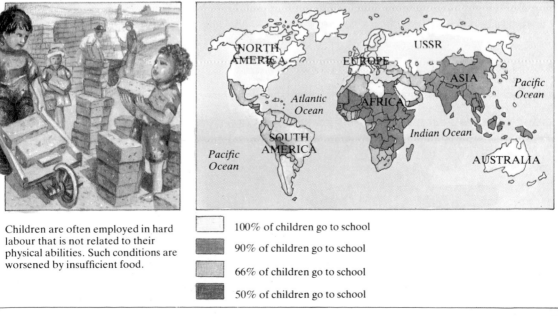

Children are often employed in hard labour that is not related to their physical abilities. Such conditions are worsened by insufficient food.

NORTH AMERICA · USSR · EUROPE · ASIA · Pacific Ocean · Atlantic Ocean · AFRICA · Indian Ocean · SOUTH AMERICA · Pacific Ocean · AUSTRALIA

▫ 100% of children go to school

▪ 90% of children go to school

▫ 66% of children go to school

▪ 50% of children go to school

The African Continent

Location in the world

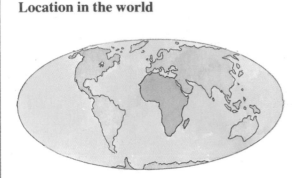

Important facts

Area: 30.6 million sq km (11.8 million sq miles)

Population: 600 million inhabitants (1987)

Density of population: 20 inhabitants per sq km (51 per sq mile).

It is the hottest continent in the world.

Africa has:

the largest desert in the world – the *Sahara*, and the longest river in the world – the *Nile* (6,693km or 4,160 miles in length).

The highest African mountain, *Kilimanjaro*, is 5,895m (19,320ft) high.

The continent is rich in natural resources but is still largely under-developed.

Africa has many human problems – food shortage, epidemics, racial discrimination (in the Republic of South Africa).

In an attempt to solve these problems, African countries have formed an organization, the OAU (Organization of African Unity), with headquarters in Addis Ababa (Ethiopia).

Many African countries use a European language for official business, but there are also thousands of different African languages.

Algeria	Angola	Benin	Botswana	Burkina Faso	Burundi
A 2,381,741 (919,595)	A 1,246,700 (481,354)	A 112,622 (43,484)	A 582,000 (224,711)	A 274,200 (105,869)	A 27,834 (10,747)
P 23,000,000	P 9,000,000	P 4,400,000	P 1,168,000	P 8,305,000	P 5,000,000
C Algiers	C Luanda	C Porto-Novo	C Gaborone	C Ouagadougou	C Bujumbura
M Dinar	M Kwanza	M CFA franc	M Pula	M CFA franc	M Burundi franc
L Arabic, French	L Portuguese, African	L French, Fon	L English, Setswana	L French, Mossi	L Kirundi, French

Cameroon	Cape Verde	Central African Rep.	Chad	Comoros	Congo
A 475,442 (183,569)	A 4,033 (1,557)	A 622,984 (240,535)	A 1,284,000 (495,750)	A 1,862 (719)	A 342,000 (132,046)
P 10,822,000	P 334,000	P 2,740,000	P 5,129,000	P 412,000	P 2,180,000
C Yaoundé	C Praia	C Bangui	C N'Djamena	C Moroni	C Brazzaville
M CFA franc	M Cape Verde escudo	M CFA franc	M CFA franc	M CFA franc	M CFA franc
L French, English	L Portuguese, Crioulo	L French, Sangho	L French, Arabic	L French, Arabic	L French, Lingala

Djibouti	Egypt	Equatorial Guinea	Ethiopia	Gabon	Gambia
A 23,200 (8,950)	A 997,739 (385,229)	A 28,051 (10,830)	A 1,223,600 (472,435)	A 267,667 (103,346)	A 11,295 (4,361)
P 483,000	P 50,740,000	P 328,000	P 46,184,000	P 1,206,000	P 737,000
C Djibouti	C Cairo	C Malabo	C Addis Ababa	C Libreville	C Banjul
M Franc	M Pound	M Ekuele	M Birr	M CFA franc	M Dalasi
L French, Arabic	L Arabic	L Spanish, Fang	L Amharic, Arabic	L French, African	L English

Ghana	Guinea	Guinea-Bissau	Ivory Coast	Kenya	Lesotho
A 238,537 (92,099)	A 245,857 (94,925)	A 36,125 (13,948)	A 322,462 (124,503)	A 580,367 (224,081)	A 30,355 (11,720)
P 13,892,000	P 6,380,000	P 943,000	P 11,150,000	P 21,415,000	P 1,619,000
C Accra	C Conakry	C Bissau	C Abidjan	C Nairobi	C Maseru
M Cedi	M Syli	M Peso	M CFA franc	M Shilling	M Maloti
L English, Asante	L French, Soussou	L Portuguese, Crioulo	L French, Dioula	L Swahili, English	L Sesotho, English

A = area in square kilometres and (in brackets) square miles, P = population, C = capital, M = money unit, L = Language

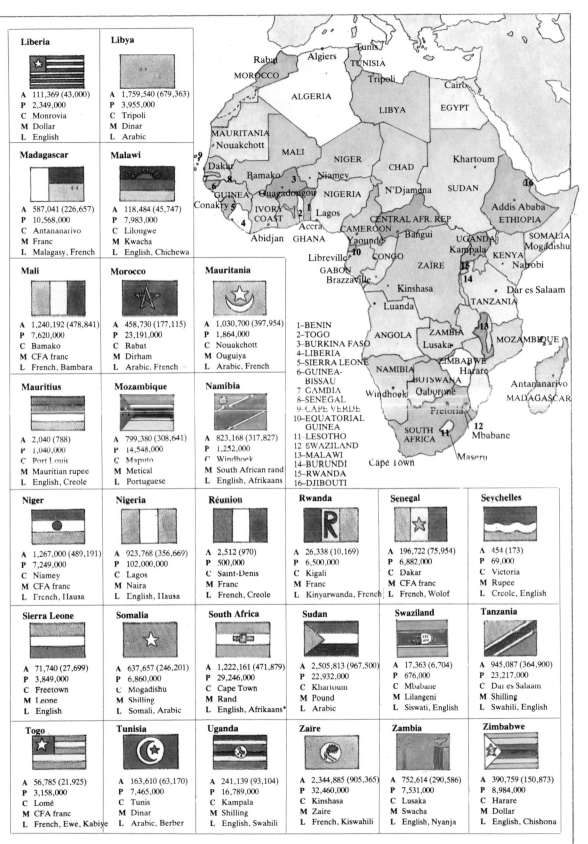

Liberia
A 111,369 (43,000)
P 2,349,000
C Monrovia
M Dollar
L English

Libya
A 1,759,540 (679,363)
P 3,955,000
C Tripoli
M Dinar
L Arabic

Madagascar
A 587,041 (226,657)
P 10,568,000
C Antananarivo
M Franc
L Malagasy, French

Malawi
A 118,484 (45,747)
P 7,983,000
C Lilongwe
M Kwacha
L English, Chichewa

Mali
A 1,240,192 (478,841)
P 7,620,000
C Bamako
M CFA franc
L French, Bambara

Morocco
A 458,730 (177,115)
P 23,191,000
C Rabat
M Dirham
L Arabic, French

Mauritania
A 1,030,700 (397,954)
P 1,864,000
C Nouakchott
M Ouguiya
L Arabic, French

Mauritius
A 2,040 (788)
P 1,040,000
C Port Louis
M Mauritian rupee
L English, Creole

Mozambique
A 799,380 (308,641)
P 14,548,000
C Maputo
M Metical
L Portuguese

Namibia
A 823,168 (317,827)
P 1,252,000
C Windhoek
M South African rand
L English, Afrikaans

Map legend:
1–BENIN
2–TOGO
3–BURKINA FASO
4–LIBERIA
5–SIERRA LEONE
6–GUINEA-BISSAU
7 GAMBIA
8–SENEGAL
9–CAPE VERDE
10–EQUATORIAL GUINEA
11–LESOTHO
12 SWAZILAND
13–MALAWI
14–BURUNDI
15–RWANDA
16–DJIBOUTI

Niger
A 1,267,000 (489,191)
P 7,249,000
C Niamey
M CFA franc
L French, Hausa

Nigeria
A 923,768 (356,669)
P 102,000,000
C Lagos
M Naira
L English, Hausa

Réunion
A 2,512 (970)
P 500,000
C Saint-Denis
M Franc
L French, Creole

Rwanda
A 26,338 (10,169)
P 6,500,000
C Kigali
M Franc
L Kinyarwanda, French

Senegal
A 196,722 (75,954)
P 6,882,000
C Dakar
M CFA franc
L French, Wolof

Seychelles
A 454 (173)
P 69,000
C Victoria
M Rupee
L Creole, English

Sierra Leone
A 71,740 (27,699)
P 3,849,000
C Freetown
M Leone
L English

Somalia
A 637,657 (246,201)
P 6,860,000
C Mogadishu
M Shilling
L Somali, Arabic

South Africa
A 1,222,161 (471,879)
P 29,246,000
C Cape Town
M Rand
L English, Afrikaans*

Sudan
A 2,505,813 (967,500)
P 22,932,000
C Khartoum
M Pound
L Arabic

Swaziland
A 17,363 (6,704)
P 676,000
C Mbabane
M Lilangeni
L Siswati, English

Tanzania
A 945,087 (364,900)
P 23,217,000
C Dar es Salaam
M Shilling
L Swahili, English

Togo
A 56,785 (21,925)
P 3,158,000
C Lomé
M CFA franc
L French, Ewe, Kabiye

Tunisia
A 163,610 (63,170)
P 7,465,000
C Tunis
M Dinar
L Arabic, Berber

Uganda
A 241,139 (93,104)
P 16,789,000
C Kampala
M Shilling
L English, Swahili

Zaire
A 2,344,885 (905,365)
P 32,460,000
C Kinshasa
M Zaire
L French, Kiswahili

Zambia
A 752,614 (290,586)
P 7,531,000
C Lusaka
M Swacha
L English, Nyanja

Zimbabwe
A 390,759 (150,873)
P 8,984,000
C Harare
M Dollar
L English, Chishona

*Krio, Mende, Xhosa, Zulu and Sesotho are also spoken in South Africa.

The American Continent

Location in the world

The American continent spreads over many latitudes and extends 15,120km (9,400 miles) from north to south. This is why there is such a variety of land forms.

America contains the most important river as measured by its rate of flow – the *Amazon* (in Brazil).

The highest American mountain, *Mount Aconcagua* (at the border of Argentina and Chile), reaches 7,035m (23,080ft) above sea-level.

The Americas are characterized by a great variety of population and by great social inequalities. Racial groups include whites, blacks, Native Americans, and many people of mixed background including Mestizos and Amerindians.

The continent is greatly influenced by the *United States*, the leading agricultural and industrial power of the world. The United States is a federation of 50 states.

Canada, the world's second largest country, is made up of ten provinces and two territories. Many countries of Central and South America suffer from social tensions and civil wars.

Important facts

Area	in millions of sq kilometres (miles)	
North America	22.0	(8.50)
Central America	2.7	(1.05)
South America	17.6	(6.81)
Total	42.3	(16.36)

Population	in millions of inhabitants
North America	300
Central America	90
South America	260
Total	650

Density of population: 15 inhabitants per sq km (40 per sq mile).

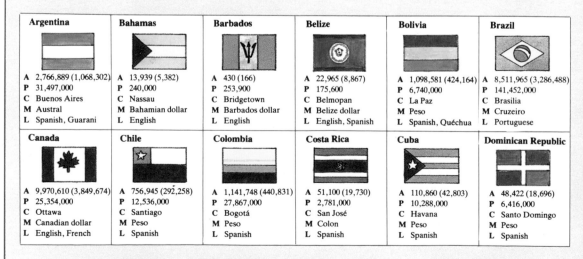

Argentina
A 2,766,889 (1,068,302)
P 31,497,000
C Buenos Aires
M Austral
L Spanish, Guarani

Bahamas
A 13,939 (5,382)
P 240,000
C Nassau
M Bahamian dollar
L English

Barbados
A 430 (166)
P 253,900
C Bridgetown
M Barbados dollar
L English

Belize
A 22,965 (8,867)
P 175,600
C Belmopan
M Belize dollar
L English, Spanish

Bolivia
A 1,098,581 (424,164)
P 6,740,000
C La Paz
M Peso
L Spanish, Quéchua

Brazil
A 8,511,965 (3,286,488)
P 141,452,000
C Brasilia
M Cruzeiro
L Portuguese

Canada
A 9,970,610 (3,849,674)
P 25,354,000
C Ottawa
M Canadian dollar
L English, French

Chile
A 756,945 (292,258)
P 12,536,000
C Santiago
M Peso
L Spanish

Colombia
A 1,141,748 (440,831)
P 27,867,000
C Bogotá
M Peso
L Spanish

Costa Rica
A 51,100 (19,730)
P 2,781,000
C San José
M Colon
L Spanish

Cuba
A 110,860 (42,803)
P 10,288,000
C Havana
M Peso
L Spanish

Dominican Republic
A 48,422 (18,696)
P 6,416,000
C Santo Domingo
M Peso
L Spanish

A = area in square kilometres and (in brackets) square miles, P = population, C = capital, M = money unit, L = language

Ecuador
A 270,670 (104,506)
P 10,204,000
C Quito
M Sucre
L Spanish

El Salvador
A 21,393 (8,260)
P 5,009,000
C San Salvador
M Colon
L Spanish

French Guiana
A 90,976 (35,126)
P 78,536
C Cayenne
M Franc
L Creole

Grenada
A 344 (133)
P 98,000
C St George's
M Caribbean dollar
L English

Guadeloupe
A 1,779 (687)
P 300,000
C Basse-Terre
M Franc
L French, Creole

Guatemala
A 108,889 (42,042)
P 8,434,000
C Guatemala City
M Quetzal
L Spanish

Guyana
A 214,969 (83,000)
P 825,000
C Georgetown
M Dollar
L English, Hindi

Haiti
A 27,750 (10,714)
P 5,707,000
C Port-au-Prince
M Gourde
L French, Creole

Honduras
A 112,088 (43,277)
P 4,051,000
C Tegucigalpa
M Lempira
L Spanish

Jamaica
A 10,991 (4,244)
P 2,355,000
C Kingston
M Dollar
L English

Martinique
A 1,116 (431)
P 300,000
C Fort-de-France
M Franc
L French, Creole

Mexico
A 1,958,201 (756,066)
P 82,735,000
C Mexico City
M Peso
L Spanish

Nicaragua
A 120,254 (46,430)
P 3,384,000
C Managua
M Cordoba
L Spanish, Miskito

Panama
A 77,082 (29,762)
P 2,274,000
C Panama City
M Balboa
L Spanish

Paraguay
A 406,752 (157,048)
P 3,922,000
C Asunción
M Guarani
L Spanish, Guarani

Peru
A 1,285,216 (496,225)
P 20,727,000
C Lima
M Sol
L Spanish, Quechua

St Pierre/Miquelon
A 241 (93)
P 6,041
C St Pierre
M Franc
L French

Suriname
A 163,265 (63,037)
P 395,000
C Paramaribo
M Guilder
L Dutch, Sranang Togo

Trinidad/Tobago
A 5,130 (1,981)
P 1,217,000
C Port of Spain
M Dollar
L English

United States
A 9,372,614 (3,618,770)
P 245,602,000
C Washington, DC
M Dollar
L English

Uruguay
A 176,215 (68,037)
P 3,058,000
C Montevideo
M New peso
L Spanish

Venezuela
A 912,050 (352,144)
P 18,757,000
C Caracas
M Bolivar
L Spanish, Indian

1–BELIZE
2–GUATEMALA
3–EL SALVADOR
4–HONDURAS
5–NICARAGUA
6–COSTA RICA
7–PANAMA
8–GUYANA
9 SURINAME
10–FRENCH GUIANA
11–HAITI
12–DOMINICAN REPUBLIC
13–CUBA
14–JAMAICA
15–ANTIGUA

Alaska

CANADA

NORTH AMERICA

Ottawa

UNITED STATES

Washington, DC

MEXICO

Mexico City

CENTRAL AMERICA

Caribbean Sea

Atlantic Ocean

Caracas

VENEZUELA

COLOMBIA

Bogotá

Quito

ECUADOR

BRAZIL

Lima

PERU

Brasilia

La Paz

BOLIVIA

PARAGUAY

Asunción

URUGUAY

Montevideo

Pacific Ocean

CHILE

Santiago

Buenos Aires

ARGENTINA

SOUTH AMERICA

Cape Horn

The Asian Continent

Location in the world

Important facts

Area: 44.5 million sq km (17.2 million sq miles) not including the western part of USSR.

Population: 2,370 million inhabitants, not including the USSR.

Density of population: 53 inhabitants per sq km (138 per sq mile).

The largest continent in the world, Asia extends over one-third of the Earth's land surface.

It is also the most populated continent (containing more than half the world's population) and has the greatest population growth.

Its extent in latitude, 9,051km (or 5,625 miles) from north to south, divides the continent into three climatic zones:

- Cold Asia in the north
- Dry Asia in the centre and the west
- Monsoon Asia in the south.

Asia has the highest mountain in the world – *Mount Everest*, 8,848m (or 29,028ft) in the Himalayas.

A great variety of ethnic groups, with white, yellow, brown and black skin, live in Asia.

In Asia, over 100 languages and different dialects are spoken.

All the great religions began here: Islam, Hinduism, Buddhism, Judaism and Christianity.

Many countries in this vast continent are faced with over-population, malnutrition and under-development.

Afghanistan	Bahrain	Bangladesh	Bhutan	Brunei	Burma (Myanmar)
A 652,225 (251,773)	A 691 (297)	A 143,998 (55,598)	A 46,500 (17,954)	A 5,765 (2,226)	A 676,552 (261,218)
P 18,614,000	P 412,000	P 105,000,000	P 1,313,000	P 226,300	P 39,411,000
C Kabul	C Manama	C Dhaka	C Thimphu	C Bandar Seri Begawan	C Rangoon
M Afghani	M Dinar	M Taka	M Ngultrum	M Brunei dollar	M Kyat
L Pushto, Dari	L Arabic	L Bengali	L Dzongkha	L Malay, Chinese	L Burmese
Cambodia	**China**	**Cyprus**	**Hong Kong**	**India**	**Indonesia**
A 181,035	A 9,571,300 (3,695,500)	A 9,251 (3,572)	A 1,045 (403)	A 3,287,263 (1,269,212)	A 1,919,443 (741,101)
P 7,688,000	P 1,072,300,000	P 680,400	P 4,957,000	P 796,600,000	P 170,534,000
C Phnom Penh	C Beijing	C Nicosia	C Victoria	C New Delhi	C Jakarta
M CFA franc	M Yuan	M Pound	M Hong Kong dollar	M Rupee	M Rupiah
L Khmer, French	L Chinese	L Greek, Turkish	L Chinese, English	L Hindi, English	L Bahasa Indonesia
Iraq	**Iran**	**Israel**	**Japan**	**Jordan**	**Korea, North**
A 441,839 (170,595)	A 1,648,000 (636,296)	A 21,946 (8,473)	A 377,815 (145,874)	A 89,206 (34,443)	A 120,538 (46,540)
P 16,278,000	P 49,930,000	P 4,331,000	P 122,264,000	P 2,796,000	P 21,390,000
C Baghdad	C Tehran	C Jerusalem	C Tokyo	C Amman	C Pyongyang
M Dinar	M Rial	M Shekel	M Yen	M Dinar	M Won
L Arabic, Kurdish	L Persian (Farsi)	L Hebrew, Arabic	L Japanese	L Arabic	L Korean

A = area in square kilometres and (in brackets) square miles, **P** = population, **C** = capital, **M** = money unit, **L** = language

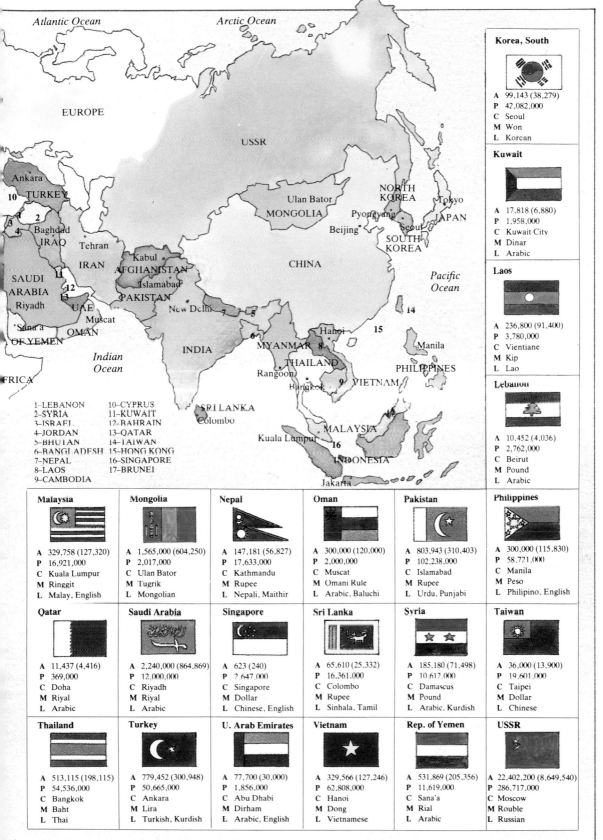

Atlantic Ocean   Arctic Ocean

EUROPE

USSR

Ankara

10 TURKEY

2
5
4 Baghdad
IRAQ   Tehran
    IRAN   Kabul
     AFGHANISTAN
SAUDI   **11**   Islamabad
ARABIA **12**   PAKISTAN
13
Riyadh   UAE
   Muscat   New Delhi   **7**   **5**
Sana'a   OMAN
OF YEMEN
AFRICA

Indian
Ocean

Ulan Bator
MONGOLIA

NORTH
KOREA
Pyongyang
Beijing   SOUTH
    KOREA

CHINA

INDIA

6
THAILAND   MYANMAR **8**
Rangoon
Bangkok   **9**   VIETNAM
   Hanoi   **15**

Tokyo
JAPAN
Seoul

Pacific
Ocean

14

Manila

PHILIPPINES

SRI LANKA
Colombo

Kuala Lumpur   MALAYSIA
16

INDONESIA

Jakarta

1—LEBANON   10—CYPRUS
2—SYRIA   11—KUWAIT
3—ISRAEL   12—BAHRAIN
4—JORDAN   13—QATAR
5—BHUTAN   14—TAIWAN
6—BANGLADESH   15—HONG KONG
7—NEPAL   16—SINGAPORE
8—LAOS   17—BRUNEI
9—CAMBODIA

Korea, South
A 99,143 (38,279)
P 42,082,000
C Seoul
M Won
L Korean

Kuwait
A 17,818 (6,880)
P 1,958,000
C Kuwait City
M Dinar
L Arabic

Laos
A 236,800 (91,400)
P 3,780,000
C Vientiane
M Kip
L Lao

Lebanon
A 10,452 (4,036)
P 2,762,000
C Beirut
M Pound
L Arabic

Malaysia
A 329,758 (127,320)
P 16,921,000
C Kuala Lumpur
M Ringgit
L Malay, English

Mongolia
A 1,565,000 (604,250)
P 2,017,000
C Ulan Bator
M Tugrik
L Mongolian

Nepal
A 147,181 (56,827)
P 17,633,000
C Kathmandu
M Rupee
L Nepali, Maithir

Oman
A 300,000 (120,000)
P 2,000,000
C Muscat
M Omani Rule
L Arabic, Baluchi

Pakistan
A 803,943 (310,403)
P 102,238,000
C Islamabad
M Rupee
L Urdu, Punjabi

Philippines
A 300,000 (115,830)
P 58,721,000
C Manila
M Peso
L Philipino, English

Qatar
A 11,437 (4,416)
P 369,000
C Doha
M Riyal
L Arabic

Saudi Arabia
A 2,240,000 (864,869)
P 12,000,000
C Riyadh
M Riyal
L Arabic

Singapore
A 623 (240)
P 2,647,000
C Singapore
M Dollar
L Chinese, English

Sri Lanka
A 65,610 (25,332)
P 16,361,000
C Colombo
M Rupee
L Sinhala, Tamil

Syria
A 185,180 (71,498)
P 10,612,000
C Damascus
M Pound
L Arabic, Kurdish

Taiwan
A 36,000 (13,900)
P 19,601,000
C Taipei
M Dollar
L Chinese

Thailand
A 513,115 (198,115)
P 54,536,000
C Bangkok
M Baht
L Thai

Turkey
A 779,452 (300,948)
P 50,665,000
C Ankara
M Lira
L Turkish, Kurdish

U. Arab Emirates
A 77,700 (30,000)
P 1,856,000
C Abu Dhabi
M Dirham
L Arabic, English

Vietnam
A 329,566 (127,246)
P 62,808,000
C Hanoi
M Dong
L Vietnamese

Rep. of Yemen
A 531,869 (205,356)
P 11,619,000
C Sana'a
M Rial
L Arabic

USSR
A 22,402,200 (8,649,540)
P 286,717,000
C Moscow
M Rouble
L Russian

The European Countries

Location in the world

Europe has great geographical variety – old mountains, great plains and high mountain chains. The highest peak is *Mont Blanc* (4,807m or 15,623ft) in France.

Located almost entirely in the temperate zone, with the exception of northern Scandinavia, Europe has three climate zones – oceanic, Mediterranean and continental.

Densely populated, its population nevertheless is not growing as fast as that of the rest of the world.

A mix of people, cultures, religions and languages make up Europe.

Attempts at unification began on 1 January 1958 when the European Economic Community (EC) was founded. Today 12 European countries are members and more have applied to join. The EC helps to make it easier for the member countries to live and do business together.

Important facts

Europe is not a separate continent, but the western part of the vast Eurasian continent. It extends from the Atlantic Ocean to the Ural mountains and includes the eastern part of the USSR.

Area: 10.4 million sq km (4 million sq miles).
Population: 761 million inhabitants.
Density of population: 73 inhabitants per sq km (190 per sq mile).

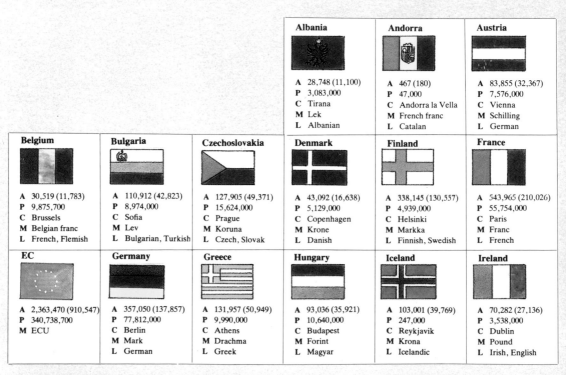

Albania	Andorra	Austria
A 28,748 (11,100)	A 467 (180)	A 83,855 (32,367)
P 3,083,000	P 47,000	P 7,576,000
C Tirana	C Andorra la Vella	C Vienna
M Lek	M French franc	M Schilling
L Albanian	L Catalan	L German

Belgium	Bulgaria	Czechoslovakia	Denmark	Finland	France
A 30,519 (11,783)	A 110,912 (42,823)	A 127,905 (49,371)	A 43,092 (16,638)	A 338,145 (130,557)	A 543,965 (210,026)
P 9,875,700	P 8,974,000	P 15,624,000	P 5,129,000	P 4,939,000	P 55,754,000
C Brussels	C Sofia	C Prague	C Copenhagen	C Helsinki	C Paris
M Belgian franc	M Lev	M Koruna	M Krone	M Markka	M Franc
L French, Flemish	L Bulgarian, Turkish	L Czech, Slovak	L Danish	L Finnish, Swedish	L French

EC	Germany	Greece	Hungary	Iceland	Ireland
A 2,363,470 (910,547)	A 357,050 (137,857)	A 131,957 (50,949)	A 93,036 (35,921)	A 103,001 (39,769)	A 70,282 (27,136)
P 340,738,700	P 77,812,000	P 9,990,000	P 10,640,000	P 247,000	P 3,538,000
M ECU	C Berlin	C Athens	C Budapest	C Reykjavik	C Dublin
	M Mark	M Drachma	M Forint	M Krona	M Pound
	L German	L Greek	L Magyar	L Icelandic	L Irish, English

A = area in square kilometres and (in brackets) square miles, P = population, C = capital, M = money unit, L = language

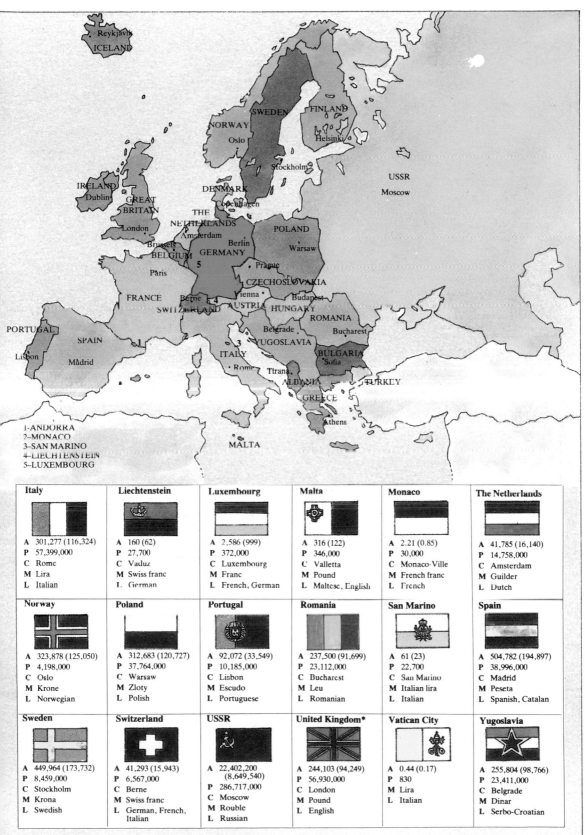

1-ANDORRA
2-MONACO
3-SAN MARINO
4-LIECHTENSTEIN
5-LUXEMBOURG

Italy
- A 301,277 (116,324)
- P 57,399,000
- C Rome
- M Lira
- L Italian

Liechtenstein
- A 160 (62)
- P 27,700
- C Vaduz
- M Swiss franc
- L German

Luxembourg
- A 2,586 (999)
- P 372,000
- C Luxembourg
- M Franc
- L French, German

Malta
- A 316 (122)
- P 346,000
- C Valletta
- M Pound
- L Maltese, English

Monaco
- A 2.21 (0.85)
- P 30,000
- C Monaco-Ville
- M French franc
- L French

The Netherlands
- A 41,785 (16,140)
- P 14,758,000
- C Amsterdam
- M Guilder
- L Dutch

Norway
- A 323,878 (125,050)
- P 4,198,000
- C Oslo
- M Krone
- L Norwegian

Poland
- A 312,683 (120,727)
- P 37,764,000
- C Warsaw
- M Zloty
- L Polish

Portugal
- A 92,072 (33,549)
- P 10,185,000
- C Lisbon
- M Escudo
- L Portuguese

Romania
- A 237,500 (91,699)
- P 23,112,000
- C Bucharest
- M Leu
- L Romanian

San Marino
- A 61 (23)
- P 22,700
- C San Marino
- M Italian lira
- L Italian

Spain
- A 504,782 (194,897)
- P 38,996,000
- C Madrid
- M Peseta
- L Spanish, Catalan

Sweden
- A 449,964 (173,732)
- P 8,459,000
- C Stockholm
- M Krona
- L Swedish

Switzerland
- A 41,293 (15,943)
- P 6,567,000
- C Berne
- M Swiss franc
- L German, French, Italian

USSR
- A 22,402,200 (8,649,540)
- P 286,717,000
- C Moscow
- M Rouble
- L Russian

United Kingdom*
- A 244,103 (94,249)
- P 56,930,000
- C London
- M Pound
- L English

Vatican City
- A 0.44 (0.17)
- P 830
- M Lira
- L Italian

Yugoslavia
- A 255,804 (98,766)
- P 23,411,000
- C Belgrade
- M Dinar
- L Serbo-Croatian

*The United Kingdom of Great Britain and Northern Ireland consists of England, Wales, Scotland and Northern Ireland.

Oceania and the Polar Lands

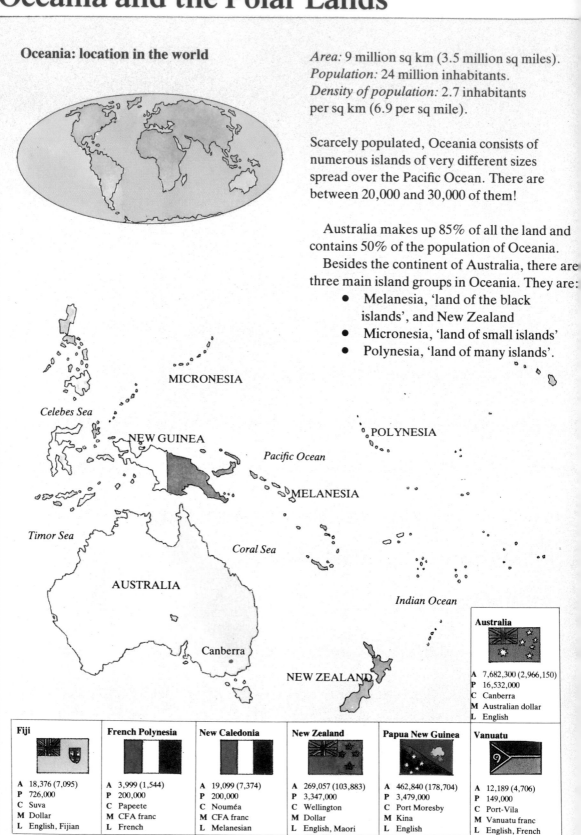

Oceania: location in the world

Area: 9 million sq km (3.5 million sq miles).
Population: 24 million inhabitants.
Density of population: 2.7 inhabitants per sq km (6.9 per sq mile).

Scarcely populated, Oceania consists of numerous islands of very different sizes spread over the Pacific Ocean. There are between 20,000 and 30,000 of them!

Australia makes up 85% of all the land and contains 50% of the population of Oceania.
Besides the continent of Australia, there are three main island groups in Oceania. They are:

- Melanesia, 'land of the black islands', and New Zealand
- Micronesia, 'land of small islands'
- Polynesia, 'land of many islands'.

Australia
A 7,682,300 (2,966,150)
P 16,532,000
C Canberra
M Australian dollar
L English

Fiji	**French Polynesia**	**New Caledonia**	**New Zealand**	**Papua New Guinea**	**Vanuatu**
A 18,376 (7,095)	A 3,999 (1,544)	A 19,099 (7,374)	A 269,057 (103,883)	A 462,840 (178,704)	A 12,189 (4,706)
P 726,000	P 200,000	P 200,000	P 3,347,000	P 3,479,000	P 149,000
C Suva	C Papeete	C Nouméa	C Wellington	C Port Moresby	C Port-Vila
M Dollar	M CFA franc	M CFA franc	M Dollar	M Kina	M Vanuatu franc
L English, Fijian	L French	L Melanesian	L English, Maori	L English	L English, French

A = area in square kilometres and (in brackets) square miles, **P** = population, **C** = capital, **M** = money unit, **L** = language

Polar lands: location in the world

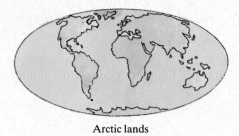

Arctic lands

Antarctic lands

The climate of the polar lands is extremely harsh. In summer, the average temperature does not rise above 10°C (50°F) because of the high degree of slanting of the rays of the Sun.

A difference between the poles

The North Pole is a dot in the middle of the Arctic Ocean. It is surrounded by islands and lands.

The South Pole is a dot located on the continent of Antarctica.

Arctic area

This vast region includes the largest island in the world – *Greenland*, a Danish territory with an area of 2,212,000 sq km (845,000 sq miles) and a population of 53,000 inhabitants. Of its surface, 90% is covered by a sheet of ice averaging 1,500m (5,000ft) thick. The Arctic area also includes Spitzbergen (Norway), Lapland (the northern part of Scandinavia, Finland and the north-western USSR), Alaska, and northern Canada.

Antarctica

This is the largest ice desert in the world (more than 13 million sq km or 5 million sq miles). The environment is very harsh. The coldest temperature on record was reached here: *minus* 88.3°C (–191°F) in 1960.

The sheet of ice has a thickness of about 4,000m (13,000ft). There are very strong winds (record speed: 328kph or 204mph).

Human beings live only in a few recently opened scientific stations.

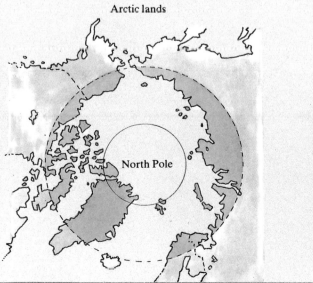

Arctic lands

North Pole

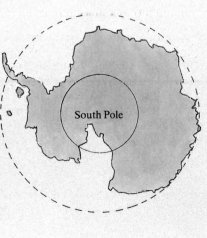

Antarctic lands

South Pole

Expressing Oneself – Communicating

Speech and language

A sequence of sounds, organized into words or sentences, is called speech, which allows human beings to express themselves and to communicate. Human speech varies according to countries and people. Each variety of speech is called a *language*. There are close to 4,000 spoken languages in the world.

Major languages

The table below shows the most common languages in the world. Nearly 5,000 million human beings speak them.

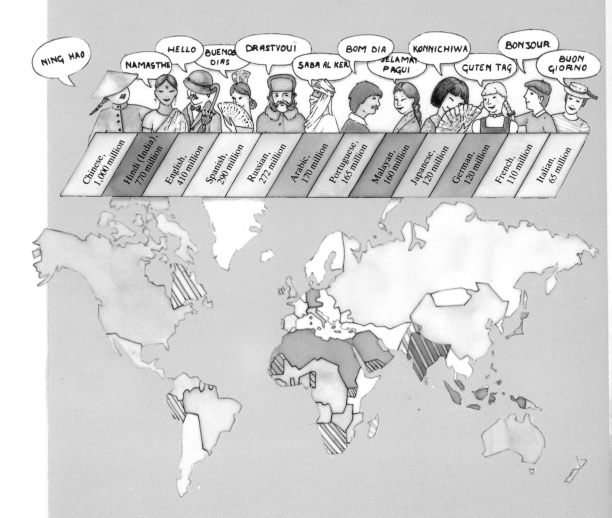

A common language

For better communication between people, some people have felt that a common language was needed. Ever since the 1700s, hundreds of languages have been developed to enable people all over the world to communicate, but none has had great success.

The most famous of these is *Esperanto*, which is used by about three million people in 100 countries. Today, English is the language most often used for international communication.

Written language

In the 1700s, a famous writer claimed that 'writing is the painting of the voice'. For over 5,000 years, humans have used signs or symbols to express themselves and to communicate.

3000 BC: The Sumerians carved pictographs on clay tablets.

Original	Modified	Babylonian	Assyrian
Bird			
Fish			
Sun/day			
Seed			
Orchard			

Evolution of pictographs in the Near East. They became more and more abstract (less like real objects).

Original	4th to 3rd century BC	Modern
Man		
Hill		
Tree		
Dog		
Moon		

Evolution of Chinese pictographs. A pictograph became an ideograph or a symbol. Chinese writing has more than 3,000 ideographs!

One symbol, one idea

The Egyptian pictograph ▭ (sky) which was used to mean both 'clouds' and 'paradise' is an *ideograph*.

One symbol, one sound

In later Egyptian writing, each symbol also had a phonetic value and represented one, two or three sounds. There were no vowels, only consonants. For instance: ⬯ (mouth) means 'r', ⬠ (loaf of bread) means 't', ⌐ (throne) means 's + t' and is pronounced 'set'.

Today, in order to indicate how a word sounds, we use phonetic symbols that are grouped together in an alphabet, called the International Phonetic Alphabet (IPA).

EXAMPLE
[ʌp] = up [lɔk] = lock [dei] = day
[iːzi] = easy

The alphabet

The introduction of the alphabet simplified writing considerably. The Phoenicians were the first to use it about 1000 BC.

Finally the invention of the printing press by Johann Gutenberg in the 1400s increased the number of books and made them more widespread and available.

North-Semitic	Early Phoenician	𐤊 𐤂 𐤁 ◁ 𐤄 Y	I 𐤄 ⊕ 𐤆	↓ ⸦ 𐤔 𐤎 𐤈 O 𐤍	𐤆 W +
	Phoenician	𐤊 𐤂 𐤁 𐤃 𐤄 𐤅	I 𐤄 ⊗ Z	𐤙 ⸦ 𐤌 𐤍 O 𐤐 𐤑 𐤒 𐤔 w t X
Greek	Early	△ 𐤂 𐤁 △ 𐤄 𐤅	I 𐤄 ⊗ ᒢ	𐤙 𐤠 𐤌 𐤍 O 𐤐 M 𐤒 𐤠 𐤆 X
	Classical	A B Γ △ E	Z H θ I	K Λ M N Ξ O Π P Σ T Y
Etruscan	Classic	A 𐤠 𐤂 𐤄	𐤙 B O I	𐤙 𐤠 M 𐤮 M Q 𐤠 𐤆 𐤯 V
Latin	Early	A	▽ 𐤂 𐤄	目 I	𐤙 M 𐤠 O Γ	𐤠 V
	Classical	A B C D E F G	H I	K L M N O P Q R S T V
Modern capitals	Roman	A B C D E F G	H I J	K L M N O P Q R S T U V W

Signs and Symbols

The spoken and written word are not the only ways to communicate. Visual symbols can also be used.

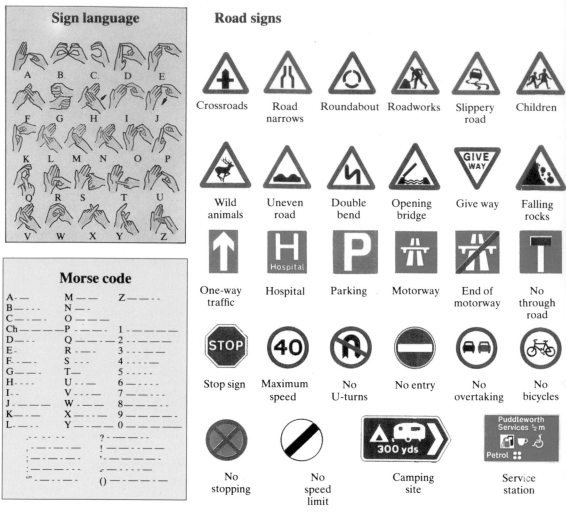

Sign language

Morse code

A .—	M ——	Z ——..
B —...	N —.	
C —.—.	O ———	
Ch ————	P .——.	1 .————
D —..	Q ——.—	2 ..———
E .	R .—.	3 ...——
F ..—.	S ...	4 ....—
G ——.	T —	5 .....
H	U ..—	6 —....
I ..	V ...—	7 ——...
J .———	W .——	8 ———..
K —.—	X —..—	9 ————.
L .—..	Y —.——	0 —————

Road signs

Crossroads · Road narrows · Roundabout · Roadworks · Slippery road · Children

Wild animals · Uneven road · Double bend · Opening bridge · Give way · Falling rocks

One-way traffic · Hospital · Parking · Motorway · End of motorway · No through road

Stop sign · Maximum speed · No U-turns · No entry · No overtaking · No bicycles

No stopping · No speed limit · Camping site · Service station

Semaphore

Arm signals are usually given with two small flags, one in each hand.

A B C D E F G H I J
K L M N O P Q R S T
U V W X Y Z attack cancelled end of signal

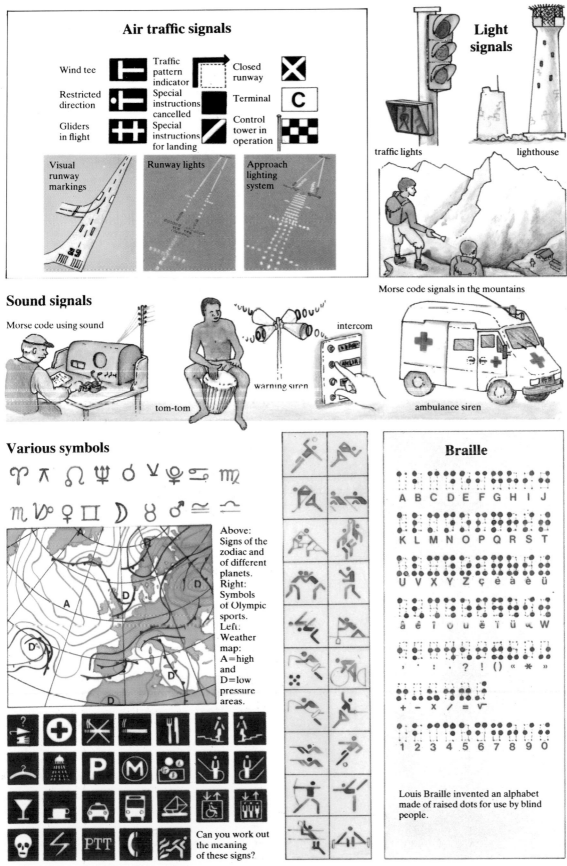

Air traffic signals

Wind tee

Traffic pattern indicator

Closed runway

Restricted direction

Special instructions cancelled

Terminal

Gliders in flight

Special instructions for landing

Control tower in operation

Visual runway markings

Runway lights

Approach lighting system

Light signals

traffic lights

lighthouse

Morse code signals in the mountains

Sound signals

Morse code using sound

tom-tom

warning siren

intercom

ambulance siren

Various symbols

Above: Signs of the zodiac and of different planets.
Right: Symbols of Olympic sports.
Left: Weather map: A=high and D=low pressure areas.

Can you work out the meaning of these signs?

Braille

Louis Braille invented an alphabet made of raised dots for use by blind people.

The English Language

cwædon þæt he wære Wyruld-cyninga
manna mildust ond mon·þwærust,
leodum liðost ond lof-geornost.

Old English from the poem *Beowulf* can be translated:

> 'It's said that of all the world's kings he was the mildest and gentlest of men, the kindest to his people, and most eager for praise'.

The beginning of English

About the year AD 449, bands of Anglo-Saxon warriors came from Europe to conquer the British Isles. They spoke a language called *Old English,* which was very different from the English we now speak. They used some words they learned from the Celtic people they had defeated. Some of these new words were Latin which had been taught to the Celts by the Roman soldiers who once occupied England. English is a language that grows and develops by bringing in words from other languages.

Middle English and modern English

When the Normans from France conquered England in 1066, hundreds of words came into the language, and English continued to grow and develop into what we now call *Middle English.*

The Normans defeat the English in 1066. Note the Latin words on this Bayeux tapestry. Latin was used in the Church and for official purposes.

The English Bible, 1611

An example of Middle English is the line:

'Soune ys noght but eyre ybroken'

which means: 'Sound is nothing but air broken'. By the year 1500, English, as we now speak it, was well established. This modern English became widely used when the English Bible (the King James version) was published in 1611. Modern spelling, of course, did not begin to be established until Dr Samuel Johnson published his famous dictionary in 1755.

English words from other languages

Like no other language in the world, English is a mixture of all languages. More than half of our words come from Latin; for example, *memorandum, orbit* and *item*.

Here is a list of some 'English' words from the languages of other countries:

French: *baton, fruit.*
Spanish: *barbecue, alligator.*
Italian: *violin, soprano.*
Indian: *dungarees, shampoo.*

German: *pretzel, frankfurter.*
Hebrew: *cherub, kosher.*
Persian: *caravan, bazaar.*
Hawaiian: *ukulele.*

Japanese: *ju-jitsu, samurai.*
Chinese: *kowtow, lychee.*
African: *banana, yam.*
Scandinavian: *muggy, ski.*

English spoken around the world

More people speak Chinese than any other language. That is because there are 1,000 million Chinese people – a quarter of the world's population. The next most widely spoken language is English, which is the main language in the United States, Canada, Great Britain, Ireland, Australia, South

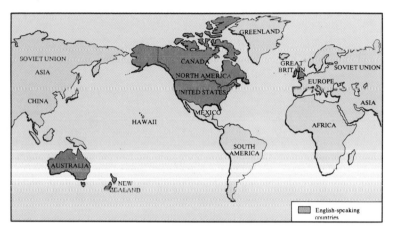

Countries where the main language is English

Africa and New Zealand. In other countries, most people who decide to learn a second language choose English. It is the official language for all aircraft controllers and is used all over the world in business.

The oldest manuscript in English

The manuscript of the Old English poem, *Beowulf,* which was written about the year 1000 after having been composed in the 8th century, is the oldest piece of writing in English that has been found. This is very recent compared to the writings of other languages. Many pieces of Greek, Latin or Egyptian writing are over two thousand years old.

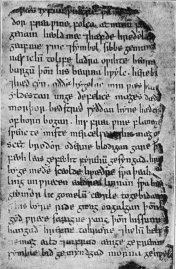

A page from the only surviving manuscript of *Beowulf*

The Meaning of Words

Homonyms

The English language can be troublesome because it contains many *homonyms* – words that sound or look the same but have different meanings.

Words with the same spelling but different meanings are called *homographs:*

- We caught a *perch* while fishing today.
- The parrot sat on its *perch*.
- The knight was protected by a coat of *mail*.
- The letter was sent by air *mail*.
- A victory would be something to *crow* over.
- The jet black *crow* flew across our path.

Other examples of *homographs* are:

state	–	particular condition/say
bar	–	pole or rod/pub
boom	–	deep sound/business growth
fine	–	excellent/punishment
hide	–	conceal/animal skin

Words with different spelling but the same pronunciation are called *homophones:*

- Dinner will be served at *eight* o'clock.
- She *ate* every piece of fruit in the bowl.
- Ben handed me a *pair* of tickets.
- The painting showed a golden *pear* on a kitchen table.
- Your cupboard is completely *bare*.
- The *bear* lived in a cave in the forest.

Other examples of *homophones* are:

pail (buckct)
pale (of little colour)

meet (to encounter)
meat (animal flesh)

whole (entire)
hole (opening)

council (law-makers)
counsel (advice)

piece (part of something)
peace (calm)

Synonyms

The English language has many words that are similar in meaning. These words are called *synonyms*.

- I was *glad* to hear from you.
(You might have used *pleased, overjoyed, happy, delighted, thrilled.*)
- The man had a *bad* character.
(You might have used *wicked, evil, corrupt, vile, rotten, unpleasant.*)

Note the many possible synonyms of these words. Can you suggest others?

hungry	–	starving, famished
angry	–	enraged, upset, cross
huge	–	big, large, enormous
strong	–	powerful, sturdy, muscular
stubborn	–	obstinate, inflexible, hard-headed
beautiful	–	attractive, lovely, delightful
cold	–	freezing, chilly, cool
funny	–	humorous, comic, amusing

As writers know, most synonyms present a different shading, a more specific way of making a point. It's one thing, for example, to say that you have a *big* job to do, but it's something else to describe that job as *immense, overwhelming, brutal, titanic, monstrous, crushing*, etc.

Antonyms

An *antonym* is a word that is opposite in meaning to another. *Tall* and *short, backwards* and *forwards, rich* and *poor, courage* and *cowardice* are all antonyms for each other.

With the addition of a *prefix* (letters added to the beginning of a word), we are able to form numerous antonyms:

possible	–	impossible	respect	–	disrespect
inform	–	misinform	similar	–	dissimilar
known	–	unknown	wise	–	unwise
correct	–	incorrect	freqent	–	infrequent
equal	–	unequal	accurate	–	inaccurate

Writing in all its Forms

Abbreviations

In order to save time, we frequently use *abbreviations* (shortened forms of words). Instead of writing out the word *Street* in an address, we often substitute *St.* Other familiar abbreviations are:

AD	anno domini (in the year of our Lord)
am	ante meridiem (before noon)
BC	before Christ
GB	Great Britain
MP	Member of Parliament
Ltd	Limited
pm	post meridiem (afternoon)
RSPCA	Royal Society for the Prevention of Cruelty to Animals
UK	United Kingdom
UN	United Nations
USA	United States of America
USSR	Union of Soviet Socialist Republics

Playing with Words

Suffixes and prefixes

Suffixes are endings added to words and prefixes are letters added to the beginnings of words. By learning the meaning of some important prefixes, suffixes and stems you will be able to expand your vocabulary as you recognize them in unfamiliar words. For example, if you are aware that *auto*=self, *bio*=life, and *graph*=to write, you will then know that an *autobiography* is a person's story of his or her own life. Here are some useful examples:

ab (away from)	–	*ab*duct
able (capable of)	–	port*able*
agri (field)	–	*agri*culture
ante (before)	–	*ante*cedent
anthrop (man)	–	phil*anthrop*ist
aqua (water)	–	*aqua*tic
aud (to hear)	–	*aud*itorium
belli (war)	–	re*belli*on
bene (good, well)	–	*bene*factor
bi (two)	–	*bi*annual
cap (head)	–	de*cap*itate
contra (against)	–	*contra*dict

Anagrams

An anagram is a word or phrase formed from another by rearranging the letters.

devil	–	lived
charm	–	march
tea	–	eat
read	–	dear
teach	–	cheat

Exercise

What anagrams can you suggest for these words?

1 male
2 thread
3 bleat

Idioms

Idioms are phrases or expressions that cannot be understood from the ordinary meanings of their words. For example, when we say, 'I'm going to catch a train', we don't mean that we are going to *catch* a train as we would catch a ball. Over the years, idioms have gained acceptance in a language, and it is almost impossible to deal with people without an understanding of the true meanings of the idioms they use. If someone gives you 'the cold shoulder' or 'hauls you over the coals', for example, will you be happy about those two experiences?

Here are some idioms often used in English:

a pig in a poke – an item you buy without having seen it; a disappointment
a flash in the pan – promising at the start but then disappointing
to pour oil on troubled waters – to make peace
a wet blanket – one who spoils your fun
crocodile tears – insincere emotion
to rule the roost – to be in charge
to pass the buck – to avoid responsibility
red-letter day – time for rejoicing
let sleeping dogs lie – let well alone
thumbs down – sign of rejection
an axe to grind – having a selfish motive
to cool one's heels – to be kept waiting

Crossword puzzle

Across

1 Stream of water
5 Either tea ... coffee
6 Abbreviation for radium
7 Sloping edge
9 Poor

Down

1 Red-breasted bird
2 Anger
3 Old word for 'before'
4 Mass meeting
8 Compete

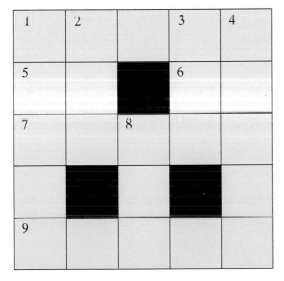

Answers

Across

1 river
5 or
6 Ra
7 bevel
9 needy

Down

1 robin
2 ire
3 ere
4 rally
8 vie

Find the animals!

Somewhere in this box of letters, reading up, down, across or diagonally, find the names of four well-known animals from children's literature.

P	S	B	I	O	R	M	D
O	B	G	F	P	X	M	A
O	A	R	L	I	O	Q	O
H	D	I	E	G	U	M	T
B	S	P	C	R	N	C	R
E	R	T	A	G	F	K	M
A	S	L	A	N	X	O	T
R	O	D	E	L	V	O	X

Answers

X	O	A	L	E	D	O	R
T	O	X	N	A	L	S	A
M	K	F	G	A	T	R	E
R	C	N	R	C	P	S	B
T	M	U	G	E	I	D	H
O	O	O	I	L	R	A	O
A	M	X	P	F	G	B	O
D	M	R	O	I	B	S	P

Funny bunny game

What's an amusing rabbit? The rhyming answer is a 'funny bunny'. Now, solve these:

1 an improved woollen pullover
2 a huge hog
3 the most important cot
4 an angry boy

Answers

1 better sweater
2 big pig
3 head bed
4 mad lad

Literature

What is literature?

Literature consists of the body of written works, in prose or verse, that expresses the ideas of a particular culture. Western literature includes modern works as well as those that have survived from the Middle Ages and ancient Rome and Greece.

From the spoken to the written word

At first, legends and stories were transmitted by word of mouth. Starting mainly in the 15th century, with the development of the printing press, literary works were put down in permanent form and widely distributed.

The writer and language

Not every written work is classified as literature. Only a few great writers can convey precisely, originally and brilliantly such important ideas as those relating to life and death, love and hate, politics and society.

Among the most famous are:

Middle Ages	16th century	17th century
Petrarch	Sir Thomas More	Ben Jonson
Boccaccio	John Lyly	Robert Herrick
Malory	Niccolo Machiavelli	Sir Francis Bacon
Villon	François Rabelais	Sir Thomas Browne
Chaucer	Michel de Montaigne	Molière
Dante Alighieri	Miguel de Cervantes	Jean Racine
	William Shakespeare	René Descartes
	Edmund Spenser	John Donne
	Christoper Marlowe	John Milton

Types of literature

The many different forms of literature are usually distinguished by subject and treatment:

- The *novel* is a work of fiction, a product of the imagination. The author brings people to life, describing their feelings, their thoughts and their adventures. There are detective, historical, romantic, science-fiction and spy novels.
- The *short story* is a short narrative with a plot and characterization pertaining to a single set of circumstances and no sub-plots as in novels.
- The *essay* contains impressions and observations on a particular subject; non-fiction.
- *Satire* is writing that ridicules human faults, often with the intent of correcting them.
- *Drama* is written to be read or performed to an audience by actors.
- *Memoirs* narrate events in which the author has participated.
- *Poetry* uses intense language and images to convey strong emotions. The sounds of the words, using rhythm and often rhyme, are important.

World literature

Some authors have become internationally known. Through translations, it is possible to read and appreciate the literature of *France* (Hugo, Dumas), *Russia* (Tolstoy, Dostoevsky), *Germany* (Mann, Goethe), *Italy* (Dante) and *Spain* (Cervantes). The works of *American* authors (Faulkner, Hemingway) and *British* authors (Shakespeare, Dickens) have been translated into many different languages and are read all over the world.

Reference books

Many works such as encyclopedias, dictionaries, textbooks or guidebooks do not 'tell stories'. They are mainly used to provide knowledge.

18th century	19th century	20th century
Voltaire	Victor Hugo	Marcel Proust
Jean Jacques Rousseau	Alexandre Dumas	François Mauriac
Goethe	Honoré de Balzac	Albert Camus
Dr Samuel Johnson	Gustave Flaubert	Jean-Paul Sartre
Oliver Goldsmith	Emile Zola	Sinclair Lewis
William Blake	Georges Sand	F. Scott Fitzgerald
Daniel Defoe	Matthew Arnold	William Faulkner
Alexander Pope	Sir Walter Scott	Ernest Hemingway
John Dryden	Charles Dickens	Eugene O'Neill
Jonathan Swift	Emily Brontë	James Baldwin
	Thomas Hardy	Arthur Miller
	Nathaniel Hawthorne	Thomas Mann
	Herman Melville	Samuel Beckett
	Jane Austen	*(and the poets on page 111)*
	George Eliot	
	(and the poets on page 111)	

Poetry

Poets are writers who use words in harmonious and imaginative ways to create word pictures and gain emotional responses from readers. Poets use *meaning, sound, metre* and *rhyme* to transmit thoughts to the reader. *Prose*, unlike *poetry*, generally does not have a regular metre.

Ancient times

Poetry was very important in ancient Greece, where the great poet Homer sang of heroes – and the gods who interacted with them – in the long epic poems, the *Iliad* and the *Odyssey*.

The ancient Greeks loved drama, which was written in poetic metre by the great writers of tragedy: Aeschylus, Sophocles and Euripides.

In the golden age of Roman literature (first century BC), Virgil wrote his epic masterpiece, the *Aeneid*, as well as the *Eclogues*, poems about the charms of nature.

The blind Greek poet Homer lived in the ninth century BC.

The Middle Ages

Around the 12th century, wandering French troubadours wrote *chansons de geste* (songs about deeds) to praise legendary heroes. The best known of these was the *Song of Roland*, about King Charlemagne's nephew, a hero in the fight against the Moors.

One of the world's greatest writers, Dante Alighieri, was born in the 13th century in Italy. His long poem, *The Divine Comedy*, encompasses all the knowledge of the medieval period and dramatizes humanity's search for perfection.

Geoffrey Chaucer, in 14th century England, wrote the remarkable long work, *The Canterbury Tales,* filled with the wit and wisdom of the Middle Ages and a vast array of characters of the time.

'There came one night into that hostelry
Some nine and twenty in a company
Of sundry persons who had chanced to fall
In fellowship, and pilgrims were they all,
And toward Canterbury would they ride.'
(Modern English version)

A commoner who worked in the royal court, Geoffrey Chaucer (about 1343–1400) knew all of English society and described it brilliantly.

The Renaissance

In the 16th century, the English poet William Shakespeare, thought by many to be the greatest writer the world has ever known, began writing his extraordinary sonnets and plays, many of which were written in verse.

At this time, when new knowledge was bursting forth – the Renaissance – other English poets flourished: Edmund Spenser (c.1552–1599), author of *The Faerie Queene*, a long allegorical poem, and Christopher Marlowe (1564–1593), who wrote great plays in verse.

William Shakespeare (1564–1616)

'Shall I compare thee to a summer's day?
Thou art more lovely and more temperate:
Rough winds do shake the darling buds of May,
And summer's lease hath all too short a date.'

John Milton

The 17th century

English poetry took a new direction when John Donne (1572–1631) composed sonnets and lyrics with startling, complex images and John Milton (1607–1674) wrote a distinctive type of epic poem, *Paradise Lost,* as well as some of the world's greatest sonnets.

> *'How soon hath Time, the subtle thief of youth,*
> *Stol'n on his wings my three and twentieth year!'*
> [Quotation from one of Milton's sonnets]

In France, Jean Racine (1639–1699) is universally acknowledged as that country's greatest dramatic poet.

The 18th century

The century of the Enlightenment produced a new kind of poetry, which was mainly philosophical and satirical. Alexander Pope (1688–1744), who wrote profound and witty couplets in poems such as *Essay on Man* and *Essay on Criticism,* is thought by some to be the greatest poet of his age.

The 19th century

This century saw the emergence of the English Romantic poets, who glorified nature and the individual – William Wordsworth (1770–1850), Samuel Taylor Coleridge (1772–1834), Lord Byron (1788–1824), Percy Shelley (1792–1822) and John Keats (1795–1821). In America there appeared such great traditional poets as Henry Wadsworth Longfellow (1807–1882) and James Russell Lowell (1819–1891). There were also two American poets who blazed new trails: Walt Whitman (1819–1892), who wrote lyrical, personal outbursts of song about himself and his country, and Emily Dickinson (1830–1886), a shy New England woman whose keen observation and talent for imagery transformed American poetry. In the last part of the century, the English poets Alfred Tennyson (1809–1892) and Robert Browning (1812–1899) built on Romantic poetry to form the serious Victorian school of poetry. In France at this time, Charles Baudelaire, Paul Verlaine and Arthur Rimbaud liberated poetry by introducing a daring new style, the basis for modern poetry.

Emily Dickinson

Robert Frost

The 20th century

Poetry has continued to develop as an art form in this century. Some of the most acclaimed of the modern poets are William Butler Yeats (1865–1939), T. S. Eliot (1888–1965), Robert Frost (1874–1963), Gerard Manley Hopkins (1844–1889), Ezra Pound (1885–1972), Wallace Stevens (1879–1955), Wilfred Owen (1893–1918), e. e. cummings (1894–1962), Robert Graves (1895–1990), W. H. Auden (1907–1973), Dylan Thomas (1914–1953), Ted Hughes (1930–) and Sylvia Plath (1932–1963). Following no precise rules, this poetry plays with words, with rhythms and with sounds.

Information: Three Powerful Media

What are the 'media'?

Newspapers, magazines, radio and television are all forms of mass communication known as the media. They circulate information, opinions and entertainment all over the world. Both competing with each other and complementing one another, the media play an important and influential role in our lives.

The press

Over 400 million copies of thousands of *newspapers* are printed daily throughout the world. In addition, *magazines* cover almost every possible subject. Information has not always been so readily available

The first reporters

At first, news was circulated in the form of handwriting. Ancient Romans engraved information on wax tablets. The first printed sheets were made possible by the invention of the printing press in about 1450. The first daily newspaper, *The Daily Courant*, began publication in London in 1702. In the United States, the first newspaper, *Publick Occurrences Both Forreign and Domestick,* was published in 1690 by John Harris. This four-page newspaper was halted after one issue by the English government for being critical of government policies. Fourteen years later, a second newspaper, *The News-Letter*, appeared.

Advances in print technology during the 1800s made illustrated newspapers possible. This led to the growth of print *advertising*. Soon, newspapers and magazines became not only major business operations, but were also influential in causing political and social change.

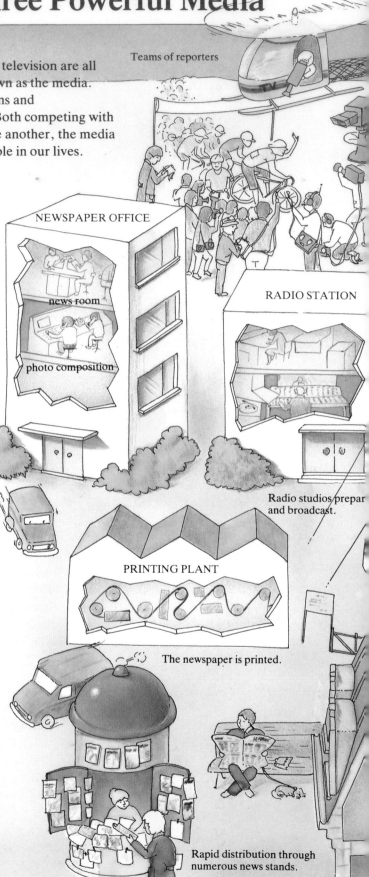

Teams of reporters

NEWSPAPER OFFICE

news room

photo composition

RADIO STATION

Radio studios prepar and broadcast.

PRINTING PLANT

The newspaper is printed.

Rapid distribution through numerous news stands.

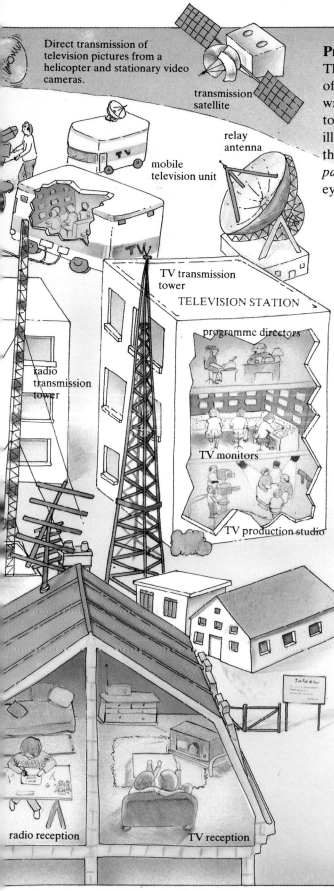

Direct transmission of television pictures from a helicopter and stationary video cameras.

transmission satellite

relay antenna

mobile television unit

TV transmission tower

TELEVISION STATION

programme directors

radio transmission tower

TV monitors

TV production studio

radio reception

TV reception

Preparing a newspaper

The newspaper is the product of a team of journalists and editors. Together they write and select articles, decide where to place them, and create headlines, illustrations and photographs. Much of their attention is focused on the *front page,* which will be the first to catch the eye of readers.

Radio broadcasting

Radio is a relatively recent invention. The first broadcasts were heard in the United States in the 1920s. Radio is the most accessible means of communication. A reporter or journalist can 'cover' an event where it happens and as it happens. This coverage is called a *news flash* or *bulletin.*

Television

Television provides sight, sound and movement. Its invention dates back to the 1920s but it did not come into use until after World War II. Television programmes are very expensive to produce. The *image,* however, seems to speak directly to the viewer in a very personal way. While radio can usually bring news of unexpected events faster, television is unequalled for live transmission of planned events, close or far away (sports competitions, the walk on the Moon, political debates, etc.). The camera sometimes transforms a televised event into recorded history. The televised assassination of President John F. Kennedy and the explosion of the space shuttle *Challenger* shocked and moved viewers who saw these events. Today, new techniques in broadcasting (satellites, cable television) pave the way for even better means of communication.

The World of Pictures

The language of pictures

All around us, pictures either *animated* (cinema, television) or *still* (photographs, cartoons, illustrations), tell stories, describe events and speak directly to our imaginations. This language is universal.

Talking and communicating through photographs

A photograph has various characteristics, depending upon its purpose.

A *family picture* or a *souvenir picture* has sentimental value to a few people and records a certain time in someone's life.

An *artistic picture*, taken to communicate a thought or feeling, uses light, colour, composition and perspective to achieve its purpose.

Newspaper photos illustrate printed text.

An *impact picture* captures our attention and forces us to think and read.

Comic strips: stories in pictures

Considered popular art, comic strips are a form of entertainment. They may be dramatic, humorous or satirical. Like the words of a text, successive pictures (text illustrations or small scenes) show action and build a story.

The story may be *silent,* where the picture by itself presents the meaning. It may be *spoken*, with some text, often a conversation, included along with the picture.

Comic strip text is written according to very specific rules.

'Balloons', which contain text, vary in their

placement and shape in order to produce different emotions – fear, excitement, love, sadness, anger, humour.

The way words are printed, their size and shape, indicate variations in voice – tone, hesitation, stuttering, yelling, whispering.

Colour also contributes to a better understanding of the comic strip by expressing moods such as happiness or fear.

Cartoon heroes

The cartoon hero is the main character in the story. He or she is meant to represent the reader's desires, ambitions or dreams and is often likeable – a model of honesty, courage and justice, such as Mighty Mouse, Superman or Wonder Woman.

Advertising pictures arouse interest and desire

These pictures are meant to grab our attention and strike our imagination. Their goal is to *sell* a product, service or idea. Advertisements use *aesthetic* means (settings, colours, space, attractive people), *technical effects* (props), and *psychological means* (types of motivation) in order to attract and keep our attention. They are designed to appeal to our dreams, our emotions and our needs. They are *'manipulated'* pictures, making us react without even thinking.

Advertising pictures are often enhanced by *slogans* or catchwords – short sentences that can be quickly understood and easily remembered.

The Cinema

Art from an invention

Motion pictures (films) were invented at the end of the nineteenth century. This invention, capable of capturing real-life images, was at first considered merely an amusement. However, films, like the theatre, have developed into an art form including many cultural masterpieces.

The 'wheel of life'
Bands of drawings were brought to life when viewed through the openings in a rotating cylinder. You can create this effect by flipping through a pile of cards with drawings on them.

The impossible became possible

Films were silent until 1927. The actors used exaggerated gestures and facial expressions to communicate their feelings. Written dialogue was projected on to the screen. An organist in the cinema provided background music.

Even without sound, films were exciting and a powerful means of communicating. Film-makers used every available means, including trick-lighting and special effects, artificial sets, unusual camera angles and editing to make the unreal seem real. Sound was first used in the film *The Jazz Singer* (1927). Later, as sound tracks improved and colour was used, film images became even more alive.

A social role

Finding sources of inspiration in all aspects of life, films entertain us, make us laugh, cry and dream, and increase our understanding of ourselves and of the world. Therefore, they have an important social function. Many of our heroes, fashions and phrases come from films.

Many fine novels and plays have been made into films. Among these were *Treasure Island* (1935) by Robert Louis Stevenson, *Gone With the Wind* (1939) by Margaret Mitchell and *The Wizard of Oz* (1939) by L. Frank Baum.

Here is a list of some popular films:

Title and year	Stars
King Kong (1932)	Fay Wray / Robert Armstrong
Gone With the Wind (1939)	Clark Gable / Vivien Leigh
An American in Paris (1951)	Gene Kelly / Leslie Caron
The Sound of Music (1965)	Julie Andrews / Christopher Plummer
The Godfather (1972)	Marlon Brando / Al Pacino
Jaws (1975)	Richard Dreyfuss / Roy Scheider
Star Wars (1977)	Mark Hamill / Carrie Fisher
E.T. (1982)	Henry Thomas

Shooting a scene in a studio

spotlights
boom operator
set assistant
actors
script girl

recording engineers
film editor

2

4

Pictures 1–4: sound and film editing

The director

The director is the creative head of the team that makes a film. He or she determines how to use actors, special effects, sets, sound, cameras and film editing to produce his or her interpretation of the script or story line. Some directors have achieved world fame: Frank Capra (United States), Steven Spielberg (United States), Alfred Hitchcock (Great Britain), Federico Fellini (Italy), Ingmar Bergman (Sweden), Jean Cocteau, François Truffaut (France).

Below is a list of some important directors and their films.

Film director	Movies	Leading actors
Frank Capra (1897–1991)	*Mr Smith Goes to Washington* (1939)	James Stewart
John Ford (1895–1973)	*The Grapes of Wrath* (1940)	Henry Fonda
		Jane Darwell
Alfred Hitchcock (1899–1980)	*Rear Window* (1954)	James Stewart
		Grace Kelly
John Huston (1906–1988)	*The African Queen* (1951)	Humphrey Bogart
		Katharine Hepburn
Steven Spielberg (1946–)	*Close Encounters of the Third Kind* (1977)	Richard Dreyfuss
Orson Welles (1915–1985)	*Citizen Kane* (1941)	Orson Welles

assistant cameraman

cameramen

film director

cinema

projection booth

screen

Awards and festivals

Beginning in 1927, the Academy of Motion Picture Arts and Sciences in Hollywood has presented annual awards, or 'Oscars', for the best picture, actor, actress, supporting actor and actress, producer, director, cinematographer, set designer, screenplay, costume designer and many other categories. There are awards from other organizations, but the Oscar is the most prestigious.

Film festivals are held in many parts of the world. New films are often premiered (first shown) at these festivals. Some festivals involve a theme such as the films of a particular director or actor. Perhaps the best known is the Cannes Film Festival in France, at which top films from all over the world are presented every year.

Animated films

Animated films are made using drawings or models. In both cases they are made by photographing still images. The drawing or model is changed a little before the next photograph is taken. When the photographs are shown quickly, one after the other, the image seems to move. Five seconds of an animated film, often called a *cartoon*, may need 60 different drawings or model movements. Making a cartoon is a very slow business, but computers can make it easier.

The Theatre

Origin

In ancient times, the Greeks enjoyed the theatre. Sitting on wooden or stone benches in the open air, spectators watched *comedies* and *tragedies* about legendary heroes. Actors wore elaborate masks and costumes so that they could be seen from high up at the back of the theatre.

The mystery plays of the Middle Ages

In the market place or in front of the cathedral, actors played out religious scenes based on the Old and New Testaments. These plays attracted large crowds, who participated actively along with the actors. In the days before most people could read, these plays were an important way of teaching the Bible stories.

The *Commedia dell'Arte*

This form of comedy started in the 16th century in Italy, where actors were also singers, musicians, dancers and acrobats.

Troupes played in castles for the nobles and in the street for others. They often played the same character in different plays, much like today's actors in film sequels. In these plays, much fun was made of human weaknesses. The actors used a bare outline of a plot and no script, making up the dialogue as they acted out the play.

A brilliant period

Writers from the European theatre produced plays of great artistic merit in the 17th century. This is called the *Classical period,* during which theatre became more sophisticated. Plays were often written in verse.

William Shakespeare (1564–1616) wrote some of the greatest plays of all time, which in his day were enjoyed by all classes of people. Many plays written since that time borrow some part of their plot from Shakespeare.

1

2

3

1   The theatre in ancient times: performance of a Greek tragedy.
2   The Middle Ages: a mystery play performed in front of a cathedral.
3   The 16th century: a clown in an Italian comedy.

4

5

6

4 The 17th century: theatre performance before a royal court.

5 The 19th century: Romantic theatre. Drama played in a formal theatre.

6 The 20th century: abstract stage of the modern theatre.

The Romantic theatre

This was the theatre of the 1800s. Playwrights gave up the rules of the classical theatre and showed human nature more realistically. The various types of drama were no longer separated. Tragedy and comedy were combined within a play to better illustrate all aspects of humans, their emotions and experiences. Prose became more commonly used than verse because it better represented real life. These changes in the theatre stirred emotional debates.

The 20th century

Theatre is still an important means of artistic expression. All sorts of subjects are used as topics for plays. Famous modern playwrights include Eugene O'Neill, Arthur Miller, Tennessee Williams, Bertolt Brecht, Samuel Beckett, Bernard Shaw and Harold Pinter. Richard Rodgers, Oscar Hammerstein II, Ira Gershwin and George Gershwin wrote some of the best-loved *musicals* of all time. Musicals are plays that include songs.

Some modern theatre involves direct contact between the audience and the actors, encouraging the audience's participation in the play. This sometimes also happens in older forms of theatre, such as pantomime.

A summary

- *Comedy* makes us laugh at amusing situations or characters.
- *Tragedy* describes the passions and the weaknesses of human beings and the unhappy, sometimes disastrous, consequences of those passions or weaknesses.
- *Tragicomedy* combines elements from both tragedy and comedy.
- *Drama* depicts violent actions or serious conflicts between people.
- *Melodrama* exaggerates emotions and conflicts in extreme and tries to stir our simplest emotions such as fear and love.
- *Pantomime* is a kind of theatre usually shown at Christmas. It tells a well-known story and may include magic tricks, special effects and songs.

Painting and Sculpture

The first artists

In prehistoric times, human beings expressed themselves by drawing and painting on the walls of caves.

About 3000 BC, the *Egyptians* decorated their tombs, temples and palaces with scenes of daily life. The *Greeks* and *Romans* became in turn sculptors and painters.

Painting and religion

For a very long time in Europe, painting, like music and theatre, expressed and encouraged *religious devotion*. Many medieval works – stained glass, sculpture, illuminated manuscripts – show this influence.

More expressive art

Slowly, under Italian influence, painting changed. Renaissance artists searched for a more human and more realistic way of painting. They studied *anatomy, perspective* and *proportion*. Religion was no longer the only source for their art. The artist was motivated by everything that excites, astonishes, or causes anxiety or enthusiasm. Landscapes, portraits, battles, still lives and scenes of daily life were now common and represented the artist's country, time and contemporaries.

Great changes

During the second half of the 1800s, artists called *Impressionists* painted directly from nature with an emphasis on movement, rich colours and intense light. That is why they painted with small touches of colour. Claude Monet, Auguste Renoir and Georges Seurat were Impressionists.

In the 1900s *Cubist* painters, such as Picasso, went further away from reality by using geometric shapes. Thereafter, some painting became *abstract*.

Today, painters sometimes avoid traditional materials or combine them with other objects.

Expression in three dimensions: sculpture

The first sculptures were made 35,000 years ago. For quite some time it remained a religious art. During the Renaissance, sculpture became *secular* (non-religious), stressing the beauty of the human body. Since the late 1800s, sculptors have been using materials ranging from steel and aluminium to glass and fluorescent lights.

FAMOUS ARTISTS AND SCULPTORS

	France and Belgium	Germany and Switzerland	Italy	Spain	Netherlands	England	United States
1400s	Froment, Le Maître de Moulins		Fra Angelico, Botticelli, Della Francesca, Donatello (sculptor)		Van Eyck brothers, Bosch		
1500s	Clouet	Dürer, Gruenwald, Holbein, Cranach	Da Vinci, Michelangelo, Raphael, Titian, Cellini (sculptor)		Brueghel		
1600s	Poussin, Le Lorrain		Caravaggio, Bernini (sculptor)	El Greco, Velázquez	Rembrandt, Hals, Vermeer, Rubens		
1700s	Watteau, Fragonard, Moudon (sculptor)	Fuseli	Canaletto, Guardi, Longhi, Tiepolo	Goya		Hogarth, Reynolds, Gainsborough	Copely, Stuart
1800s	David, Ingres, Delacroix, Daumier, Courbet, Manet, Monet, Degas, Cézanne, Gauguin, Toulouse-Lautrec, Rodin (sculptor)	Friedrich, Liebermann, Bocklin			Van Gogh	Turner, Constable	Homer, Trumbull, Harnett, Greenough (sculptor) French (sculptor)
1900s	Braque, Matisse, Chagall, Maillol (sculptor)	Ernst, Grosz, Klee	Modigliani, De Chirico, Giacometti (sculptor)	Picasso, Dali, Miró	Mondrian	Bacon, Hockney, Moore (sculptor), Hepworth (sculptor)	Sargent, Bellow, Pollock, De Kooning, Wyeth, Rothko, Warhol, Calder (sculptor)

Music and Dance

Magical power

Primitive people believed that music had power to cure diseases, cause the rain to fall, or calm the anger of the gods. Many legends are told about the good effects of music on humans, animals and nature.

Today almost everyone enjoys the music that is all around us in various forms – modern, classical, folk, jazz and rock.

An ancient Greek musician plays the lyre.

Always changing

A troubadour plays the lute.

From ancient times to the present day, music has never stopped developing. At first it was mainly religious, but in the Middle Ages *troubadours* (travelling poets) began singing about love and nature. Later, music was used for entertainment and dancing.

Great composers like Bach, Mozart, Beethoven and Chopin expressed in music many emotions, such as happiness, patriotism and hope.

Today, music is often composed on *computers* and played on *synthesizers*, which can reproduce the sounds of all instruments.

Chopin

Bach

Mozart

Beethoven

Necessary instruments

A modern symphony orchestra uses about 100 instruments, half of them *stringed instruments* (violins, violas, cellos and double basses). There are also *woodwinds* (clarinets, oboes, flutes and bassoons), *brass instruments* (trumpets, French horns, trombones, tubas), and *percussion instruments* (drums and cymbals). To learn the special sounds of these instruments, listen to Prokofiev's musical fairy tale, *Peter and the Wolf*, where a cat is represented by a clarinet, a bird by a flute, Peter by a string quartet, and the wolf by horns.

A modern rock band is usually made up of electric guitars, a synthesizer and drums, but may include other instruments.

1 Double bass   2 Drums   3 Harp   4 Bassoon
5 Recorder   6 Harmonica   7 Trumpet

Body language

Even before music existed, human beings used dancing to express their emotions. Every civilization has used dance to celebrate great events such as birth and death. Like music, dancing was at first a religious expression, and this is still true for many peoples around the world.

African dance

From folk dancing to ballroom

Dancing is also used for entertainment and fun. In Europe and America, ballroom dances include the *tango, waltz* and *foxtrot*. Folk dances include the *morris dances* of England, the *flamenco* of Spain, the *square dances* of rural America, and the *polkas* of eastern Europe. People also dance to rock bands and to jazz, which is a special form of music with its roots in African music.

Flamenco

American square dancing

Ballet

In 1661, King Louis XIV of France founded the Royal Academy of Dance to train dancers according to precise rules. From that time, dancing became a theatrical performance called *ballet*, in which stories are told by dance movements.

In the 1900s, ballet began to change. Today, although stories are still told through dance, the movements are more realistic and communicate more directly with the audience. Modern ballet does not follow the rules of classical ballet or use the classical costumes. Sometimes modern ballets do not tell a story but express strong emotions or ideas.

Classical ballet

Modern ballet

The History of Mathematics

Necessary to the social and economic life of human beings, mathematics remained purely an applied subject for a long time (a means of counting goods or of measuring length and volumes) before it became a science and achieved extraordinary theoretical development.

These primitive sticks with notches were delivered by a messenger who, upon his arrival, read aloud the number of objects or persons written on the stick.

The oldest evidence for counting

This was a bone found in Czechoslovakia and dates from about 30,000 BC! The bone is engraved with 55 lines in two sequences.

The difference between *one* and *several*

This difference is the basis of the number system. Early human beings established this difference by observing the world around them. The ancient Hindus, for example, considered the Moon and the Earth the number *one*; the wings of a bird, *two*; the leaves of a clover, *three*; the legs of a dog, *four*; and the fingers of a hand, *five*. Ultimately, the use of *ten* fingers, to which were sometimes added *ten* toes, became the most frequently used system of counting.

Mesopotamia

In 2500 BC, Babylon was a great cultural centre. Many clay tablets have been found that show the mathematical knowledge of that time. These tablets are marked with a series of numbers, with statements of

On this Babylonian clay tablet, a scribe has practised writing the sign for *one*.

problems and their solutions, and with calculations of surface areas, volumes and algebraic calculations.

India

Mathematics in India was characterized by the development of numerical and algebraic calculations. Our decimal system, with symbols for the numerals 1 to 9, was developed in India and brought to Europe by the Arabs.

Arabia

Greek and Indian discoveries in mathematics were preserved and improved by the Arabs, from whom we obtained this ancient knowledge. The Arabs were especially clever in perfecting new methods of calculation.

Egypt

A papyrus (the papyrus of Rhind) written by a scribe in 1650 BC shows that the Egyptians

This Egyptian leather roll has mathematical inscriptions.

had a good knowledge of mathematics, which they used in their daily life for agriculture, land measurements, accounting and architecture (the pyramids).

Greece

The Greeks took advantage of Babylonian and Egyptian contributions and turned mathematics into a real *science* – an activity where research is done for its own sake. Besides finding better methods of calculation, Greek mathematicians also stated, defined and demonstrated important mathematical *laws* and *principles*. These included the theory of numbers, the theory of proportions, the calculation of areas and surfaces, and geometry and algebra. *Thales of Miletus, Pythagoras* and later *Archimedes* were responsible for these important developments.

Pythagoras   Archimedes

The Far East

The Chinese and Japanese developed their own number systems. The *bead abacus*, still

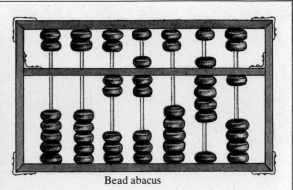

Bead abacus

used today, helps to perform many kinds of mathematical calculations.

America

The *Incas* of Peru had their own number system. Knots of *quipu* (cord) represented values in a decimal system. The *Maya* in Guatemala used the calendar and employed

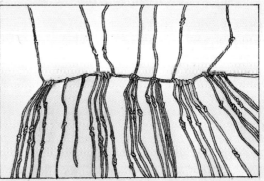

Knots of *quipu*

the zero (a symbol for nought) in their number system.

Rome

The Romans had their own way of writing numbers, but it made calculations rather difficult.

Europe

After the barbarian invasions of Europe that began about AD 400, the science of mathematics was not taken up again until the Middle Ages. The Renaissance was an important time for the development of algebra, trigonometry and geometry.

Later on, developments in mathematics increased and knowledge spread rapidly. Today no one can be an expert in all fields.

Early Methods of Counting

We have seen that learning how to count was the first mathematical problem to occupy the attention of human beings. Through time and various civilizations, different systems of numeration (of counting and numbering) were invented and developed.

Primitive human beings

They used *oral numeration*. For example, the ancient Sumerians used the words:

man for 1
woman for 2
several for 3.

The Mesopotamians

Written signs were carved into a wet clay tablet that was later baked.

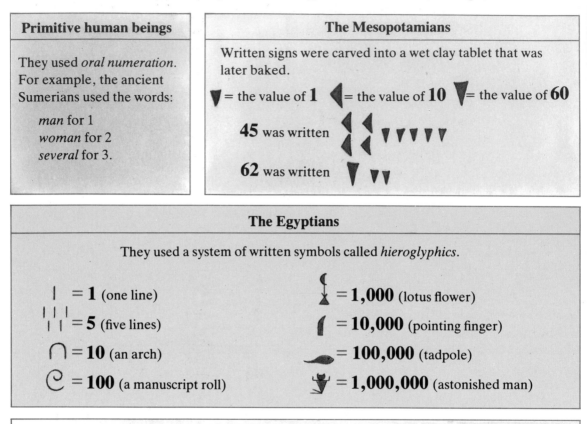

▼ = the value of **1**   ◀ = the value of **10**   ▼ = the value of **60**

45 was written

62 was written

The Egyptians

They used a system of written symbols called *hieroglyphics*.

| = **1** (one line)

||| || = **5** (five lines)

∩ = **10** (an arch)

℃ = **100** (a manuscript roll)

= **1,000** (lotus flower)

= **10,000** (pointing finger)

= **100,000** (tadpole)

= **1,000,000** (astonished man)

The Greeks

They used two principal systems: the *Attic* and the *Herodianic* systems. These were used often in Athenian inscriptions. Later, in the 5th century BC, they also used the *Ionic* or *alphabetical* system.

Attic numerals

| = 1

|| = 2

||| = 3

|||| = 4

Γ = 5

△ = 10

Η = 100

╳ = 1,000

Μ = 10,000

Ionic numeral system

Units

A α 1	B β 2	Γ γ 3	Δ δ 4	E ε 5	Ϛ δ 6	Z ζ 7	H η 8	Θ θ 9

Tens

I ι 10	K κ 20	Λ λ 30	M μ 40	N ν 50	Ξ ξ 60	O ο 70	Π π 80	Ϛ ς 90

Hundreds

P ρ 100	Σ σ 200	T τ 300	Y υ 400	Φ φ 500	X χ 600	Ψ ψ 700	Ω ω 800	↗ 900

The Romans

They used a numcration system where numbers were repeated and added together to make larger numbers.

I = 1   II = 2   III = 3   IV = 4   A sign placed to the left of a higher sign is subtracted from it.

V = 5   VI = 6   X = 10   L = 50

C = 100   D = 500   M = 1,000 $\overline{V}$ = 5,000   One line above a letter indicates thousands.

$\overline{\overline{V}}$ = 5,000,000   Two lines above a letter indicate millions.

The Maya

They used a numeration system with a base of 20 and with vertical writing.

• = 1   — = 5   = = 10   ⋮̇̇ = 13

The Chinese

They used a base 10 multiplication system.

= 1	= 2	= 3	= 4	= 5	= 6	= 7	= 8	= 9	= 10

= 100	= 1,000	= 10,000	= 100,000	= 1,000,000	= 10,000,000
(10^2)	(10^3)	(10^4)	(10^5)	(10^6)	(10^7)

A few comparisons

	Mesopotamia	Egypt	Greece	Rome	Maya	China
1	▼	I	α'	I	•	一
5	▼ ▼ ▼ ▼ ▼	ꞌ ꞌ ꞌ	$\mathcal{E}'$	V	—	五
10	◀	∩	L'	X	=	十
15	◀▼▼▼▼▼	∩ ꞌꞌꞌ	$L\mathcal{E}'$	XV	≡	十五
18	◀ ▼▼▼▼▼	∩ ‖‖‖	$\iota\eta'$	XVIII	⋮̇̇̇̇	十八
100	▼◀◀◀◀	℃	ρ'	C	⋯̇	百

In fact, numeration systems fall into two main groups:

A system using combinations of symbols
This system is not very practical because many signs had to be used to write larger numbers (Mesopotamian and Egyptian systems).

A system using position
It is the position of the number that determines its value. (An example is our decimal system.)

Modern Methods of Counting

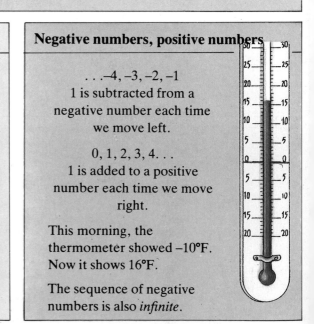

Muslim scholars from the Arab world brought the decimal number system to the Western world. Slowly, it replaced the former Roman number system. The decimal numerals (1–9) were first used to count beads on the abacus (calculation table).

There are two kinds of abacus: the bead abacus and one with three rods. Both can be used to carry out arithmetical calculations.

Numeral, digit and number

A numeral is a symbol for a number. XVI is a Roman numeral; 16 is a decimal numeral; both are symbols for the number sixteen.

A digit is one of the symbols 0, 1, 2, 3, 4, 5, 6, 7, 8 and 9 in the decimal system.

Base 10

$9+1=10$ $99+1=100$ $999+1=1,000$

This base of numeration allows us to represent any number by using only ten digits:

$$0 \quad 1 \quad 2 \quad 3 \quad 4 \quad 5 \quad 6 \quad 7 \quad 8 \quad 9$$

According to its *position* from right to left, each digit corresponds to a specific unit ten times greater than the one before it.

3	**2**	**5**	**4**	**8**
tens of thousands	thousands	hundreds	tens	units

Whole numbers (or integers)

125 pages, 12 eggs, 3,585 inhabitants: 125, 12, 3,585 are natural whole numbers.

These numbers that we commonly use for counting form an *infinite sequence*:

0,1,2,3. . .15. . .170. . .4,624. . .

because it is always possible to add 1 to any number to get the next one in the sequence.

Negative numbers, positive numbers

. . .–4, –3, –2, –1
1 is subtracted from a negative number each time we move left.

0, 1, 2, 3, 4. . .
1 is added to a positive number each time we move right.

This morning, the thermometer showed –10°F. Now it shows 16°F.

The sequence of negative numbers is also *infinite*.

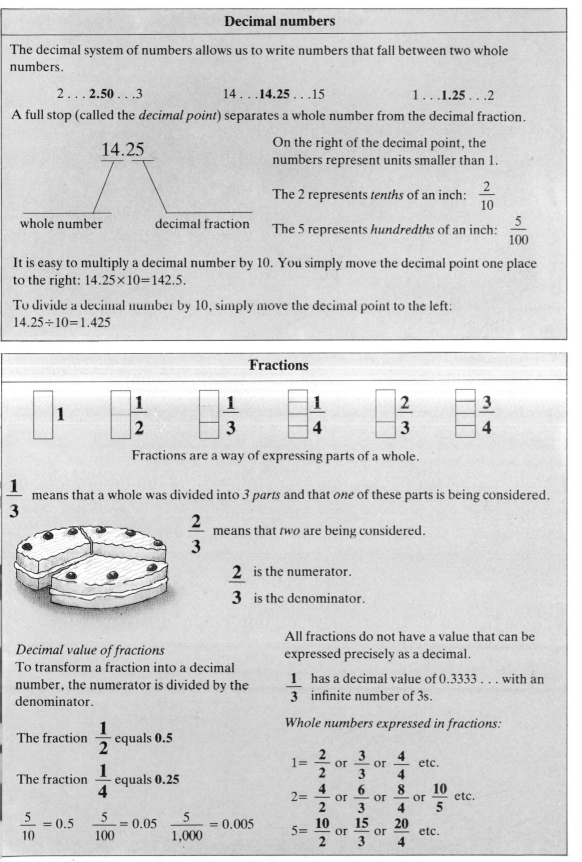

Decimal numbers

The decimal system of numbers allows us to write numbers that fall between two whole numbers.

    2 . . . **2.50** . . .3   14 . . .**14.25** . . .15   1 . . .**1.25** . . .2

A full stop (called the *decimal point*) separates a whole number from the decimal fraction.

14.25

whole number   decimal fraction

On the right of the decimal point, the numbers represent units smaller than 1.

The 2 represents *tenths* of an inch: $\dfrac{2}{10}$

The 5 represents *hundredths* of an inch: $\dfrac{5}{100}$

It is easy to multiply a decimal number by 10. You simply move the decimal point one place to the right: $14.25 \times 10 = 142.5$.

To divide a decimal number by 10, simply move the decimal point to the left: $14.25 \div 10 = 1.425$

Fractions

1      $\dfrac{1}{2}$ $\dfrac{1}{3}$ $\dfrac{1}{4}$ $\dfrac{2}{3}$ $\dfrac{3}{4}$

Fractions are a way of expressing parts of a whole.

$\dfrac{1}{3}$ means that a whole was divided into *3 parts* and that *one* of these parts is being considered.

$\dfrac{2}{3}$ means that *two* are being considered.

2 is the numerator.

3 is the denominator.

Decimal value of fractions
To transform a fraction into a decimal number, the numerator is divided by the denominator.

The fraction $\dfrac{1}{2}$ equals **0.5**

The fraction $\dfrac{1}{4}$ equals **0.25**

$\dfrac{5}{10} = 0.5$ $\dfrac{5}{100} = 0.05$ $\dfrac{5}{1,000} = 0.005$

All fractions do not have a value that can be expressed precisely as a decimal.

$\dfrac{1}{3}$ has a decimal value of 0.3333 . . . with an infinite number of 3s.

Whole numbers expressed in fractions:

$1 = \dfrac{2}{2}$ or $\dfrac{3}{3}$ or $\dfrac{4}{4}$ etc.

$2 = \dfrac{4}{2}$ or $\dfrac{6}{3}$ or $\dfrac{8}{4}$ or $\dfrac{10}{5}$ etc.

$5 = \dfrac{10}{2}$ or $\dfrac{15}{3}$ or $\dfrac{20}{4}$ etc.

Other Counting Bases

We usually count with a base of 10. The Babylonians counted mainly with a base of 60, a base which we use today to measure time. The Maya counted with a base of 20. It is possible to use any whole number starting with 2 as a base.

Base 2

To write a number in base 2, only two digits are used: **0** and **1**. This is the *binary system*. It is used for computers.

Thus, 7 (base 10) is written **111** (*read one, one, one*) in base 2.

One way to write the number in base 2 is to form possible groups of 2 and powers of 2, that is, of 2, 4, 8, 16 and so on.

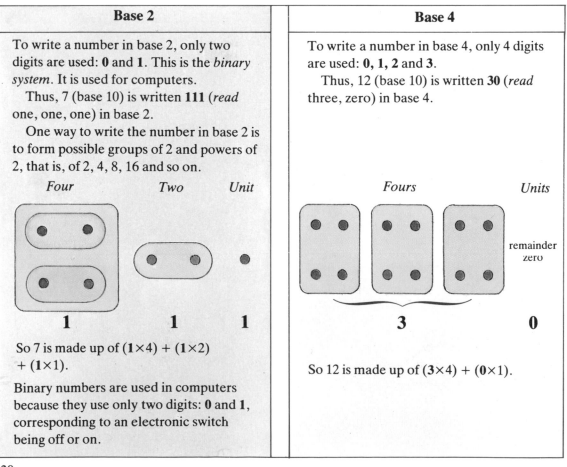

Four *Two* *Unit*

1 **1** **1**

So 7 is made up of $(1 \times 4) + (1 \times 2) + (1 \times 1)$.

Binary numbers are used in computers because they use only two digits: **0** and **1**, corresponding to an electronic switch being off or on.

Base 4

To write a number in base 4, only 4 digits are used: **0, 1, 2** and **3**.

Thus, 12 (base 10) is written **30** (*read three, zero*) in base 4.

Fours *Units*

remainder zero

3 **0**

So 12 is made up of $(3 \times 4) + (0 \times 1)$.

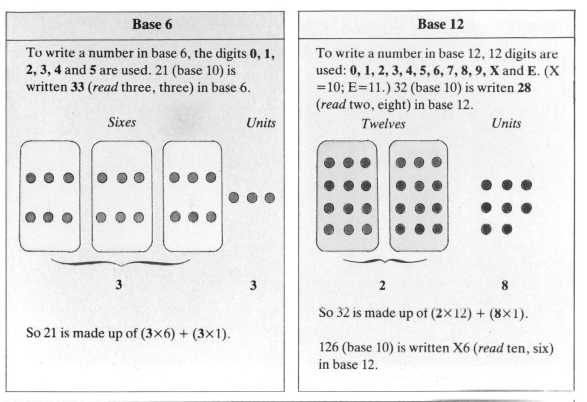

Base 6

To write a number in base 6, the digits **0, 1, 2, 3, 4** and **5** are used. 21 (base 10) is written **33** (*read* three, three) in base 6.

Sixes   *Units*

3   **3**

So 21 is made up of $(3 \times 6) + (3 \times 1)$.

Base 12

To write a number in base 12, 12 digits are used: **0, 1, 2, 3, 4, 5, 6, 7, 8, 9, X** and **E**. (X =10; E=11.) 32 (base 10) is written **28** (*read* two, eight) in base 12.

Twelves   *Units*

2   **8**

So 32 is made up of $(2 \times 12) + (8 \times 1)$.

126 (base 10) is written X6 (*read* ten, six) in base 12.

To change back to base 10

Write the values of each column for the base the number is in.

Value of each column   **Base 2:** 2^3 2^2 2^1 1

$$= 8 \quad 4 \quad 2 \quad 1$$

101 (base 2)→   **1**   **0**   **1** $= (1 \times 4) + (0 \times 2) + (1 \times 1) = 5$ (base 10)

Value of each column   **Base 4:** 4^3 4^2 4^1 1

$$= 64 \quad 16 \quad 4 \quad 1$$

131 (base 4)→   **1**   **3**   **1** $= (1 \times 16) + (3 \times 4) + (1 \times 1)$
$= 16 + 12 + 1 = \mathbf{29}$ (base 10)

From one base to another

Base 10	0	1	2	3	4	5	10	20	50	60
Base 2	0	1	10	11	100	101	1,010	10,100	110,010	111,100
Base 4	0	1	2	3	10	11	22	110	302	330
Base 6	0	1	2	3	4	5	14	32	122	140
Base 12	0	1	2	3	4	5	10	18	42	50
Base 60	0	1	2	3	4	5	10	20	50	10

Computers

What is a computer?

It is an electronic device that stores instructions (words, numbers, drawings, music) for processing data (information) and then follows these instructions at high speed when requested.

A computer is not intelligent. It processes data only according to the instructions it is given.

The first modern computers, built around 1950, were very large, took up a great deal of space, and were very expensive. Today, computers are small in size, relatively inexpensive, and a thousand times faster. PCs (personal computers) are becoming common in schools, workplaces and homes.

A very helpful machine

With the help of computers, great technical progress has become possible in various fields.

Now, we can use a computer to:

- control the flight of a rocket or a plane or the movement of a train
- operate a robot
- diagnose and treat patients
- produce pictures
- compose music
- teach.

Computers can also be used to create and operate military weapons.

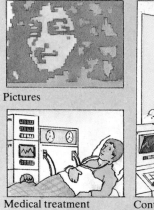

Pictures

Medical treatment   Controls

How do they work?

All computers do four things: *input, store information* in a memory, *process* and *output*.

During *input*, data is entered into the computer. It is then stored in a *memory*. The data is then *processed* according to instructions in the *central processing unit*, the brain of the machine. During *output*, processed data, or information that results from the computer's calculations, is displayed on a screen and can be printed.

Communication between the different elements is done by *electric currents*.

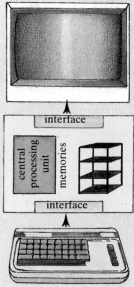

monitor

interface

central processing unit

memories

interface

keyboard

The conductor

This is a tiny *microprocessor* or *microchip* within the computer that handles the flow of data and is capable of processing several million operations per second.

microprocessor

It is the development of the *microchip* that has enabled smaller and smaller computers to be built.

Main unit and other devices

It is possible to connect the main unit with devices other than the keyboard and the screen.

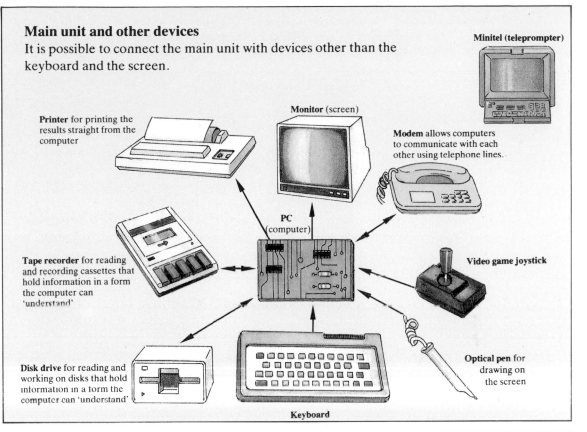

Minitel (teleprompter)

Printer for printing the results straight from the computer

Monitor (screen)

Modem allows computers to communicate with each other using telephone lines.

PC (computer)

Tape recorder for reading and recording cassettes that hold information in a form the computer can 'understand'

Video game joystick

Disk drive for reading and working on disks that hold information in a form the computer can 'understand'

Optical pen for drawing on the screen

Keyboard

Computer language

The computer does not understand human language and uses only a machine language – electrical impulses flowing through the different circuits. This language is coded by means of two digits, **0** and **1**.

    0   the current docs not pass.
    1   the current passes.

This is called a *binary code*. All information received is translated into this language.

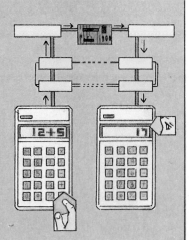

Computer programming

This means to give a list of instructions to the computer for processing.

    Various *computer language programs* have been invented. With the help of a *compiler*, a kind of interpreter, the program translates words of complex languages into binary numbers 0 and 1.

    To understand a computer language program, one has to learn its words and grammar.

    The most frequently used language is BASIC. The easiest to learn is LOGO.

    Other computer languages are:

        FORTRAN
        ALGOL
        APL
        PASCAL
        ASSEMBLY
        FORTH.

Writing Large Numbers

Texas has a surface area of about 267,000 square miles.
The Sun is about 93,000,000 miles away from the Earth.
The Earth will soon number 6,000,000,000 inhabitants.

Thousands, millions, billions

It is easy to read whole numbers of 4, 5 or 6 digits (**2,965**; **34,254**; **987,672**), but that is not the case for larger numbers.

The reading and writing of these large numbers follows certain rules.

The number **597643275** written like this is difficult to read.

It is much easier to read when written like this: **597,643,275**.

Starting from the right, the number is divided by commas into segments that consist of three digits and indicate units, thousands and millions.

597643275 reads: **597** million, **643** thousand, **275**.

In Europe a *billion* is a million million but in the United States it means only a thousand million. This can be confusing.

How are these large numbers read?

128 534 217 000   24 609 240 000 000   398 215 132 024 013

Answers

In the US:
128,534 billion, 534 million, 217 thousand
24,609 billion, 240 million
398,215 billion, 132 thousand, 24 thousand, and 13

In Europe:
128,534 million, 217 thousand
24 billion, 609,240 million
398 billion, 215,312 million, 24 thousand, and 13

Eliminating zeros

To make calculations easier, mathematicians do not write:

1,000 but 10^3 (which reads *ten to the power three*), that is
$$10 \times 10 \times 10, \text{ or 1 thousand.}$$

1,000,000 but 10^6 (which reads *ten to the power six*), that is
$$10 \times 10 \times 10 \times 10 \times 10 \times 10, \text{ namely 1 million.}$$

1,000,000,000,000 but 10^{12} (which reads *ten to the power twelve*), that is
$$10 \times 10 \times 10 \times 10 \times 10 \times 10 \times 10 \times 10 \times 10 \times 10 \times 10 \times 10, \text{ namely 1 billion.}$$

3, 6 and **12** in the numbers above are *exponents*. They indicate the number of zeros that must be written after the 1.

Going back to the examples at the top of the page, we can write:

Texas has (267×10^3) square miles of surface area.
The Sun is at a distance of (93×10^6) miles from the Earth.
The Earth will soon number (6×10^9) inhabitants.

The advantage of exponents

When multiplying a number several times by itself, exponents can be used.

Instead of writing $4 \times 4 \times 4 \times 4 \times 4$, we write 4^5
$$2^4 = 2 \times 2 \times 2 \times 2$$

To write large numbers with the help of exponents

$$4,585,278,000 = 4,000,000,000 + 585,000,000 + 278,000$$

$$= 4 \times 10^9 + 585 \times 10^6 + 278 \times 10^3$$

Thus $4,585,278,000$ can be written:

$$(4 \times 10^9) + (585 \times 10^6) + (278 \times 10^3)$$

What number is this?

$$(275 \times 10^9) + (834 \times 10^6) + (173 \times 10^3)$$

Answer

275,834,173,000

The Romans and large numbers

To write large numbers, the Romans introduced the symbols ‾ and ☐ which have the values of 1,000 and 100,000 respectively.

So:

$$\overline{VII} = 7,000 \quad \boxed{III} = 300,000 \quad \overline{L} = 50,000 \quad \boxed{XV} = 1,500,000$$

What are these numbers?					In Roman writing, how did one write?				
C	IV	CX	X	LV	6,000	900,000	12,000	10,010	511,000

Answers

$\overline{VI} = 6,000$ $\boxed{IX} = 900,000$ $\overline{XII} = 12,000$ $\overline{X}X = 10,010$ $\boxed{V}\overline{XI} = 511,000$
$\overline{C} = 100,000$ $IV = 4$ $\overline{CX} = 110,000$ $\boxed{X} = 1,000,000$ $\boxed{LV} = 5,500,000$

Game

Which is the largest number that one can write with 3 digits?

Answer

It is a number composed of three 9s written as follows: $9(9^9)$, which means 9×9^9.
This number includes 369,693,101 *digits!* The first 7 are
9,431,549 . . . the last digit is 9.

From Coins to Credit Cards

Money

The *pound sterling* (£) is the basic unit of currency in the United Kingdom. It has a value of 100 pence (100p). Bank notes and coins together are called *legal tender*. Paying with notes and coins is called *paying cash*.

Coins in circulation:
1p 2p 5p 10p 20p 50p £1

Bank notes:
£50 £20 £10 £5

Paying with a cheque

To pay large amounts, cheques are commonly used.

Cheque books are issued to people who open a *bank* or *building society account*, called a current account, and deposit money in the bank.

On the cheque, the amount to be paid is written in numbers and words, and the word *Pay* is followed by the name of the person or company to whom the cheque is written. The cheque is dated and signed by the owner of the current account.

Postal orders can be bought in post offices and used, like cheques, instead of cash.

Cheque book

Postal order

Credit cards

Credit cards have become popular all over the world. They are used instead of cash or cheques to pay for many goods or

services. A bill is sent monthly to the owner of the card.

There are many issuers of credit cards: Visa, MasterCard, American Express,

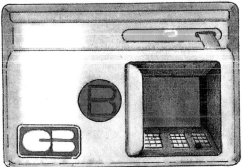

department stores and petrol companies are the most common ones.

A *cashpoint card* can be used to *withdraw* or *deposit money* at cashpoint machines.

Cheque cards

A cheque card guarantees that a cheque you write will be paid by your bank up to a certain value (usually £50 or £100). The number of the cheque card must be written on the back of the cheque.

Foreign currencies

People know by experience what their currency is worth in their own country. They can go to a shop, for example, and find out how much bread they can buy with £1.

But when they want to travel abroad, they have to use their own currency to buy the currency of another country. How much of a foreign currency can be bought with £1 is determined by the *rate of exchange*.

The rate of exchange can change very often. This is not too much of a problem for someone going on holiday, but for companies selling and buying goods from another country, it can cause huge difficulties.

The European Monetary System tries to make sure that the rate of exchange between EC countries does not vary much.

ECU (European Currency Unit)

The European Monetary System came into effect on 13 March 1979. The value of the currency (the ECU) is calculated from a 'basket' of the currencies of the members of the European Community. The currency is not at the moment used as cash but is a way of referring to amounts of money within Europe.

Measuring Lengths

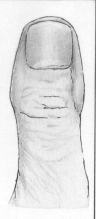
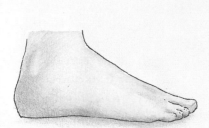
Units of measurement

The units of measurement described above were used for hundreds of years but they were not very easy to use for calculations.

12 **inches** (in) = 1 **foot** (ft)
3 **feet** = 1 **yard** (yd)
1,760 **yards** = 1 **mile**

A distance of 1ft 6in was often written 1′ 6″.

Today, metric measurements, which are widely used in Europe, are common in the United Kingdom. They are much easier to use because they are based on a decimal system (a system of tens).

10 **millimetres** (mm) = 1 **centimetre** (cm)
100 **centimetres** = 1 **metre** (m)
1,000 **metres** = 1 **kilometre** (km)

All of these metric units of measurement are now in common use except for kilometres. Although the length of races is now usually described in kilometres, signposts and road markings still use miles. Eventually, though, it is likely that these too will be brought into line with other European countries.

Using units of measurement

It is important to use the best unit of measurement for the length that you want to measure. If you wanted to say how far it was from London to New York, for example, you *could* use millimetres, but you would end up with an enormous number. It would be far better to use kilometres or miles for this measurement.

Which units would you use to measure the following?

1 A length of material to make a shirt
2 The height jumped by an Olympic high-jumper
3 The length of a football pitch
4 The length of an exercise book
5 The thickness of a piece of glass
6 The distance between Edinburgh and Dublin

Answers
1 metres
2 metres
3 metres
4 centimetres
5 millimetres
6 kilometres

Expressing measurements

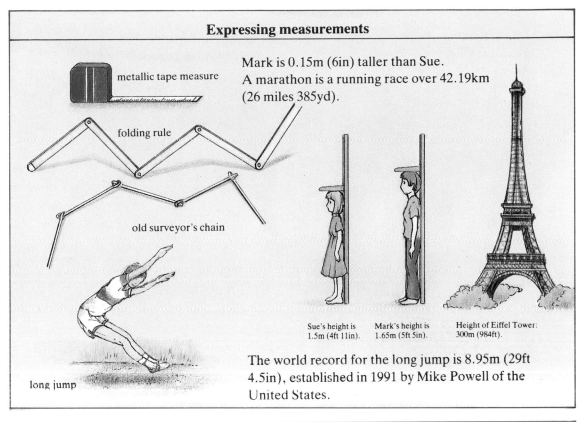

metallic tape measure

folding rule

old surveyor's chain

long jump

Mark is 0.15m (6in) taller than Sue.
A marathon is a running race over 42.19km (26 miles 385yd).

Sue's height is 1.5m (4ft 11in).

Mark's height is 1.65m (5ft 5in).

Height of Eiffel Tower: 300m (984ft).

The world record for the long jump is 8.95m (29ft 4.5in), established in 1991 by Mike Powell of the United States.

Converting units of measurement

To convert **in** to **mm**, multiply by 25.4

To convert **in** to **cm**, multiply by 2.54

To convert **ft** to **m**, multiply by 0.3048

To convert **yd** to **m**, multiply by 0.9144

To convert **miles** to **km**, multiply by 1.609

Rough conversions

When you don't need to be so accurate, it is worth remembering that:

1m is about 3in (7.5cm) longer than 1 yd.

2.5cm are about the same as 1in.

5 miles are about the same as 8km.

Measuring Masses

Because of the Earth's attraction, each body presses upon whatever supports it from below. This pressure is the *weight* of the body.

This weight varies according to the location of the body. When the body is located at a *higher* elevation, the attraction of the Earth *decreases* and the body weighs *less*.

On the other hand, the *mass* of a body does not change according to its location. Mass depends upon the quantity and the nature of materials that form the body, and thus the mass of a body is *constant*. Nevertheless, the distinction between mass and weight is not usually made for everyday measurements.

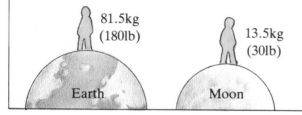

81.5kg (180lb)

13.5kg (30lb)

Earth

Moon

The Moon attracts bodies less than the Earth (one-sixth as much). An astronaut weights only 13.5kg (30lb) on the Moon although his mass has not changed.

Units of measurement for weights

Again, both metric and imperial weights are used.

16 **ounces** (oz) = 1 **pound** (lb)
14 **pounds** = 1 **stone** (st)
160 **stones** = 1 **ton**

1,000 **grams** (g) = 1 **kilogram** (kg)
1,000 **kilograms** = 1 **tonne**

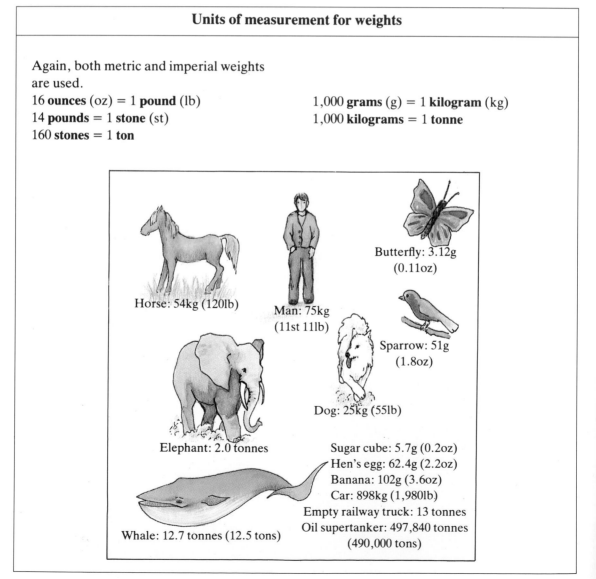

Horse: 54kg (120lb)

Man: 75kg (11st 11lb)

Butterfly: 3.12g (0.11oz)

Sparrow: 51g (1.8oz)

Dog: 25kg (55lb)

Elephant: 2.0 tonnes

Sugar cube: 5.7g (0.2oz)
Hen's egg: 62.4g (2.2oz)
Banana: 102g (3.6oz)
Car: 898kg (1,980lb)
Empty railway truck: 13 tonnes
Oil supertanker: 497,840 tonnes (490,000 tons)

Whale: 12.7 tonnes (12.5 tons)

American units of measurement

On the whole, the United States uses imperial units and has not yet moved over to metric measurement, but beware of units that sound like British imperial units but are slightly different.

1 **ton** (US) = 2,000lb
1 **ton** (UK) = 2,240lb

Large masses

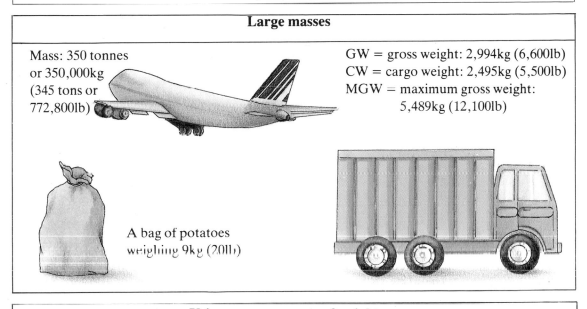

Mass: 350 tonnes or 350,000kg (345 tons or 772,800lb)

GW = gross weight: 2,994kg (6,600lb)
CW = cargo weight: 2,495kg (5,500lb)
MGW = maximum gross weight: 5,489kg (12,100lb)

A bag of potatoes weighing 9kg (20lb)

Using measurements of weight

If you look at packets of food, you will find that some of them give the weight in imperial *and* metric units. When food started to be labelled with metric weights, manufacturers had to decide whether to sell the same size packets or change to a size that came to a round figure in metric weights. By looking at the weights on the packets, you will soon see which has happened.

In the United States, weights of people are given in pounds, rather than stones and pounds. It is easy to convert from stones and pounds to pounds. You simply multiply the stones by 14 and add on any extra pounds.

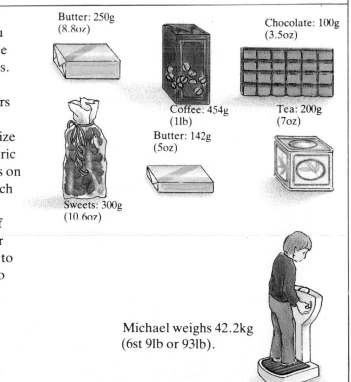

Butter: 250g (8.8oz)

Chocolate: 100g (3.5oz)

Coffee: 454g (1lb)

Tea: 200g (7oz)

Butter: 142g (5oz)

Sweets: 300g (10.6oz)

Michael weighs 42.2kg (6st 9lb or 93lb).

Units of Volume (Liquids)

Units of measurement of liquids

Although we still talk about pints of milk and gallons of petrol, which are imperial units, metric units are now being used much more widely.

20 **fluid ounces** (fl oz) = 1 **pint** (pt)
8 **pints** = 1 **gallon**

10 **millilitres** (ml) = 1 **centilitre** (cl)
100 **centilitres** = 1 **litre** (l)

The most common liquid units of measurement are millilitres and litres. Centilitres are not used very often.

Converting units of liquid measurement

To convert **pints** to **litres**, multiply by 0.5683
To convert **gallons** to **litres**, multiply by 4.546

For a quick, rough conversion from **pints** to **litres,** multiply by 3 and divide by 4.

For very large quantities

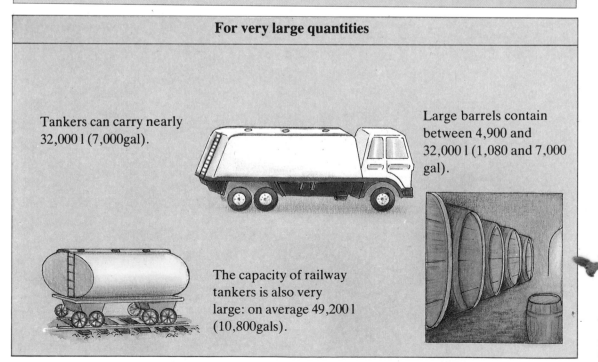

Tankers can carry nearly 32,000 l (7,000gal).

Large barrels contain between 4,900 and 32,000 l (1,080 and 7,000 gal).

The capacity of railway tankers is also very large: on average 49,200 l (10,800gals).

All kinds of containers

For small quantities

75ml
glass

5ml
vial

30ml (1fl oz)

10ml

60ml

small bottles

150ml

250ml

500ml

bottles

1 l (1.76pt)
mineral water
bottle

500ml
(0.88pt)
milk carton

5 l
(1.1gal)
oil can

70cl
(1.2pt)
wine bottle

For larger quantities

8 l (14pt)
watering can

23 l (5gal)
petrol can

250 l
(55gal)
oil drum

The Metric and Imperial Systems

The metric system is a different system of measuring units from the imperial sytem that used to be used in the United Kingdom. The metric system is used in most other countries of the world and for scientific work all over the world.

Metric measures

Each system of metric measurement is based on a basic unit. All the other units of measure are either 10, 100 or 1,000 times larger or smaller than the basic unit. The names of these other units are made up by attaching special prefixes to the front of the basic unit to show how many times its size they are. These prefixes are:

mili for $\dfrac{1}{1,000}$ **deka** for 10 times

centi for $\dfrac{1}{100}$ **hecto** for 100 times

deci for $\dfrac{1}{10}$ **kilo** for 1,000 times

Thus, a **millimetre** (mm) is $\dfrac{1}{1,000}$ of a metre

a **centimetre** (cm) is $\dfrac{1}{100}$ of a metre

a **decimetre** (dm) is $\dfrac{1}{10}$ of a metre

a **dekametre** (dkm) is 10 times the size of a metre

a **hectometre** (hm) is 100 times the size of a metre

a **kilometre** (km) is 1,000 times the size of a metre

Since we multiply by 10 by moving a decimal point one place to the right and divide by 10 by moving a decimal point one place to the left, the metric system makes it very easy to change from one unit to another by simply moving the decimal point. For example, 483 metres = 48.3 dekametres or 4.83 hectometres or 0.483 kilometres or 4,830 decimetres or 48,300 centimetres or 483,000 millimetres.

The metre and measures smaller than a metre

This line measures 1**dm** (decimetre) or 10**cm** (centimetres) or 100**mm** (millimetres)

The double-decimetre = 2dm
2**dm** or 20**cm** or 200**mm**

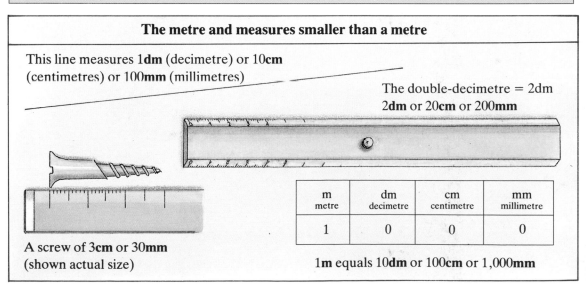

m metre	dm decimetre	cm centimetre	mm millimetre
1	0	0	0

A screw of 3**cm** or 30**mm**
(shown actual size)

1**m** equals 10**dm** or 100**cm** or 1,000**mm**

Basic units in the metric system

metre (length)
litre (liquid volume)
gram (weight)
sq metre *or* **m²** *or* **hectare** (surface area)
cubic metre *or* **m³** (volume, cubic area)

Other units of measurement

For scientific purposes there is an internationally recognized system of units called SI units. The metric units above are the SI units that we use every day. Other, more specialized, units are:

ampere (A) electric current
kelvin (K) temperature
mole (mol) amount of substance
candela (cd) luminous intensity
joule (j) energy

The standard unit of time is the **second**.

Conversions from metric to imperial system

To convert **mm** to **in**, multiply by 0.03937
To convert **m** to **ft**, multiply by 3.2808
To convert **m** to **yd**, multiply by 1.0936
To convert **km** to **miles**, multiply by 0.6214

To convert **g** to **oz**, multiply by 0.03527
To convert **g** to **lb**, multiply by 0.002205
To convert **kg** to **lb**, multiply by 2.205
To convert **tonnes** to **tons**, multiply by 0.9842

To convert **sq cm** to **sq in**, multiply by 0.155
To convert **sq m** to **sq ft**, multiply by 10.764
To convert **sq m** to **sq yd**, multiply by 1.196
To convert **sq miles** to **sq km**, multiply by 2.59

To convert **cubic cm** to **cubic in**, multiply by 0.06102
To convert **cubic m** to **cubic ft**, multiply by 35.32
To convert **cubic m** to **cubic yd**, multiply by 1.308

To convert **gal** to **l**, multiply by 4.546
To convert **pt** to **l**, multiply by 0.5683

Constructing Figures

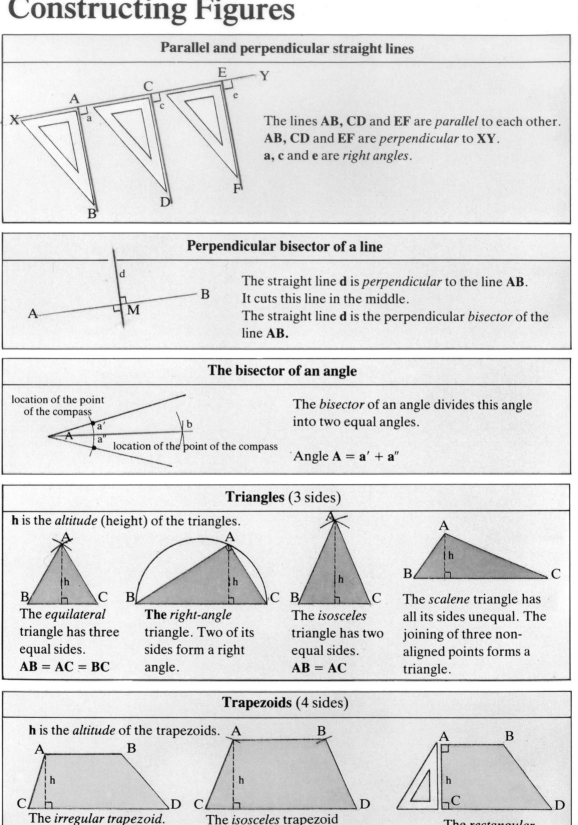

Parallel and perpendicular straight lines

The lines **AB**, **CD** and **EF** are *parallel* to each other. **AB**, **CD** and **EF** are *perpendicular* to **XY**. **a**, **c** and **e** are *right angles*.

Perpendicular bisector of a line

The straight line **d** is *perpendicular* to the line **AB**. It cuts this line in the middle. The straight line **d** is the perpendicular *bisector* of the line **AB**.

The bisector of an angle

location of the point of the compass

location of the point of the compass

The *bisector* of an angle divides this angle into two equal angles.

Angle **A** = **a′** + **a″**

Triangles (3 sides)

h is the *altitude* (height) of the triangles.

The *equilateral* triangle has three equal sides. **AB = AC = BC**

**The *right-angle* triangle. Two of its sides form a right angle.

The *isosceles* triangle has two equal sides. **AB = AC**

The *scalene* triangle has all its sides unequal. The joining of three non-aligned points forms a triangle.

Trapezoids (4 sides)

h is the *altitude* of the trapezoids.

The *irregular trapezoid*. **AB** (its small base) is parallel to **CD** (its large base).

The *isosceles* trapezoid has two equal sides: **AC** and **BD** (the non-parallel sides).

The *rectangular* trapezoid has two right angles.

146

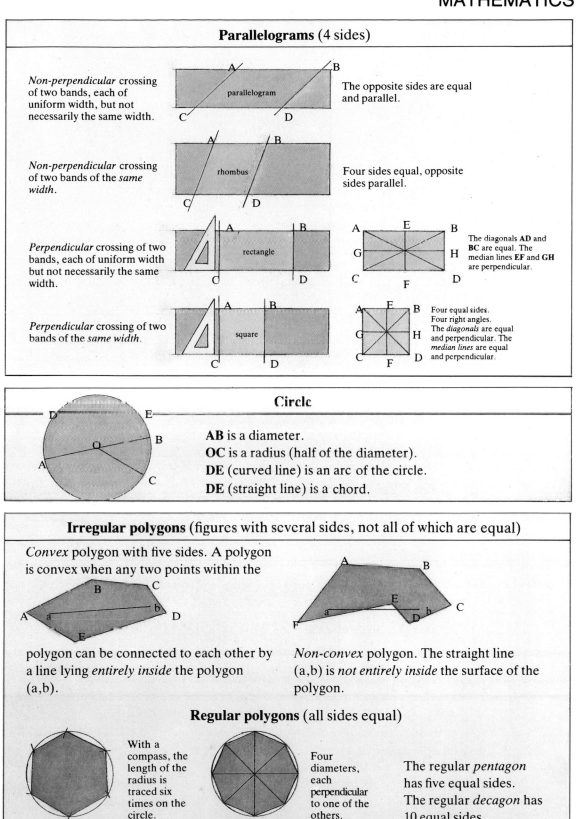

Parallelograms (4 sides)

Non-perpendicular crossing of two bands, each of uniform width, but not necessarily the same width.

parallelogram

The opposite sides are equal and parallel.

Non-perpendicular crossing of two bands of the *same width*.

rhombus

Four sides equal, opposite sides parallel.

Perpendicular crossing of two bands, each of uniform width but not necessarily the same width.

rectangle

The diagonals **AD** and **BC** are equal. The median lines **EF** and **GH** are perpendicular.

Perpendicular crossing of two bands of the *same width*.

square

Four equal sides. Four right angles. The *diagonals* are equal and perpendicular. The *median lines* are equal and perpendicular.

Circle

AB is a diameter.
OC is a radius (half of the diameter).
DE (curved line) is an arc of the circle.
DE (straight line) is a chord.

Irregular polygons (figures with several sides, not all of which are equal)

Convex polygon with five sides. A polygon is convex when any two points within the polygon can be connected to each other by a line lying *entirely inside* the polygon (a,b).

Non-convex polygon. The straight line (a,b) is *not entirely inside* the surface of the polygon.

Regular polygons (all sides equal)

With a compass, the length of the radius is traced six times on the circle.

The regular hexagon
Polygon with six equal sides.

Four diameters, each perpendicular to one of the others.

The regular octagon
Polygon with eight equal sides.

The regular *pentagon* has five equal sides.
The regular *decagon* has 10 equal sides.
The regular *dodecagon* has 12 equal sides.

Measuring Areas and Volumes

Units of area

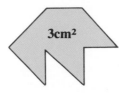

1 sq cm = 1cm²

1cm / 1cm

A square cm (cm²) is a unit of area measurement equal to a square measuring 1cm on each side.

Different units of measurement are used for areas. Very small areas may be measured in **square millimetres** (sq mm *or* mm²). Slightly

3cm²

The area of this figure is 3cm². It occupies the same space as three squares measuring 1cm on each side.

larger areas may be measured in **square centimetres** (sq cm *or* cm²) or **square inches** (sq in *or* in²). The floor area of rooms and warehouses used to be measured in **square feet** (sq ft *or* ft²) but is now usually measured in **square metres** (sq m *or* m²). For most measurements, square metres are now used instead of square yards. The area of a farm may be given in **acres** (1 acre = 43,560ft²) or **hectares** (1 hectare = 10,000m²).

Calculation of surface areas

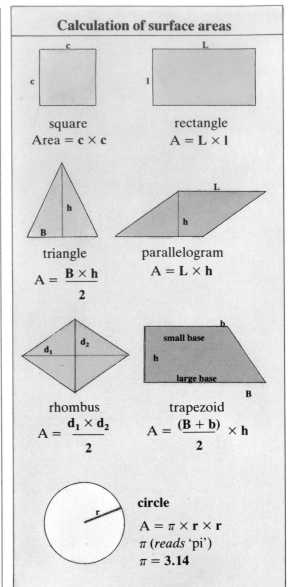

square
Area = $c \times c$

rectangle
$A = L \times l$

triangle
$A = \dfrac{B \times h}{2}$

parallelogram
$A = L \times h$

rhombus
$A = \dfrac{d_1 \times d_2}{2}$

trapezoid
$A = \dfrac{(B + b)}{2} \times h$

circle
$A = \pi \times r \times r$
π (*reads* 'pi')
$\pi = 3.14$

Converting units of area

To convert **sq in** to **sq mm**, multiply by 645.2
To convert **sq in** to **sq cm**, multiply by 6.452
To convert **sq ft** to **sq m**, multiply by 0.0929
To convert **sq yd** to **sq m**, multiply by 0.8361
To convert **sq miles** to **sq km**, multiply by 2.59
To convert **acres** to **hectares (ha)**, multiply by 0.4047

Area measure

One square metre (m²) equals a square measuring one metre on each side.

 = 100

100mm²	=	1cm²
100cm²	=	1dm²
100dm²	=	1m²
10,000m²	=	1ha
100ha	=	1km²

Units of volume

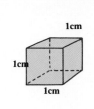

Volumes may be expressed in cubic inches (in³), cubic feet (ft³), cubic yards (yd³), cubic centimetres (cm³ *or* cc) or other cubic forms of metric measurements.

A cubic centimetre is a unit that corresponds to the volume of a cube with sides of 1cm.

Calculation of volumes

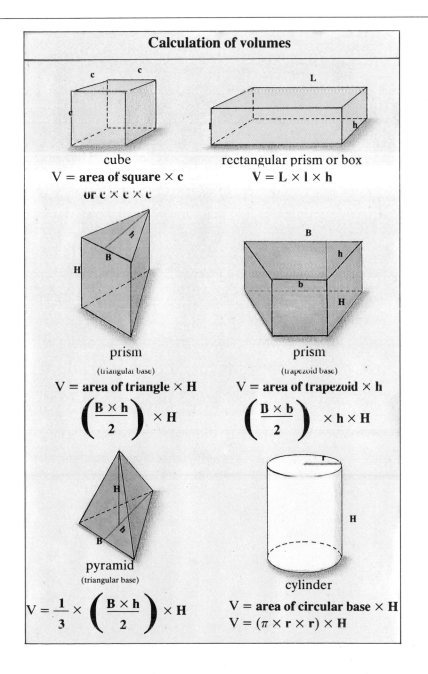

cube
$$V = \textbf{area of square} \times c$$
or c × c × c

rectangular prism or box
$$V = L \times l \times h$$

prism
(triangular base)
$$V = \textbf{area of triangle} \times H$$
$$\left(\frac{B \times h}{2}\right) \times H$$

prism
(trapezoid base)
$$V = \textbf{area of trapezoid} \times h$$
$$\left(\frac{B \times b}{2}\right) \times h \times H$$

pyramid
(triangular base)
$$V = \frac{1}{3} \times \left(\frac{B \times h}{2}\right) \times H$$

cylinder
$$V = \textbf{area of circular base} \times H$$
$$V = (\pi \times r \times r) \times H$$

Constructing Solids

Polyhedrons are solids bounded by *faces*. The lines limiting these faces are *edges*. The intersection (meeting) of two or several edges forms a *vertex* (corner).

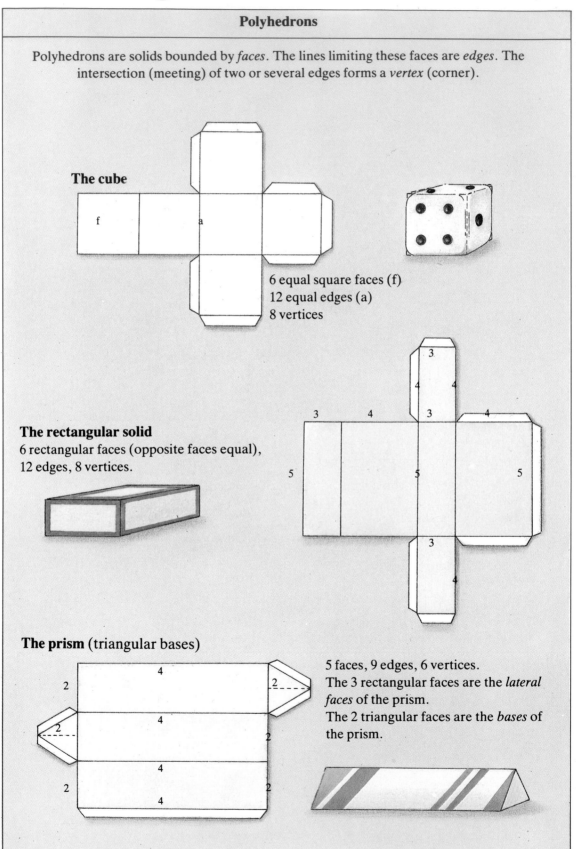

The cube

6 equal square faces (f)
12 equal edges (a)
8 vertices

The rectangular solid

6 rectangular faces (opposite faces equal),
12 edges, 8 vertices.

The prism (triangular bases)

5 faces, 9 edges, 6 vertices.
The 3 rectangular faces are the *lateral faces* of the prism.
The 2 triangular faces are the *bases* of the prism.

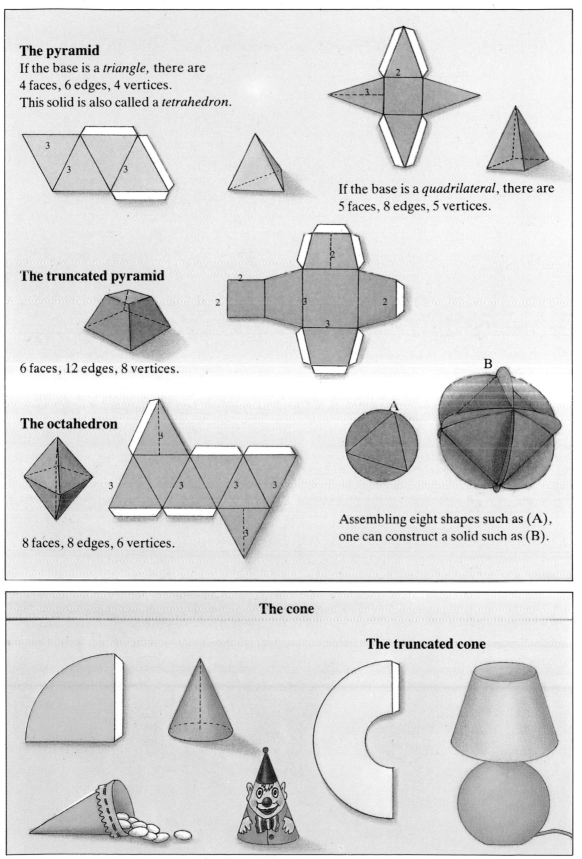

The pyramid

If the base is a *triangle,* there are
4 faces, 6 edges, 4 vertices.
This solid is also called a *tetrahedron.*

If the base is a *quadrilateral*, there are
5 faces, 8 edges, 5 vertices.

The truncated pyramid

6 faces, 12 edges, 8 vertices.

The octahedron

8 faces, 8 edges, 6 vertices.

Assembling eight shapes such as (A),
one can construct a solid such as (B).

The cone

The truncated cone

Plans, Maps and Scales

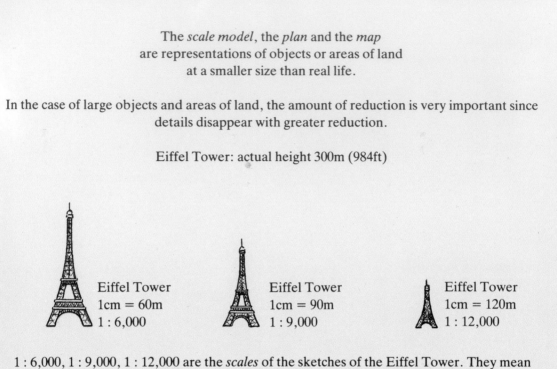

The *scale model*, the *plan* and the *map*
are representations of objects or areas of land
at a smaller size than real life.

In the case of large objects and areas of land, the amount of reduction is very important since details disappear with greater reduction.

Eiffel Tower: actual height 300m (984ft)

Eiffel Tower
1cm = 60m
1 : 6,000

Eiffel Tower
1cm = 90m
1 : 9,000

Eiffel Tower
1cm = 120m
1 : 12,000

1 : 6,000, 1 : 9,000, 1 : 12,000 are the *scales* of the sketches of the Eiffel Tower. They mean that 1cm represents 60m, 90m and 120m respectively.

Plans

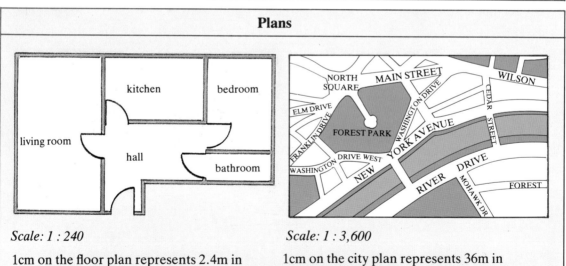

Scale: 1 : 240

1cm on the floor plan represents 2.4m in the flat. 1in = 20ft or 240in.

Scale: 1 : 3,600

1cm on the city plan represents 36m in the city. 1in = 100yd or 3,600in.

Graphic scale

Many maps and plans have a scale like the ones below.

| 0   500 miles   0   5m   10m   0   600km |

Maps

In order to be accurate, a map must be drawn to scale. The scale of a map shows how much of the Earth's surface is represented by a given measurement on the map. The scale on the map enables you to measure the distances on the map so that you can work out the real distance on the Earth's surface.

Maps show places in different sizes. A map the size of this page could show the whole world or only one country. The map scale on each of these maps would obviously be different. Thus, a centimetre on each map would stand for a different distance. For example, a centimetre on a map of a city could stand for a kilometre or even less. But a centimetre on a map of the world could stand for 50,000 kilometres. To find out what a centimetre stands for, you must find the scale on the map.

The scale may be expressed in three different ways. Many maps use a *graphic scale*. The scale consists of a straight line on which distances are marked off. The marks stand for a certain number of kilometres on the Earth's surface. For example, $\overset{\llcorner\quad\quad\quad\lrcorner}{\underset{0\quad\;150\quad\;300}{}}$ means that one centimetre on the map stands for 150 kilometres on the Earth's surface.

The map scale may be *written in words:* one-cm-to-one-km, or 1cm = 1km. This

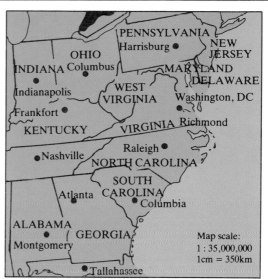

Map scale:
1 : 35,000,000
1cm = 350km

means that 1cm on the map equals 1km on the surface of the Earth.

The map scale is often expressed by a *fraction or a ratio.* 1 : 36,000. This means that one unit of measurement on the map represents 36,000 of the same units on the surface shown on the map. Thus 1cm on the map could equal 36,000 cm on the ground. The larger the scale's denominator, the smaller the scale of the map. Thus 1 : 1,000,000 is a smaller scale than 1 : 100,000. Moreover, the larger the scale, the more detailed the map: 1 : 25,000 is a large scale; 1 : 1,000,000 is a small scale.

How to find the scale

1cm on the plan represents 20m on the

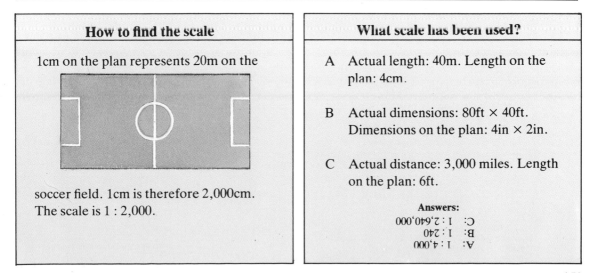

soccer field. 1cm is therefore 2,000cm. The scale is 1 : 2,000.

What scale has been used?

A   Actual length: 40m. Length on the plan: 4cm.

B   Actual dimensions: 80ft × 40ft. Dimensions on the plan: 4in × 2in.

C   Actual distance: 3,000 miles. Length on the plan: 6ft.

Answers:
C: 1 : 2,640,000
B: 1 : 240
A: 1 : 4,000

Percentages and Graphic Representations

14% increase in serious crime

[newspaper text]

Government leads by 4% in opinion poll

[newspaper text]

£23.75
OFF THE
MARKED
PRICE

25% OFF

REIMBURSED 8% INCOME TAX

[newspaper text]

70%
OF WILDLIFE

8% INFLATION

[newspaper text]

33% MORE IN CANS

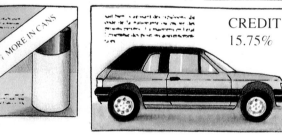

CREDIT
15.75%

Understanding and calculating percentage discounts

$$25\% = 25 \text{ per cent and can be written } 25/100 \text{ or } \frac{25}{100}$$

A discount of 25% means that for £100 worth of goods, the amount reduced is £25. £100 worth of goods therefore costs £100 − £25 = £75.

For a coat costing £95, the reduction is £95 × 25/100 or £95 × 0.25 = £23.75. The coat on sale thus costs: £95 − £23.75 = £71.25.

One operation can be omitted!

25% reduction means that you have to pay 75% of the marked price.

Therefore, 75% of £95 = £95 × 75/100 or £95 × 0.75 = £71.25.

Understanding and calculating percentage increases

An increase of 5% after 1 April.

This means that for every £100, the increase is £5
(£100 → £105).

For £3.00, the increase is £3.00 × 0.05 = £0.15.
The new price of the magazine: £3.00 + £0.15 = £3.15,
or directly: £3.00 × 105/100 or £3.00 × 1.05 = £3.15.

What is the percentage of the discount?

1 The amount of the reduction is:
£1.80 – £1.44 = £0.36.

The amount of the reduction for £1 is
0.36/1.80 = £0.20.

The reduction for £100 is
0.20 × 100 = £20, or
20%.

Answers 2 = 30% 3 = 12%

Percentages and graphs

Graphs provide easier and often more
dramatically revealing presentations of
comparative information. Several types of
graphs can be used.

Among the most common:
Bars of various heights represent the
people polled.

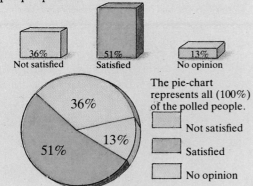

The pie-chart
represents all (100%)
of the polled people.

☐ Not satisfied

☐ Satisfied

☐ No opinion

Poll of public opinion

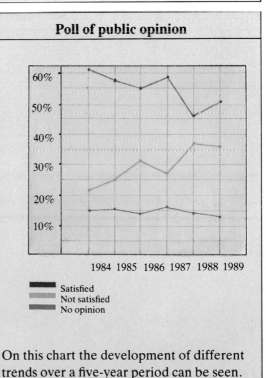

1984 1985 1986 1987 1988 1989

■ Satisfied
■ Not satisfied
■ No opinion

On this chart the development of different
trends over a five-year period can be seen.

Logic Games

What is the next item in the series?

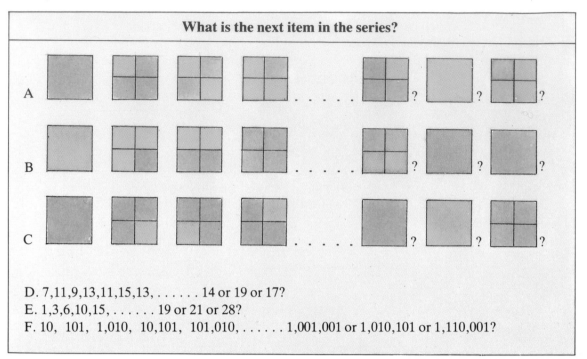

A

B

C

D. 7,11,9,13,11,15,13, ... 14 or 19 or 17?

E. 1,3,6,10,15, ... 19 or 21 or 28?

F. 10, 101, 1,010, 10,101, 101,010, ... 1,001,001 or 1,010,101 or 1,110,001?

Missing letters

Fill in the missing letters.

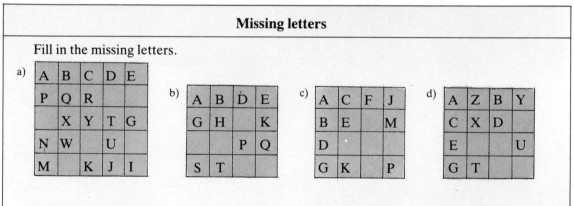

a)

A	B	C	D	E
P	Q	R		
	X	Y	T	G
N	W		U	
M		K	J	I

b)

A	B	D	E
G	H		K
		P	Q
S	T		

c)

A	C	F	J
B	E		M
D	.		
G	K		P

d)

A	Z	B	Y
C	X	D	
E			U
G	T		

Logic

What completes these sequences?

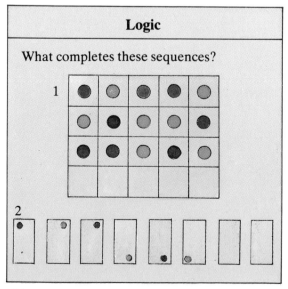

1

2

The hidden sides

How many spots are on the side of the dice opposite to the sides shown?

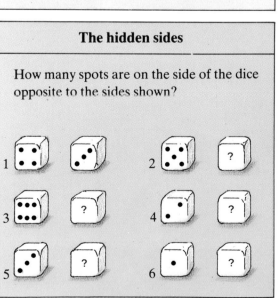

1

2

3

4

5

6

156

Missing pieces

Which is the missing part?

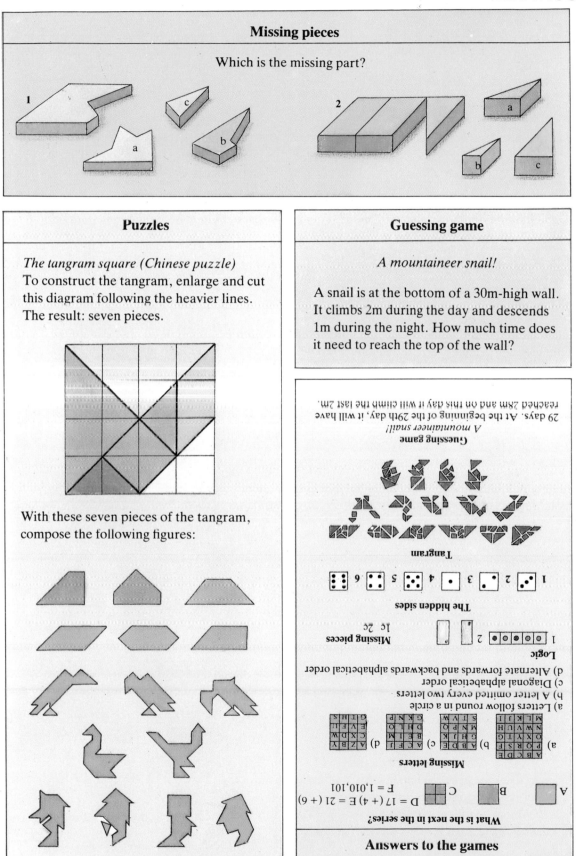

Puzzles

The tangram square (Chinese puzzle)
To construct the tangram, enlarge and cut this diagram following the heavier lines. The result: seven pieces.

With these seven pieces of the tangram, compose the following figures:

Guessing game

A mountaineer snail!

A snail is at the bottom of a 30m-high wall. It climbs 2m during the day and descends 1m during the night. How much time does it need to reach the top of the wall?

Answers to the games

What is the next in the series?

A   B   C   D = 17 (+ 4) E = 21 (+ 6) F = 1,010,101

Missing letters

a)
A	B	C	D	E
P	O	R	S	E
O	X	Y	I	G
N	M	L	K	J

b)
A	B	D	E
G	H	J	K
B	E	I	M
O	T	V	A
U	H	N	V

c)
A	C	E	F
D	H	L	O
M	N	P	Q
S	T	V	W
G	K	N	P

d)
A	Z	B	Y
C	X	D	W
E	V	F	U
G	T	H	S

a) Letters follow round in a circle
b) A letter omitted every two letters
c) Diagonal alphabetical order
d) Alternate forwards and backwards alphabetical order

Logic

Missing pieces 1 [....] 2 [ ][ ]
1c 2c

The hidden sides
1 [die] 2 [die] 3 [die] 4 [die] 5 [die] 6 [die]

Tangram

Guessing game
A mountaineer snail!
29 days. At the beginning of the 29th day, it will have reached 2km and on this day it will climb the last 2m.

Mathematical Games

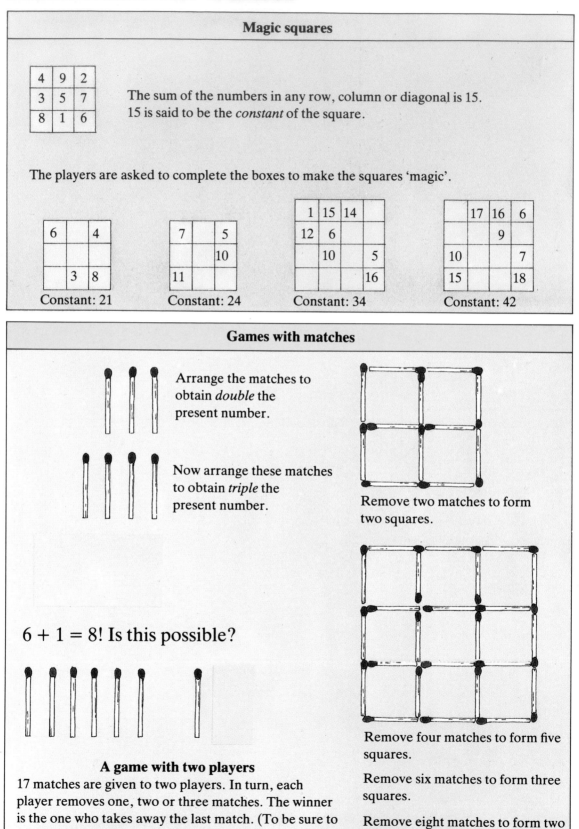

Magic squares

4	9	2
3	5	7
8	1	6

The sum of the numbers in any row, column or diagonal is 15.
15 is said to be the *constant* of the square.

The players are asked to complete the boxes to make the squares 'magic'.

6		4
	3	8

Constant: 21

7		5
		10
11		

Constant: 24

1	15	14	
12	6		
	10		5
			16

Constant: 34

	17	16	6
		9	
10			7
15			18

Constant: 42

Games with matches

Arrange the matches to obtain *double* the present number.

Now arrange these matches to obtain *triple* the present number.

6 + 1 = 8! Is this possible?

Remove two matches to form two squares.

Remove four matches to form five squares.

Remove six matches to form three squares.

Remove eight matches to form two squares.

A game with two players

17 matches are given to two players. In turn, each player removes one, two or three matches. The winner is the one who takes away the last match. (To be sure to win, he or she must remove the 13th match.)

Tricks

How is the number 23 written by using only the digit 2?
How is the number 45 written by using only the digit 4?
How is the number 1,000 written by using only the digit 9?

A shortcut

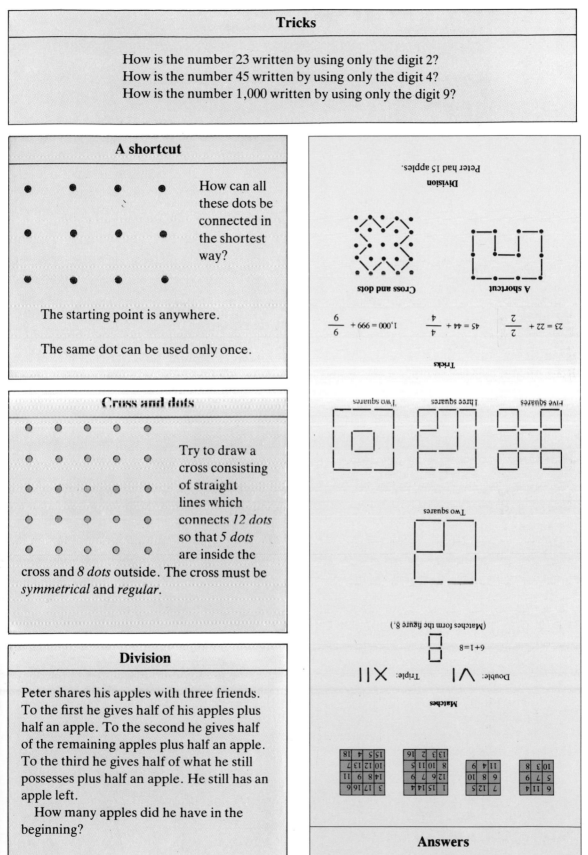

How can all these dots be connected in the shortest way?

The starting point is anywhere.

The same dot can be used only once.

Cross and dots

Try to draw a cross consisting of straight lines which connects *12 dots* so that *5 dots* are inside the cross and *8 dots* outside. The cross must be *symmetrical* and *regular*.

Division

Peter shares his apples with three friends. To the first he gives half of his apples plus half an apple. To the second he gives half of the remaining apples plus half an apple. To the third he gives half of what he still possesses plus half an apple. He still has an apple left.

How many apples did he have in the beginning?

Answers

Division
Peter had 15 apples.

Cross and dots

A shortcut

Tricks

$$23 = 22 + \frac{2}{2}$$ $$45 = 44 + \frac{4}{4}$$ $$1,000 = 999 + \frac{9}{9}$$

Five squares   **Three squares**   **Two squares**

Two squares

Matches

Double: VI Triple: XII

$9 + 1 = 8$

(Matches form the figure 8.)

8	3	10
6	7	5
4	11	9

11	4	6
6	8	10
7	12	5

16	2	13	3
8	10	11	5
12	6	7	9
1	14	15	4

18	4	5	15
10	13	12	7
14	8	9	11
3	17	16	6

159

Water

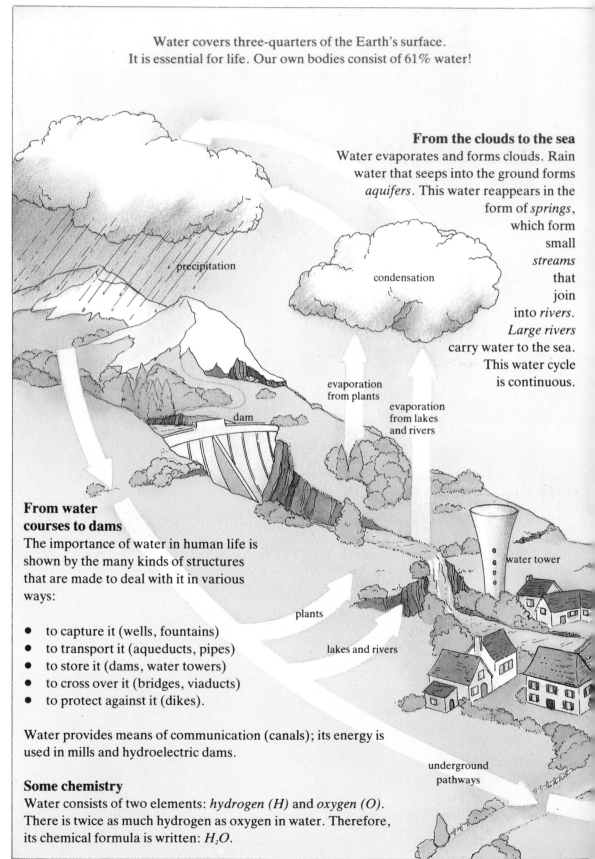

Water covers three-quarters of the Earth's surface.
It is essential for life. Our own bodies consist of 61% water!

precipitation

condensation

From the clouds to the sea
Water evaporates and forms clouds. Rain water that seeps into the ground forms *aquifers*. This water reappears in the form of *springs*, which form small *streams* that join into *rivers*. *Large rivers* carry water to the sea. This water cycle is continuous.

evaporation from plants

evaporation from lakes and rivers

dam

water tower

plants

lakes and rivers

underground pathways

From water courses to dams
The importance of water in human life is shown by the many kinds of structures that are made to deal with it in various ways:

- to capture it (wells, fountains)
- to transport it (aqueducts, pipes)
- to store it (dams, water towers)
- to cross over it (bridges, viaducts)
- to protect against it (dikes).

Water provides means of communication (canals); its energy is used in mills and hydroelectric dams.

Some chemistry
Water consists of two elements: *hydrogen (H)* and *oxygen (O)*.
There is twice as much hydrogen as oxygen in water. Therefore, its chemical formula is written: H_2O.

160

Water that does not flow!

When cooling, water becomes solid. This tranformation starts at 0°C, which is 32°F.

Solid water takes up more space than liquid water. This is why the glass of a bottle filled with water shatters when the water freezes.

Some very cold regions in the world are completely covered with ice (Arctic, Antarctic). The layer of ice may reach a thickness of 4km.

When tiny droplets of water in the form of clouds meet currents of cold air, these droplets change into solid water: snow (flakes) or ice (hail).

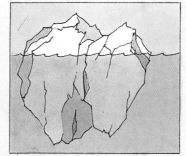

Water that floats on water

The submerged part (under water) of an iceberg is much larger than the visible part.

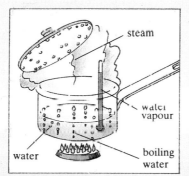

Invisible water!

When laundry dries, the water seems to disappear. It evaporates.

Water vapour is an invisible gas that mixes with the air.

Heat and wind speed evaporation. Every second, millions of tonnes of water evaporate from the surface of the Earth! When water vapour meets cold surfaces or currents of cold air, it condenses into droplets and becomes visible as *clouds, fog* or *dew*.

How to make a cloud
Metal tray with ice cubes. Container with hot water.

Observation in the dark with a torch.

What is the weight of water?

At sea-level, one cubic cm of water weighs exactly 1g.

Water changes into ice at 0°C which is 32°F.

At what temperature does water boil?

At sea-level, water boils at 100°C, which is 212°F.

At an altitude of five km or three miles, it boils at 80°C, or 176°F.

Is it true that bodies are lighter in water?

They seem lighter because the water helps to lift them.

---

evaporation from the ocean

dike

ocean

Air

Air everywhere

Air is an invisible gas with no colour or smell, but we always know it is there.

The Earth is surrounded by a layer of air 97km (60 miles) thick, called the *atmosphere*. This atmosphere protects the Earth against the strong rays of the Sun. It acts as a screen.

Without air, life would be impossible

Most living things die when they are without air because they stop breathing. Without air, fire does not burn and sounds cannot be heard.

A bottle is never empty

Air spreads out to fill all spaces. When you pour liquid from a bottle, air rushes in. The bottle that seems to be empty is really full of air. Here are three experiments to prove it:

1 Air in a bottle offers resistance that prevents a balloon from being blown up.

3 Under water, air from a bottle can be transferred into another container.

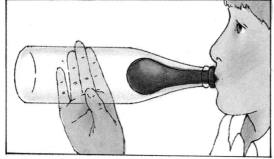

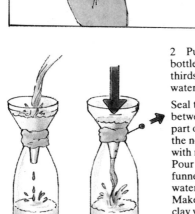

2 Put a funnel in a bottle that is two-thirds filled with water.

Seal the space between the lower part of the funnel and the neck of the bottle with modelling clay. Pour water into the funnel. Almost no water filters through. Make a hole in the clay with a needle. The water flows through because the hole lets the air out.

Some chemistry

Air consists of several gases, the most important of which are nitrogen (78%), oxygen (21%), and small amounts of other gases such as argon, carbon dioxide and water vapour (1%).

A deep-sea diver's tank of air contains about 400 gallons of compressed air.

Air is heavy

A balloon full of air is heavier than a balloon without air.

Make a notch in the middle of a stick so that you can easily attach a thin string to it. Blow up two balloons of the same size and tie them at the ends and at the same distance from the middle of the stick. Hold the string with one hand. The stick should remain horizontal. With the other hand, pierce one of the balloons with a needle. The scale tips to the side of the balloon full of air.

To make liquid air

It can be done by compressing and deep freezing air (at about −190°C or −372°F).

Liquid air is blue. It is stored in thermos bottles.

Why do high-altitude mountain climbers use oxygen bottles?

The higher the elevation, the thinner the air. Above 4,500m (15,000ft) breathing becomes very difficult. Any physical effort is very tiring.

In planes flying at high altitudes (3,050m or 10,000ft and more), the air provided for passengers is pressurized.

What is there beyond the atmosphere?

A vacuum.
Rockets and satellites travel in it.

The bottle is full of water. It is impossible to reduce the volume of water by pressing strongly on the cork. Liquids cannot be compressed.

Air can be compressed

It is possible to reduce the space occupied by air by compressing it. A bottle full of air can be sealed by pushing in a cork. This is not possible with a bottle full to the top with water. Water, like all liquids, cannot be compressed.

Fire

Wild and violent . . .

Fire occurs naturally in various places on the Earth. Roaring torrents of hot, glowing matter rise through fractures in the Earth's crust.

Volcanoes, mouths of fire that remain unpredictable for long periods, often cause great destruction.

Lava consisting of partially molten (melted) rocks may reach temperatures above 1,000°C, or 1,832°F.

. . . but essential for life

Fire is the greatest discovery made by humans. Some 750,000 years ago, they learned to create and use it. Ever since then, fire has always been present in our lives. With fire we can provide heat, cook food, melt metals, produce light and burn waste.

What is combustion?

Combustion is the tranformation into light and heat of the energy stored in fuel. Anything that can burn is said to be *combustible*.

Early humans making fire

Metal-casting

burning gas

escaping gas

hot fuel

Combustibles may be:
      solid – plastics, wood, coal
      liquid – cooking oil, petrol, alcohol, diesel
      gaseous – illuminating gas, propane.

To burn, a combustible needs the oxygen of the air. When it burns, it produces carbon dioxide and water vapour.

Barbecue

Fireplace

Gas cooker

Furnace

Types of lamp

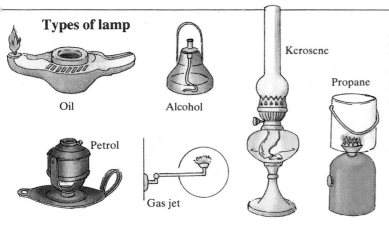

Oil

Alcohol

Petrol

Gas jet

Kerosene

Propane

A ball of fire that provides heat and light

Although 150 million km (93 million miles) away, the Sun can sometimes burn our skin! Its temperature reaches 10,800°F on its surface; in the centre it is between 16 and 20 *million* degrees! It gets so hot because it is not really a fire – it is a *nuclear reaction*.

All kinds of flames

Flames are not all the same. According to the fuel, they have different colours: yellow, yellow and red, red and blue, blue. The bluer the flame, the hotter it is. A yellow flame is less hot. It contains substances that have not burned. These substances may appear in the form of smoke.

Some fuels burn without a flame, like the tobacco in a cigarette.

Fire hazard!

This sign shows the dangers of fire. Our friend can become our enemy. Indeed, every year large areas of forest are destroyed. Fires in homes or theatres can turn into catastrophes with many victims. Modern firefighting equipment is efficient and firefighters are well trained. Fires are often due to negligence, but sometimes the Sun on dry grass can begin a fire.

Fire prevention

- Do not start a fire in a forest.
- Do not open bottles containing flammable liquids close to a flame (petrol, for instance).
- Do not restart a fire with a flammable liquid.
- If there is a gas leak, do not make a spark or flame close by.
- Do not run with your clothes on fire, because air currents will make them burn faster.

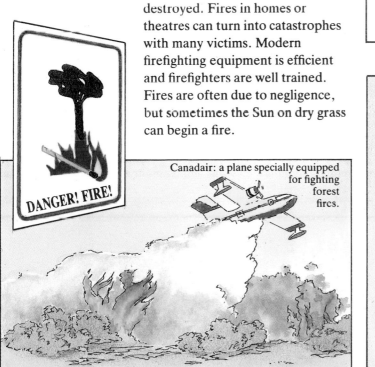

DANGER! FIRE!

Canadair: a plane specially equipped for fighting forest fires.

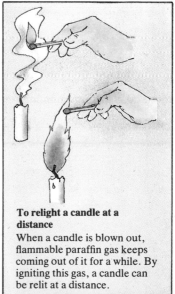

To relight a candle at a distance

When a candle is blown out, flammable paraffin gas keeps coming out of it for a while. By igniting this gas, a candle can be relit at a distance.

Weather Station

What is a weather station?

A weather station is a place where data is collected with the help of very precise measuring instruments for the purpose of weather forecasting.

Today, there are about 10,000 weather stations in the world.

The accuracy of forecasting has increased in the last 10 years from 24 hours to 72 hours. In 15 years, it may be possible to forecast weather 10 days ahead. Besides the data collected on the ground, additional information comes from balloons, marine buoys, planes and especially satellites, which transmit excellent pictures of the upper atmosphere at various places above the Earth.

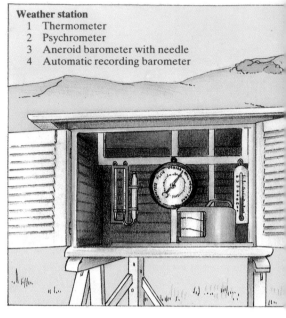

Weather station
1 Thermometer
2 Psychrometer
3 Aneroid barometer with needle
4 Automatic recording barometer

The thermometer

This measures the lowest *temperature* at night and the highest during daytime to calculate the average daily temperature. This measure is expressed in degrees Centigrade (Celsius) or Fahrenheit.

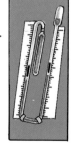

Thermometer measuring maximum and minimum temperatures.

The psychrometer

This measures the humidity of the air by the reading of two thermometers – one dry and the other kept moist with a wet cheesecloth. The wet-bulb thermometer is cooled by the evaporation of water; the drier the air, the faster the water evaporates and the lower the thermometer reads.

The barometer

This instrument measures the weight of the air, called *atmospheric pressure*. This pressure drops when bad weather is approaching and rises when the weather improves. The average atmospheric pressure is equivalent to the weight of a column of mercury about 760mm or 30in high. A simple barometer can be made as follows:

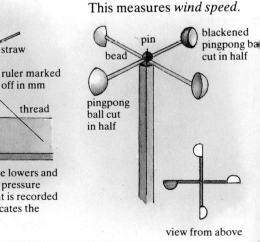

arm holding pulley
straw
rubber membrane
rubber band
can
ruler marked off in mm
thread

The stretched membrane lowers and rises as the atmospheric pressure changes. This movement is recorded by the straw, which indicates the pressure.

Wind vane

This indicates the *direction* of the wind.

cardboard   pin   cardboard
bead   wooden stick
stand
N   S
cardboard disc

Anemometer

This measures *wind speed*.

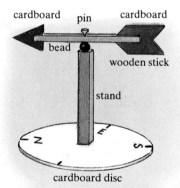

pin   blackened pingpong ball cut in half
bead
pingpong ball cut in half

view from above

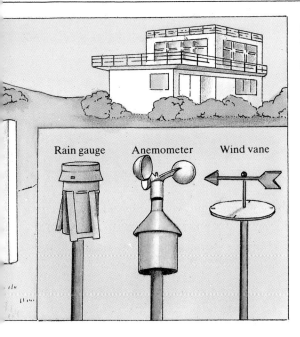

Observation data sheets

These show the different recorded data and allow certain weather forecasts.

Here is a model that can be used:

	temperature: maximum minimum	pressure: morning evening	wind: direction/speed	hygrometry	rain gauge	description of the sky
Monday						
Tuesday						
Wednesday						
Thursday						
Friday						
Saturday						
Sunday						

Rain gauge

The *amount of rainfall* during a given time is measured with this instrument. It is possible to make a rain gauge yourself using materials you have at home. To make one, cut down a plastic drinks bottle. Then place a ruler by it. The amount of rainfall is measured in inches or millimetres.

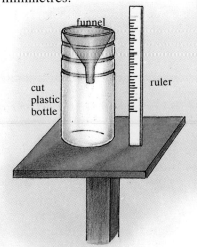

Hygrometer

This measures the amount of *humidity* in the air. It is marked from 0 to 100. The higher the value, the more water vapour is in the air. You can make a hygrometer using simple materials.

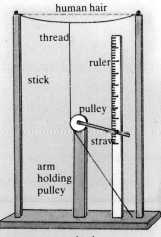

According to the humidity in the air, hair shortens (air is drier) or lengthens (more humid air), a movement recorded by the straw, which moves in front of a ruler marked from 0 to 100.

Where should a weather station be located?

Weather vanes and anemometers must be placed in an open space where there are no obstacles to block the wind. Barometers, thermometers and hygrometers must be protected from rain and sunshine, and placed inside a well-ventilated shelter painted white.

The white colour reflects most of the Sun's rays so that the inside of the box will not heat up.

Is meteorology a new science?

No, in 350 BC, the Greek scholar Aristotle wrote a treatise titled *Meteorologica* (Meteorology). However, it was not until the 1600s and 1700s that the first measuring instruments were perfected and meteorological science was born.

167

Electricity

In which of these cases does the bulb light up?

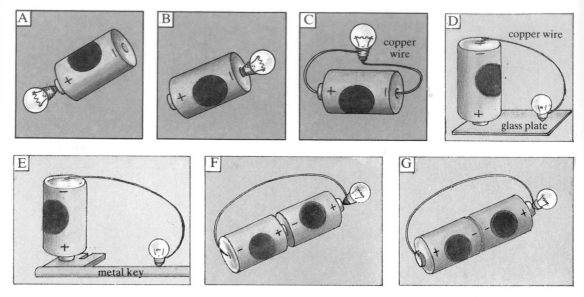

A

B

C
copper wire

D
copper wire
glass plate

E
metal key

F

G

Answer: C, E, F.

The role of the switch
In any electric installation, the current flows only when the circuit is closed, that is, when the wires that carry the current are connected. A switch opens and closes the electric circuit.

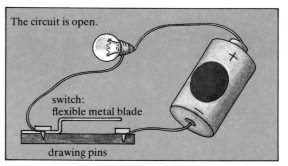

The circuit is open.

switch:
flexible metal blade

drawing pins

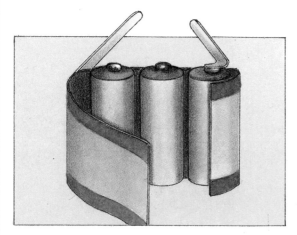

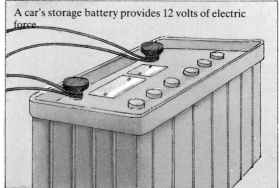

A car's storage battery provides 12 volts of electric force.

The inside of a battery.
A round battery provides 1.5 volts of electric force.

A battery consisting of three round batteries provides 4.5 volts of electric force.

The car battery
The storage battery holds electrical energy to start the motor and operate its electrical systems when the car is stopped. It is recharged when the motor runs.

The power station (thermal, hydroelectric or nuclear) provides the electric current for domestic daily use.

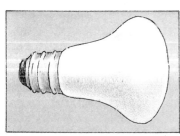

The bulb heats up
The electric current flowing through the filament of the bulb releases heat. If the temperature rises too high, the filament melts. The bulb is said to have 'burned out'. This release of heat is used in many electrical appliances.

Danger!

When the force of electricity is more than 14 volts, it can make a dangerous amount of current flow. In a home, such voltage may be fatal. Water and humidity increase the risk of electrocution.

Do not:

Change a bulb without switching off the lamp.

Use an electric appliance in the bath.

It is *very* dangerous to stick any object into a socket.

Touch an electric cooker especially when your feet are wet.

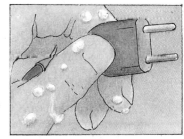

Pull a plug out with wet fingers.

Lightning
Lightning is an electric discharge between a cloud and the ground or between two clouds. Temperatures during these giant sparks may be as high as 30,000°C or 54,032°F. Lightning can kill humans and animals and start serious fires. The lightning rod, invented by Benjamin Franklin in 1752, leads the electric discharge directly to the ground.

Sources of Energy

Whenever something moves or changes in any way, energy is used. Energy occurs in many different forms.

Muscles – the first source of energy

Thousands of years ago, human beings knew no energy source except their muscular force to move around, to hunt, to lift, to carry. About 10,000 BC, they learned how to use animals, which they domesticated, as sources of energy.

Muscular energy
(chemical energy)

Water, air – natural forces

By 100 BC, the energy of flowing water was used to turn the millstones that crushed grains. Today, this form of energy is still used to produce another kind of energy – electricity (dams, hydroelectric power plants).

Aeolian energy (after the name of the god of winds, Aeolus) turns windmills and, since prehistoric times, moves sailing boats.

Mechanical energy

The spring of a wind-up clock and the weights of an old clock provide energy to mechanical parts that in turn produce movement.

Windmill
(Aeolian energy)

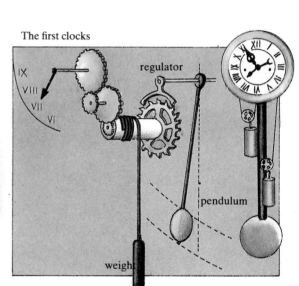

The first clocks

regulator

pendulum

weight

Natural energy sources

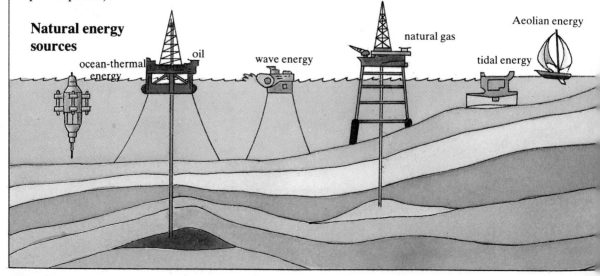

ocean-thermal energy

oil

wave energy

natural gas

tidal energy

Aeolian energy

Fuel energy

Wood and, above all, *coal* were used for the first engines that improved the lives of human beings.

The use of *oil* and *gas* to run engines revolutionized industry. Today, the energy produced during combustion of certain gases propels rockets.

Electrical energy

Produced and used in great quantities (lighting, heating, to run motors), electrical energy is sent through wires quickly and easily.

Electrical energy

The need for electricity keeps growing. The demand doubles every ten years!

Since fuel resources will not last forever, humans are searching for new sources of energy.

Solar energy

Captured with mirrors or special panels, the heat of solar radiation operates high-temperature furnaces (up to 3,800°C, or 6,872°F) to heat houses and produce electricity.

Geothermal energy

At a certain depth in the ground, aquifers of hot water are sometimes found. This water can be pumped and used inexpensively for the heating of houses or buildings.

Thus, at the Geysers geothermal energy plant in California, water comes out of the ground at a temperature of 175°C, or 350°F.

Ocean energy

A plant to use the energy of tides was built in 1934 at Passamaquoddy Bay in Maine in the United States, but it did not work well. There is an operating plant in France, however.

Today, other means are being tested to use the energy of waves and marine currents.

Nuclear energy

The first nuclear reactor was completed at the University of Chicago in 1942, and hundreds have been built since.

The use of this type of energy is being fully developed, although some people are worried about the radioactive waste products of the process.

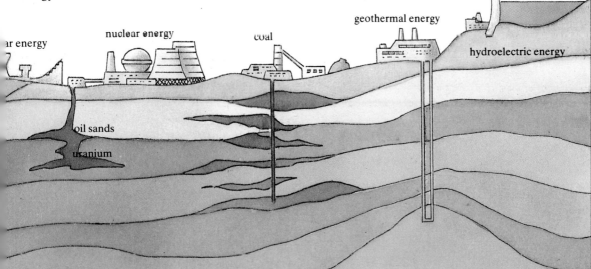

geothermal energy

nuclear energy

coal

ar energy

hydroelectric energy

oil sands

uranium

Nuclear Power: a New Energy

This form of energy is produced with a fuel called uranium. One gram of uranium releases the same energy as 2.5 tonnes of coal!

Nuclear fission

protons

neutrons

chain reaction

uranium nucleus

The nucleus of a uranium atom consists of neutrons and protons. If the nucleus is bombarded with neutrons, it breaks into smaller nuclei and releases a large amount of energy.

How is nuclear energy produced?
This is done inside a leak-proof container, the *reactor*. When uranium is introduced, a very strong nuclear reaction occurs. Each splitting uranium nucleus releases neutrons that split other uranium nuclei. This 'chain reaction' releases an enormous amount of heat.

Where is uranium found?
It is extracted from very large mines in the United States, Canada, South Africa, Australia and South America.

The atomic bomb
This is the military use of nuclear energy. With the instant release of energy contained in an atomic bomb, a target is destroyed by the blast of the explosion, by the released heat and by the spread of deadly radioactive materials.

In August 1945, two bombs were dropped by the United States on Japan, at *Hiroshima* and *Nagasaki*. Over 170,000 people were killed in a few seconds. This disaster forced Japan to surrender and ended World War II.

Mask and protective suit against radiation.

Is it dangerous?
Yes. For that reason nuclear reactors are well protected and continuously monitored. Indeed, the production of nuclear energy releases a great deal of *radioactivity*, radiation which can be fatal to most living things. Very sensitive instruments, kept close to the reactors, measure this radioactivity constantly.

atomic explosion

production of electricity

cooling towers for steam

cooling of steam by river water

turbine generators

reactors

A nuclear plant
(always built on the banks of a river, lake, or by the sea)

Nuclear plants

In this peaceful use of nuclear energy, the great release of heat can transform water in a boiler into steam under pressure. This steam turns the turbines that produce electricity.

Hundreds of nuclear plants operate today all over the world.

Because of the great risks, these plants are built to resist violent shocks (a plane crash, for instance) or earthquakes.

People protest against a nuclear power plant.

For or against nuclear power?

To date, nuclear power plants have been built in 22 countries. However, many people are *opposed* to nuclear power. Because of the dangers involved in radioactivity, they say life is in danger and that even strict controls in these plants cannot prevent serious accidents.

Breakdowns and accidents (for instance, the fire in a reactor in April 1986 at the nuclear plant at Chernobyl, in the Soviet Union) have caused fears about the safety of nuclear power. They have raised questions about the future of nuclear power plants. Some communities refuse to allow construction of nuclear plants on their lands. Public protests occur frequently.

Those people who favour the protection of nature (*ecologists*) raise strong protests against nuclear power plants because they produce radioactive wastes. The safe disposal of these wastes is a problem and ecologists are concerned about the means used to dispose of radioactive waste. They are concerned about the possible effect the disposal of radioactive wastes may have on humans, beaches and wildlife.

However, people in favour of nuclear power stress the extraordinary progress for humankind achieved by the use of this energy, which they believe to be clean, less polluting and less dangerous than certain chemical industries.

The World of Sound

Every vibrating object produces a sound (the string on a guitar, our vocal cords, etc.). The air carries sound waves to our ears. In space, on the Moon and in other places without air, sounds cannot be heard.

Lightning and thunder

Why is there often a certain lapse of time between the strike of lightning and the sound of thunder, although both actually occur at the same time?

This is so because light waves travel faster in the air than sound waves – *3,000km (186,000 miles) per second* for light, *332m (1,120ft) per second* for sound!

The sonar of a fishing boat allows it to locate a shoal of fish.

Sonar

Certain boats carry this instrument for detecting and locating objects under water. When sound waves emitted by the sonar strike an object, they bounce back through the water towards the ship.

The string telephone

Material needed: two cardboard or plastic cups or cartons and a few metres of string. This experiment shows that sound also travels through solids. Here, the sound waves follow the string, but the string must be stretched tight.

Another example is the doctor's *stethoscope*, which allows him or her to listen to a person's heartbeat and breathing. The speed of sound is faster in solids than in the air. In steel, for instance, it is 4,877m (16,000ft) per second. In water, about 1,524m (5,000 ft) per second.

HELLO-O-O

The echo

Sound waves are reflected by an obstacle and produce an echo – repetition of emitted sounds.

HELLO-O-O

Counting the number of seconds between lightning and thunder, you can tell the distance of the thunderstorm. Every 5 seconds = 1 mile.

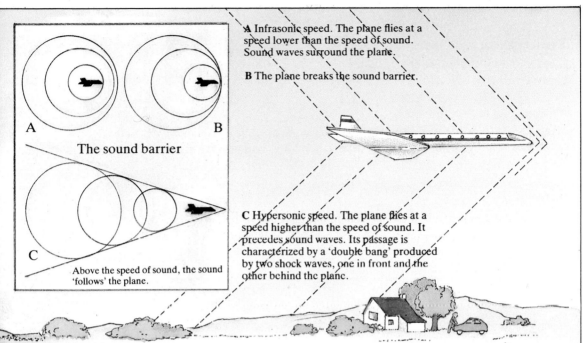

A Infrasonic speed. The plane flies at a speed lower than the speed of sound. Sound waves surround the plane.

B The plane breaks the sound barrier.

C Hypersonic speed. The plane flies at a speed higher than the speed of sound. It precedes sound waves. Its passage is characterized by a 'double bang' produced by two shock waves, one in front and the other behind the plane.

The sound barrier

Above the speed of sound, the sound 'follows' the plane.

Stethoscope

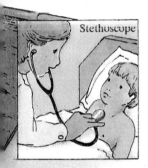

To make a toy flute:
rubber band
cigarette-
paper

plastic pipe
(inside
diameter
about
20mm,
length
12cm)

Put
your
lips
here
and
hum
a tune.

Faster than the speed of sound

Certain aircraft called *supersonic planes* fly faster than the speed of sound. When their speed reaches about 1,100kph (700mph), they run into strong resistance called the *sound barrier* or *sonic wall*. If they can overcome this resistance, they break the sound barrier. On the ground this is heard as a tremendous 'double bang'. *Concorde* flies at twice the speed of sound! The first planes that reached this speed fell apart under the effect of vibrations. The sound barrier was broken for the first time on 14 October 1947 by Charles Yeager.

How many decibels?

Depending on the vibrating object, sound waves have a greater or lesser intensity, or loudness. This intensity can be measured with certain instruments. The unit of measure is called the *decibel* (dB).

Below is a table indicating the intensity of some sounds at points close to the source:

rustling of leaves: 0–10 dB
quiet conversation: 20–50 dB
loud conversation: 50–65 dB
a train passing by: 65–90 dB
thunder: 90–110 dB
jet plane at take-off: 110–140 dB
space rocket take-off: 140–190 dB

Noise becomes painful to the ears from about 120 decibels.

Are there sounds that we cannot hear?

Yes, our ears do not hear every sound. For instance, ultrasounds are too high pitched and infrasounds too low to be heard by human ears.

Sonars of boats emit ultrasounds that cannot be perceived by humans.

Bats find their way and locate flying insects with the help of ultrasounds which they emit and which return to them as echoes. A *dolphin* uses this method in the sea.

Magnetism

The lodestone

Discovered more than 2,500 years ago, a rock called *magnetite* has the property of being able to attract iron and steel objects and to give them its power of attraction. Magnetite draws its magnetic property from the largest known magnet – the Earth.

A special magnet – the compass

This consists of a magnetic needle mounted so that it can rotate freely over a card indicating the cardinal points (N, S, E, W). The needle

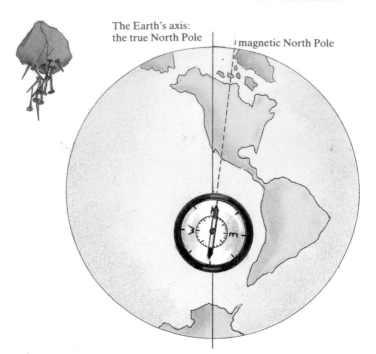

The Earth's axis: the true North Pole

magnetic North Pole

Attracted or not?

Only metals containing iron, steel or nickel are attracted to magnets. Objects consisting of glass, wood, plastic, copper or silver are not attracted to magnets.

comes to rest pointing approximately northward.

The Chinese were the first to use the compass. They taught its use to the Arabs, who transmitted it to the western world during the Middle Ages.

Artificial magnets

Today, magnets no longer consist of a natural rock, magnetite, but are made artificially. They are made in special shapes according to their use.

Which objects are not attracted to a magnet?

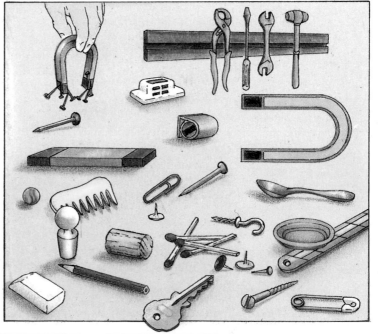

The poles of a magnet

There are certain places on any magnet where magnetism is strongest. Bar magnets suspended from a string all line up in the same direction. One end points north (the north-pointing pole) and the other end points south.

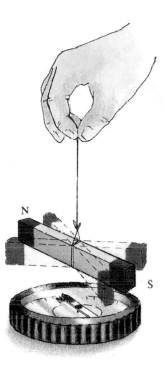

If two bar magnets are brought near each other, we see that poles of the same nature (north, for example) repel each other; they cannot be joined. Poles of different nature (north and south) attract each other.

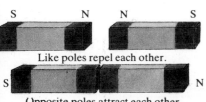

Like poles repel each other.

Opposite poles attract each other.

To make objects magnetic

Metal objects made of steel and certain alloys can be made magnetic by stroking them with a magnet.

Every magnetized object then immediately has two poles – a north-pointing pole and a south-pointing pole.

Making a picture of a magnetic field

The magnetic force can be found in the space around the magnet – a magnetic field. To make a picture of the field, cover the magnet with a piece of paper and sprinkle iron filings on the paper.

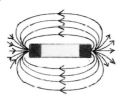

Iron filings around a magnet form loops.

Two different poles. The lines join.

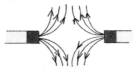

Two identical poles. The lines diverge.

Electricity and magnets

An electric wire is wrapped around a large nail and the ends of the wire are connected to an electric battery.

When the electric current flows, the nail becomes magnetic. An electromagnet has been made. Some industrial electromagnets can lift great weights.

A simple electromagnet

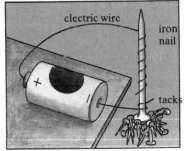

electric wire

iron nail

tacks

Can magnetism disappear?

Yes, if the magnet is heated, if it is given shocks, or if its poles are not carefully protected. A needle can be demagnetized by heating it.

What instruments use electromagnets?

Electric bells, the telegraph, all electric motors and cassette recorders use electromagnets.

cassette recorder

Levers and Balances

Large force with little effort

It is relatively easy to lift and move heavy objects, or to raise water from the bottom of a well with the help of a very simple instrument called a *lever*. The use of levers goes back to very ancient times. The Greek Archimedes (287–212 BC) first discovered and studied them.

All kinds of levers

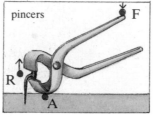
pincers

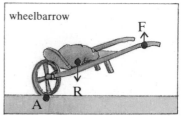
wheelbarrow

Use of a lever in acrobatics

The usefulness of this lever depends on the position of its point of support.

lifting weight with pulley

pulley

Some technical points

A lever always has three essential points:

- the point of support or fulcrum (**A**)
- the point of resistance (**R**)
- the point where force is applied (**F**)

The longer the distance **AF**, the less force is needed to lift the weight at **R.**

A practical use – the balance

Balances have been known since ancient times. In 2000 BC, the Egyptians were already using them. The first balances were made of wood.

A balance is a lever in which the fulcrum is usually located exactly half-way between the force (**F**) and the resistance (**R**). The arms of the lever, **AR** and **AF**, are therefore equal. When weighing something, you adjust the balance so it is level. Then **F** and **R** are equal.

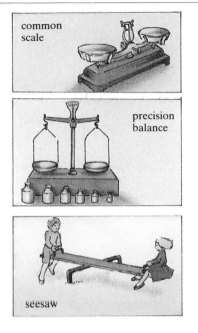

common scale

precision balance

seesaw

Balances with equal arms

The *common scale* was invented in 1670. It is still widely used.

The *precision balance* is used by jewellers and chemists. It is capable of giving accurate readings of very small weights.

The children's *seesaw* works according to the same principle as the common scale and the precision balance. If the children weigh the same, the beam is horizontal.

Everything is automatic!

Some balances allow immediate reading of the weight of an object. Examples are commercial automatic balances or scales such as postage scales and household scales.

Some sturdy balances, called *platform weighing machines*, weigh masses up to several tonnes.

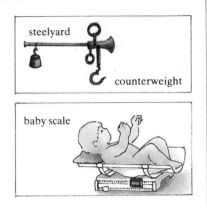

steelyard

counterweight

baby scale

A strange balance

Already known in China by 1000 BC, the *steelyard* consists of two unequal arms. For weighing, a counterweight is moved on the longer arm, which is marked off in pounds. When equilibrium is reached, the weight can be read directly.

A baby scale is a balance with cursors, a moving slide that can be read.

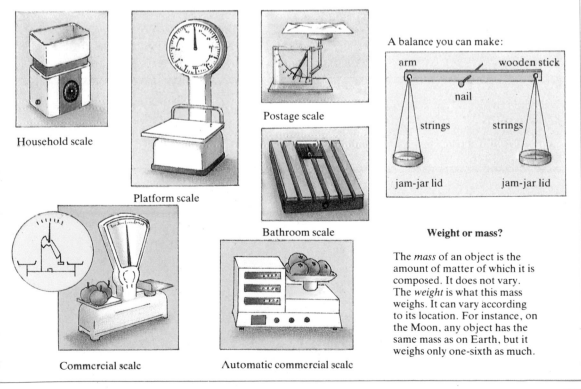

Household scale

Platform scale

Commercial scale

Postage scale

Bathroom scale

Automatic commercial scale

A balance you can make:

arm — wooden stick

nail

strings — strings

jam-jar lid — jam-jar lid

Weight or mass?

The *mass* of an object is the amount of matter of which it is composed. It does not vary. The *weight* is what this mass weighs. It can vary according to its location. For instance, on the Moon, any object has the same mass as on Earth, but it weighs only one-sixth as much.

179

The World of Colours

The colours we see are a property of light.

A little magic

When a beam of white light (daylight) crosses a glass prism, many different colours appear!

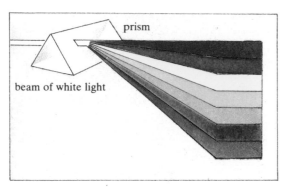

Dispersion of light through Newton's prism

The white light consists of many colours – red, orange, yellow, green, blue, indigo and violet shade into each other.

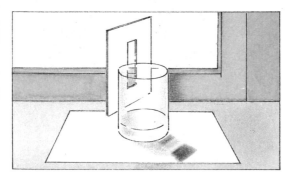

To obtain a solar spectrum

Put a glass of water on a sheet of white paper and add a small piece of cardboard with a 1cm slit. Put everything in front of a window in the sunlight.

All these colours represent the *light spectrum*. Three hundred years ago, Isaac Newton explained the composition of light based on the experiment shown above.

Only white is visible!

The cardboard disc contains some of the colours of the spectrum. If it is spun rapidly, our eyes can no longer distinguish the separate colours. If the colours are carefully chosen, they will blend together and look white.

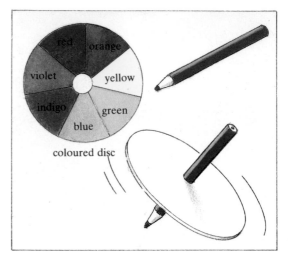

coloured disc

Our eyes are most sensitive to the colours red, green and blue.

The rainbow

All the colours of the spectrum are displayed in a rainbow. Droplets of water in the atmosphere act like many tiny glass prisms.

On a chair, with your back to the Sun, you can see a rainbow. It is interrupted by your shadow.

Why do we see a red cherry, a green apple and a white page?

All the objects that surround us absorb certain colours of the spectrum and reflect others. Our eye sees only the reflected colours. Therefore, a cherry appears red because it absorbs all the colours except red, which it reflects. A green apple reflects green and absorbs all other colours. The sheet of paper reflects all the colours of the spectrum and appears white. Eyes that are blue or brown do not absorb those colours.

The cherry appears red because it reflects only the red colour.

And black?

Any object that appears black (coal, fabric etc.) absorbs all the colours of the spectrum and reflects none. This object can thus be seen only by contrast with surrounding objects. Black is in reality the *absence* of colour.

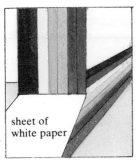

A sheet of paper reflects all the colours and appears white.

piece of coal

Black absorbs all colours.

sheet of white paper

From one colour to another

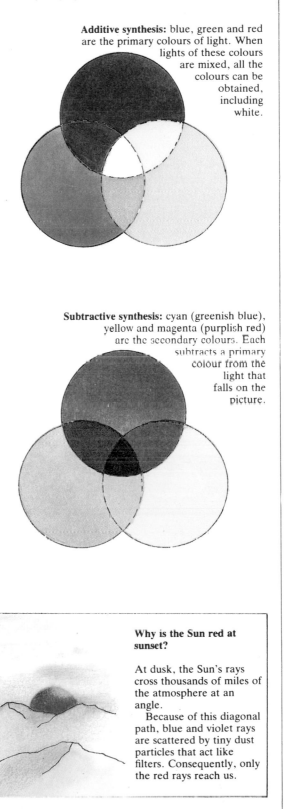

Additive synthesis: blue, green and red are the primary colours of light. When lights of these colours are mixed, all the colours can be obtained, including white.

Subtractive synthesis: cyan (greenish blue), yellow and magenta (purplish red) are the secondary colours. Each subtracts a primary colour from the light that falls on the picture.

Why is the Sun red at sunset?

At dusk, the Sun's rays cross thousands of miles of the atmosphere at an angle.

Because of this diagonal path, blue and violet rays are scattered by tiny dust particles that act like filters. Consequently, only the red rays reach us.

Observing the Sky

Ever since ancient times, humans have observed the sky and tried to understand its mysteries and explain its organization.

Who was right?

In the second century AD, the Greek astronomer *Ptolemy* described a universe of small size, with the Earth motionless in the middle. The Sun, the planets and the stars revolved, or turned around, the Earth.

In the 16th century, the Polish astronomer *Copernicus* revolutionized this view of the universe. He proposed that the Earth and the other planets revolved around the Sun, while each rotated around itself.

In the 17th century, the Italian astronomer *Galileo* confirmed Copernicus' discovery. At that time, Galileo was condemned by the Church. Today, we know that he was right.

Do we know the dimensions of the universe?

No, because the universe is huge. Even the most powerful telescopes and satellites cannot see the end of it.

Uranus

The universe contains *galaxies*. Seen from the Earth, millions of them have already been counted.

Each galaxy is formed by stars and planets grouped together into *systems*. There are *billions* of such systems in each galaxy.

Thus, the planet Earth belongs to the *solar system* which is included in 'our' galaxy – the *Milky Way*.

Star or Planet

A star *produces* light energy whereas a planet is a cold body which *reflects* received light.

A few years ago, it was discovered that celestial bodies also emit radio waves and hence radio telescopes 'with large ears' were built to listen to these celestial bodies.

Saturn

Jupiter

powerful radio telescope

path of a comet

Pluto

Neptune

artificial
satellite

What forms our Solar System?
A star, the Sun, is in the middle and nine main planets with
their satellites revolve around it.

Planets	Symbols	Diameter in miles	Average distance to Sun in millions of miles	Period of rotation	Period of revolution around the Sun
Mercury	☿	3,000	27	59 days	88 days
Venus	♀	7,630	68	243 days	224 days
Earth	⊕	8,000	93	24 hours	365.24 days
Mars	♂	4,500	156	24.5 hours	687 days
Jupiter	♃	87,500	488	10 hours	11 years
Saturn	♄	75,000	875	1 hour	30 years
Uranus	♅	30,000	1,810	216 hours	84 years
Neptune	♆	31,250	2,800	218 hours	165 years
Pluto	♇	3,750	3,700	6.4 days	248 years

What is a light year?
It is a unit of measurement used to express the enormous
distances in the universe. Light travels at a speed of
3,000km (186,000 miles) per second. A light year is the
distance travelled by light in one year, that is, 9.3 billion
km (5.8 billion miles). At
this speed, sunlight reaches
us in a little over 8 minutes!

Sun

Mercury

Venus

Earth

astronaut

What is a shooting star?

These are *meteorites* that
revolve around the Sun and
sometimes cross the orbit of the
Earth. When they enter the
atmosphere, they heat and burn
up. The light produced by their
combustion is a white streak
called a meteor.

Is there life on the other planets of the Solar System?

It is very unlikely because
atmospheric conditions
are often very extreme
(frozen or burning ground).
But there might be
life in other
systems.

And the Moon?
Located 386,100km (240,000
miles) from the Earth, the Moon
is a satellite of our planet, that is,
it revolves around the Earth in a
little over 29 days. Because of
these revolutions, we do not
always see the Moon in the same
way. Sometimes it appears full
(full Moon); sometimes partly full
(the various quarters of the
Moon). American astronauts
landed on the Moon in 1969.

At what speed does the Earth revolve around the Sun?

At the incredible speed of
106,000kph (66,000mph), or
about 29km or 19 miles per
second!

The phases of the Moon

last quarter   full Moon   first quarter

Star Charts

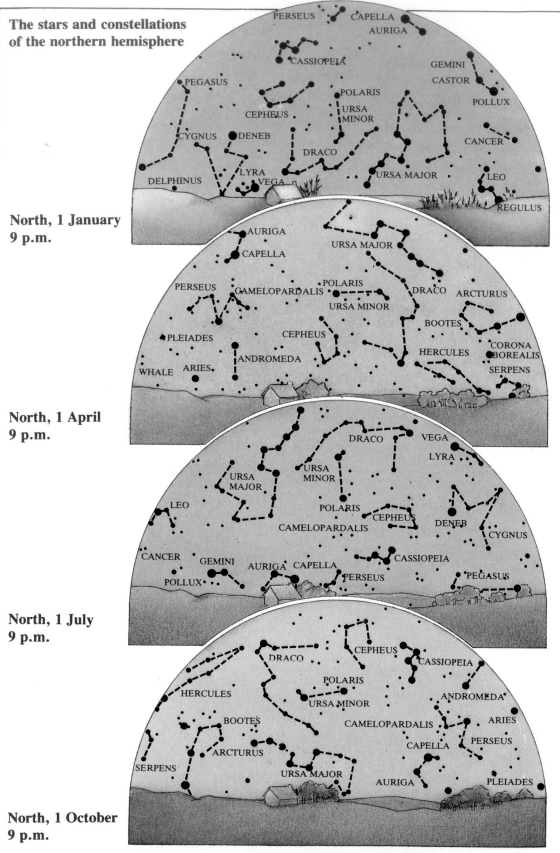

The stars and constellations of the northern hemisphere

North, 1 January 9 p.m.

North, 1 April 9 p.m.

North, 1 July 9 p.m.

North, 1 October 9 p.m.

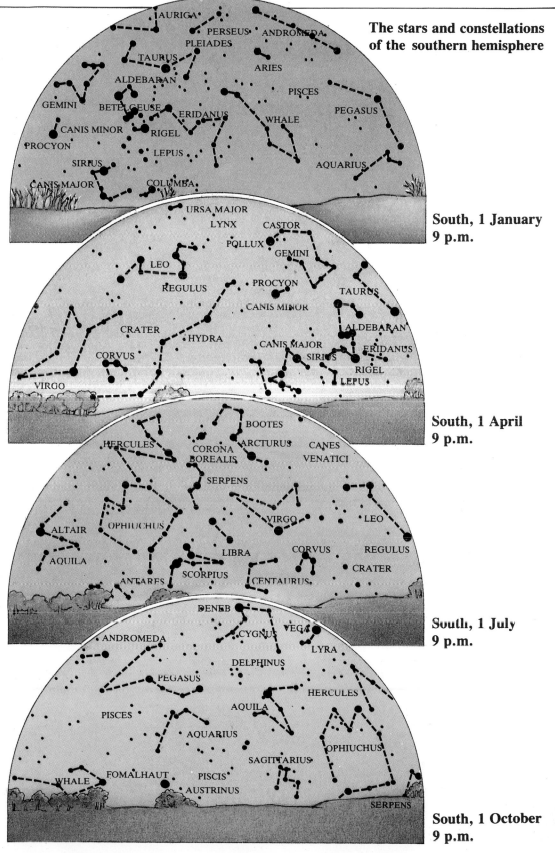

The stars and constellations of the southern hemisphere

South, 1 January
9 p.m.

South, 1 April
9 p.m.

South, 1 July
9 p.m.

South, 1 October
9 p.m.

Measuring Time

There have not always been watches, pendulums and clocks. Since they did not have such instruments for many thousands of years, humans measured the passing of time by observing natural events – the succession of days and nights, the different positions of the Sun in the sky, the phases of the Moon or the tides.

East West

Sunrise The Sun at noon Sunset

One of the first instruments – the sundial

At different times of the day, the length and the direction of the shadow cast by an object placed vertically into the ground was indicated by the *sundial*. These measurements provided an approximate reading of time.

Most ancient civilizations used this instrument. They came into general use in the 13th century. Sundials were still used in many countries at the beginning of this century.

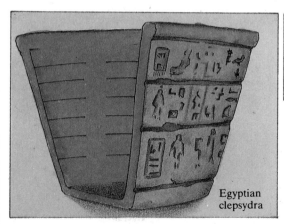

Egyptian clepsydra

These devices were called *clepsydrae*, or water clocks. Used mainly at night, they were easily made but not very precise.

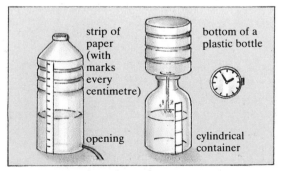

strip of paper (with marks every centimetre)

bottom of a plastic bottle

opening

cylindrical container

Two clepsydrae that are easy to make. On the right, the watch helps to make the measuring instrument (with a marked-off ruler).

Clever Egyptians!

In 3500 BC, the first time-measuring devices appeared in Egypt. These were strange containers with an opening at their base. Time was measured by how long it took for water in the container to drip through.

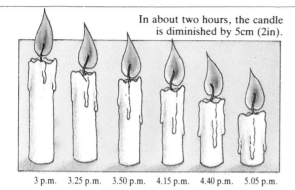

In about two hours, the candle is diminished by 5cm (2in).

3 p.m.   3.25 p.m.   3.50 p.m.   4.15 p.m.   4.40 p.m.   5.05 p.m.

The 'wax clock' of the Middle Ages

A burning candle was marked at regular intervals. Thus it was possible to measure time (a quarter of an hour, half an hour, one hour) according to how far down the candle had burnt.

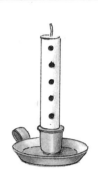

Still in use: the hourglass

Using the same principle as the clepsydra, the hourglass shows how long it takes for fine sand to flow from the top to the bottom, which varies according to the amount of sand and the size of the opening.

hourglass

Mechanical clocks

The first clocks appeared in the 14th and 15th centuries. However, they were not very precise. It was not until the 17th century that the use of the *pendulum* provided a regular movement that was more accurate.

Main parts of a mechanical clock

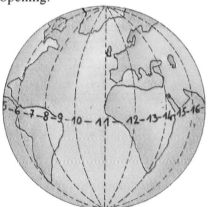

The Earth is divided into slices called *time zones*.

digital watch

cuckoo clock

chronometer

calendar

FEBRUARY

29

Today

Time is measured today with great precision. Watches with hands, digital watches and chronometers are all instruments that regulate our daily life. Switzerland is famous for its watches.

British Summer Time (BST) means that watches are set *ahead* in spring when the days become longer and set *back* in autumn.

The Earth revolves around the Sun in 365.24 days. To account for the odd 0.24 day, one day is added to the month of February every four years. These are the *leap years*.

Faster and Faster!

Using their legs, human beings were able to cross great distances although speed remained limited to about 16kph (10mph) and could not be kept up for too long. Nevertheless, this was the only way humans were able to travel for thousands of years.

Roman chariot

Little by little, with the help of their imagination, they invented and perfected techniques that enabled them to become masters of the space surrounding them.

Today, we cross great distances with tremendous speed and no effort.

Animals were the first 'vehicles'
Captured and domesticated, the donkey, the ox and later the horse became the first means of transport.

Team of oxen

The invention of the wheel – a great step
The wheel was invented about 3500 BC, most likely in Mesopotamia, and has been used in many different ways over the centuries.

An original invention – the bicycle
This was the first vehicle with two wheels in line.

1875: a bicycle with pedals, called the 'penny-farthing' bicycle, was used for the first time.

1818: the invention of the bicycle

1770: one of the first steam-powered vehicles by Cugnot.

1876: the first petrol car. The picture shows an open touring car in 1923

The Car
With the appearance of the car, a new era began. It evolved very rapidly and its role became more and more important, leading to a new way of life and completely changing urban and country landscapes.

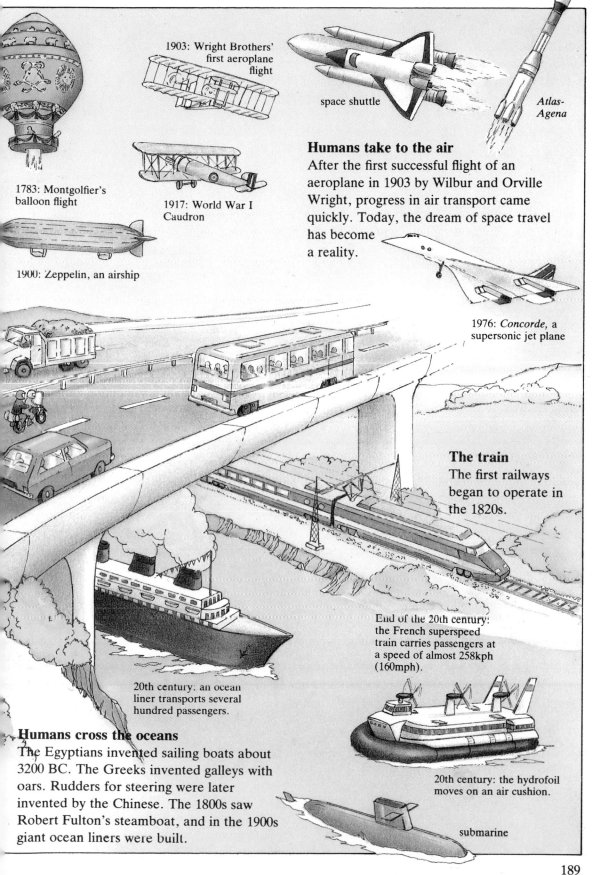

1903: Wright Brothers' first aeroplane flight

space shuttle

Atlas-Agena

1783: Montgolfier's balloon flight

1917: World War I Caudron

1900: Zeppelin, an airship

Humans take to the air

After the first successful flight of an aeroplane in 1903 by Wilbur and Orville Wright, progress in air transport came quickly. Today, the dream of space travel has become a reality.

1976: *Concorde*, a supersonic jet plane

The train

The first railways began to operate in the 1820s.

End of the 20th century: the French superspeed train carries passengers at a speed of almost 258kph (160mph).

20th century: an ocean liner transports several hundred passengers.

Humans cross the oceans

The Egyptians invented sailing boats about 3200 BC. The Greeks invented galleys with oars. Rudders for steering were later invented by the Chinese. The 1800s saw Robert Fulton's steamboat, and in the 1900s giant ocean liners were built.

20th century: the hydrofoil moves on an air cushion.

submarine

189

Photography

Some history

Since ancient times, the principle of the 'dark room' was used to observe eclipses. In 1826, Nicéphore Niepce of France produced the first photograph in black and white on paper. By 1837, another French inventor, Daguerre, perfected the system. In the 1880s the American George Eastman invented the Kodak camera.

Daguerre

Eastman

dark room

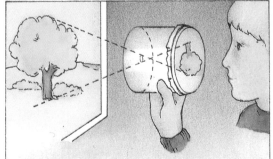
To make a pinhole camera, use a box with a tiny hole on one side and a stretched tracing paper fastened with a rubber band on the other. To observe, you must be in a dark room looking at a brightly lit object.

The ancestor of the camera – the dark room

A tiny hole in a completely dark room allows one to observe the image of what happens outside *upside down*.

During the 1500s, this method, called the *camera obscura* (dark room) was used to draw objects.

Today

The modern camera has been greatly improved. It is smaller, easy to carry, has many automatic features, and is easy to use. Inside the body of the camera, the image forms on a sheet of plastic with a light-sensitive coating – the film.

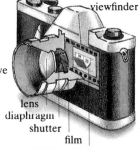
shutter release button
viewfinder
objective
lens
diaphragm
shutter
film
Modern Camera

One of the first cameras

The first cameras

They had an objective, a glass lens which concentrated all light rays. Each camera was a small camera obscura, with a lens on one end and a light-sensitive plate on the other. The lens made an image on the plate.

Some technical aspects

The *viewfinder* allows you to frame the picture to be photographed.

The *shutter* regulates the time of the film's exposure to light. It can be adjusted according to the brightness of the light and whether the object to be photographed is moving or still.

When the shutter release button is pressed, the shutter opens and closes in a fraction of a second.

The *diaphragm* regulates the amount of light to which the film is exposed.

An indispensable tool

Most sciences and technologies use photography.

It is used in medicine, in scientific research, in analysis and treatment of certain diseases, and in astronomy, for a better understanding of the universe. Aerial photography is used in drawing precise maps.

Through photography, we have been able to learn about the world beneath the sea. Photography is helpful in the study of art works.

It is present in daily life through newspapers, books, advertising and many other fields.

Development of film

Load film on spool.

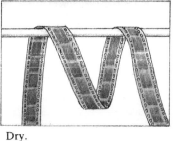
Fill with chemicals.

Empty out chemicals.

Rinse.

Dry.

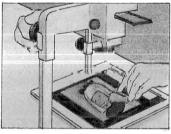
Enlarge.

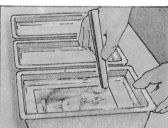
Develop.

Fix

Rinse.

Dry.

From a negative to a positive

When all the film has been exposed, it is treated with chemicals. It is dipped into several trays containing chemical fluids.

The film becomes a negative (blacks and whites reversed). The negative is used to cast an image on light-sensitive paper, which becomes the print.

The instant picture

Some cameras (Polaroid) develop the final print instantly.

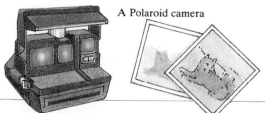
A Polaroid camera

How Life Begins

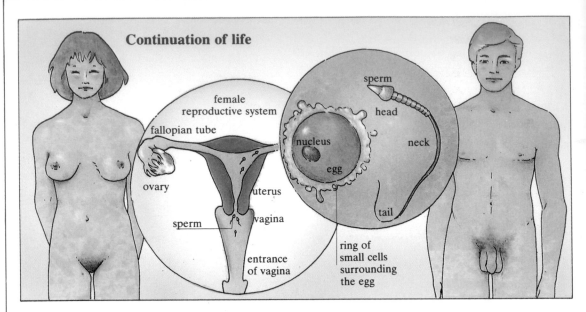

Continuation of life

female reproductive system

fallopian tube

ovary

uterus

sperm

vagina

entrance of vagina

sperm

head

neck

nucleus

egg

tail

ring of small cells surrounding the egg

Reproduction ensures the survival of the species.

Human beings, as well as most animals, reproduce when a male *sperm* enters a female *egg*. This is the first step in the generation of a new living being. It is called *fertilization* or *conception*.

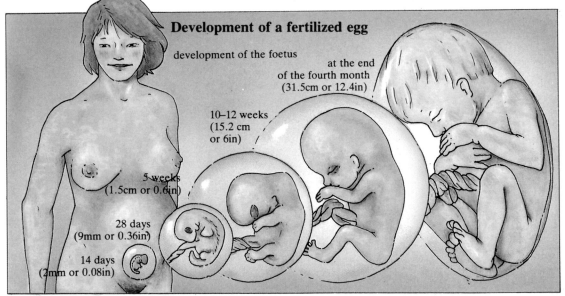

Development of a fertilized egg

development of the foetus

at the end of the fourth month (31.5cm or 12.4in)

10–12 weeks (15.2 cm or 6in)

5 weeks (1.5cm or 0.6in)

28 days (9mm or 0.36in)

14 days (2mm or 0.08in)

The fertilized egg develops and changes:
- either outside the female body, as in the case of birds, insects and most fish, that is, animals that lay eggs and often hatch them, or
- inside the body of the mother as in the case of all familiar *mammals*.

The *embryo* develops from the egg during a time that varies, according to the species, from a few days to several months. For the development of a living human being, the time is about 270 days (nine months).

A few comparisons between days of embryo development (*gestation*):

lark: 12	elephant: 620	horse: 335
rabbit: 30	hamster: 20	cow: 280
cat, dog: 56–60	lion: 110–116	
sheep: 150	monkey: 240	

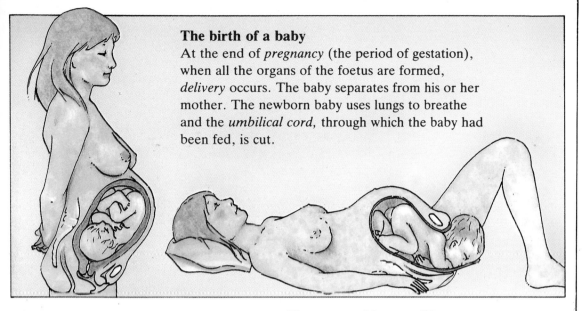

The birth of a baby

At the end of *pregnancy* (the period of gestation), when all the organs of the foetus are formed, *delivery* occurs. The baby separates from his or her mother. The newborn baby uses lungs to breathe and the *umbilical cord,* through which the baby had been fed, is cut.

Usually, a woman gives birth to only one child. *Twins* (two babies) are born sometimes, but births of *triplets* (three babies) or *quadruplets* (four babies) are rare. Mammals, such as dogs, cats and rabbits, often have 3, 6, 10 or more offspring at a time.

The stages of human life

After birth, a slow growth continues until approximately the age of 20. *Infancy* is followed by *adolescence* and then *adulthood.* The human being ages and then dies. The average life span is between 70 and 80 years.

A few average life spans (in animals)

Small flying insect = a few hours	Dog = 15 years	Crow = 50 years
Mouse = 3 years	Trout = 20 years	Elephant = 70 years
Rabbit = 8 years	Horse = 25 years	Crocodile = 80 years
	Galapagos tortoise = 100–150 years	

From tadpole to frog

Animals that lay eggs are called *oviparous* (frogs, birds). In its development, a frog goes through a complete *metamorphosis* (change). The egg is laid and fertilized in the water, where it develops into a tadpole.

Later, the tadpole grows legs and lungs, loses its gills and tail, and finally turns into a frog.

Viviparous animals are those that bring forth completely formed living young.

And the plants?

Most plants also reproduce with the help of a male organ, the *stamen,* and a female organ, the *pistil.* Pollen grains produced by the stamen fertilize the ovules of the pistil. The pistil changes into a fruit, which contains seeds. A seed contains an embryo plant, developed from the ovule. After germination, these seeds grow into new plants.

There are also other means of reproduction in plants (asexual reproduction, grafting, budding).

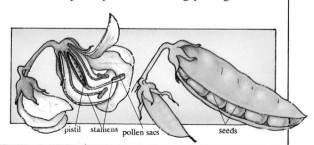

pistil   stamens   pollen sacs   seeds

Respiration

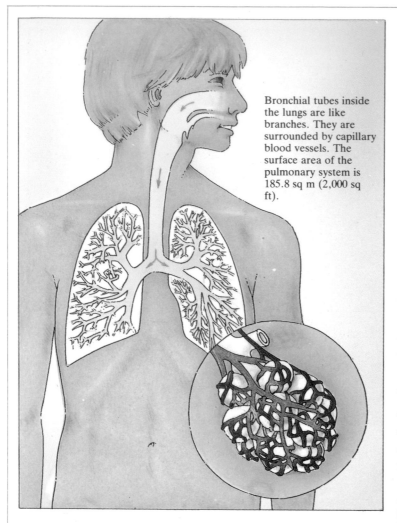

Bronchial tubes inside the lungs are like branches. They are surrounded by capillary blood vessels. The surface area of the pulmonary system is 185.8 sq m (2,000 sq ft).

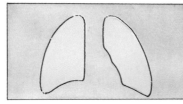

A Inhalation
The lungs are inflated with inhaled air.

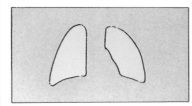

B Exhalation
Respiratory gases are expelled.

An uninterrupted circulation

Several times per minute – the number varies according to physical activity – the chest rises and lowers. We are *breathing*. At first, air enters through the *nose*. It follows the *trachea*, which branches into the *bronchi* and *bronchioles*, and thus circulates in the lungs, which expand. This is called *inhalation*.

Thereafter, air is expelled and the lungs decrease in size. This is called *exhalation*.

These two movements are *involuntary* (made without choice).

A gaseous exchange

When comparing inhaled and exhaled air, it is found that a certain amount of *oxygen* has disappeared and has been replaced, in almost the same

Gaseous exchanges occur with the help of blood.
In blue: blood carrying carbon dioxide.
In red: blood rich in oxygen.

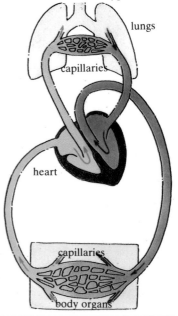

lungs

capillaries

heart

capillaries

body organs

Energy production

All our organs need *energy* to function. Oxygen from the air helps to provide such energy. Collected by the lungs during *inhalation,* oxygen is carried in the bloodstream to all parts of the body. However, when our body organs use energy, they produce a waste product – carbon dioxide – which is dangerous for cells. Carried back to the lungs by the blood, carbon dioxide is released during *exhalation*. The exchange of oxygen and carbon dioxide is called *respiration*.

proportion, with *carbon dioxide:*

- inhaled air: 21% oxygen and 0.04% carbon dioxide;
- exhaled air: 16% oxygen and 4.5% carbon dioxide.

Hence, an exchange between these two gases, or respiration, has occurred in our lungs.

Asphyxia (suffocation)

This is a failure of breathing movements. It can be caused by drowning, by electrocution or by inhaling toxic gases.

A suffocating person is in urgent need of *artificial respiration*, such as mouth-to-mouth resuscitation.

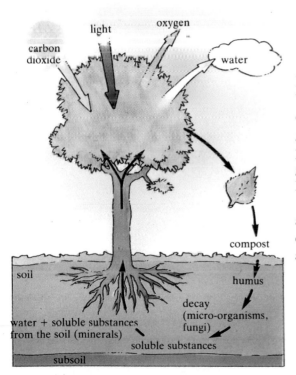

Can you survive without breathing for a long time?

No, it cannot be longer than a few minutes (in the case of divers, for instance). After a short time without oxygen, the brain is badly and permanently damaged.

Breathing in water!

Our lungs do not allow us to breathe in water. Fish have no lungs; they respire with their *gills*. As water passes over the gills,

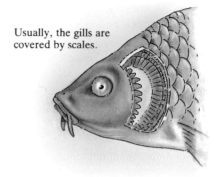

Usually, the gills are covered by scales.

oxygen moves from the water into the fish's blood. Carbon dioxide goes the other way. This is why the water of an aquarium loses oxygen rapidly and must be changed frequently.

Plants – a source of oxygen

With the help of light, gaseous exchanges occur in green plants (those that contain a green substance called *chlorophyll*). These plants absorb carbon dioxide and release great quantities of oxygen. Without plants, life would not be possible on our planet.

At night, these same plants absorb small amounts of oxygen and release carbon dioxide. At this time, they respire like animals.

Why do we get out of breath after running?

Muscular efforts produce a lot of carbon dioxide that must be rapidly released and replaced by oxygen. This is why breathing becomes faster.

At rest, we inhale and exhale about 16 times per minute.

This frequency may reach or even go beyond 60 times per minute during a fast run.

Food and Energy

Every living thing must be nourished. Food is needed for our bodies to grow and stay alive.

especially during their growing years. Too much of certain food items or a lack of others may cause serious diseases.

Food – source of energy for our bodies

Bread, meat, vegetables, milk and fruit all contain nutrients (fats, sugars, vitamins) that supply the energy necessary for movement, for the production of heat, and for the continuous functioning of our organs.

Can we eat anything?

No, humans need a *well-balanced diet*,

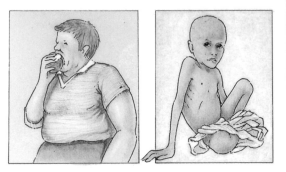

Eating food that is too rich may lead to *obesity*.

Famine, or a diet lacking in vitamins, leads to *malnutrition*.

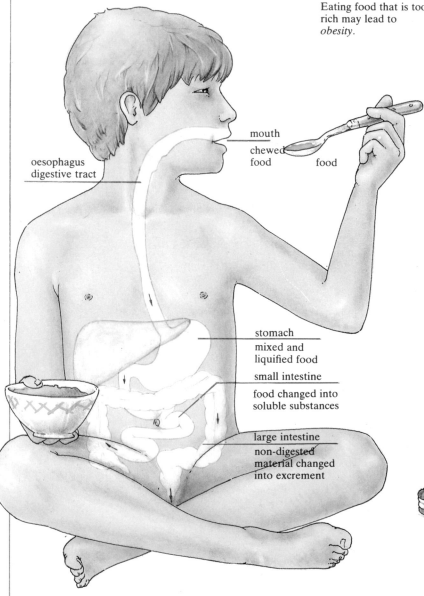

oesophagus
digestive tract

mouth
chewed food

food

stomach
mixed and liquified food

small intestine
food changed into soluble substances

large intestine
non-digested material changed into excrement

What happens during digestion?

After being chewed in the *mouth* and moistened by *saliva*, food enters the *digestive tract*. It goes through the *oesophagus* into the *stomach*. There it undergoes chemical changes and continues on its way into the *small intestine*. This is where the nutrients enter the bloodstream. Waste materials pass through the *large intestine* into the *rectum*, where they are passed from the body.

Are humans 'omnivores'?

In other words, do they eat both animal and plant foods?

insectivores

herbivores

granivores   carnivores

Certain animals eat plants only – they are called *herbivores*. Others eat only meat – they are called *carnivores*. Animals such as rodents that eat seed or grains are called *granivores*. Those such as moles, shrews and hedgehogs that eat insects are called *insectivores*. Most humans are *omnivores*, although some decide not to eat certain foods for moral, religious or health reasons. *Vegetarians* do not eat meat.

Plants also need nourishment

The most fragile plants as well as the strongest trees need food to develop and live. Their food is organic matter, made in the green leaves.

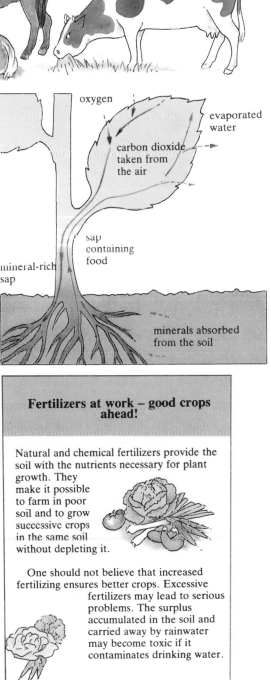

oxygen

evaporated water

carbon dioxide taken from the air

sap containing food

mineral-rich sap

minerals absorbed from the soil

The search for the natural way.

HORSE MANURE FINALLY DOMESTICATED

Horse manure is a rich natural fertilizer that is used for growing delicate plants.

The sap, the 'blood' of the plant, circulates organic matter produced by sunlight, chlorophyll, water and carbon dioxide, as well as *minerals* absorbed from the soil by the roots (iron, magnesium, phosphorus).

If the soil becomes depleted (loses minerals), plants deteriorate. They wither and die. Gardeners often fertilize the soil.

Fertilizers at work – good crops ahead!

Natural and chemical fertilizers provide the soil with the nutrients necessary for plant growth. They make it possible to farm in poor soil and to grow successive crops in the same soil without depleting it.

One should not believe that increased fertilizing ensures better crops. Excessive fertilizers may lead to serious problems. The surplus accumulated in the soil and carried away by rainwater may become toxic if it contaminates drinking water.

Good Nutrition

This represents a huge amount of food!
   We cannot stay healthy by eating whatever we please.

The choice of our meals, both in quality and quantity, is therefore very important.
   Good nutrition has to be learned.

A well-balanced meal

A poorly-balanced meal

Classification of food

According to their ingredients, foods are classified into different groups. Water is the only drink necessary for our body. Milk contains water, carbohydrates, proteins, fats, calcium and vitamins. It is a nearly complete food.

Proteins
Fish, cheese, nuts, milk, poultry, eggs, red meat.

Carbohydrates
Rice, potatoes, peas, pasta, cake, bread, chocolate, sugar.

Fats
Butter, margarine, oil, nuts.

Vitamins
Milk, whole grains, vegetables, fruit.

198

Energy that can be measured

Every item of food supplies our body with a certain amount of energy, replacing that used for our activities.

Food energy is measured in *calories*.*
Therefore:

- 1g (.04oz) of carbohydrate produces 4 calories;
- 1g of protein produces 4 calories;
- 1g of fat produces 9 calories.

The daily energy requirement varies according to age and activity.

For instance, a teenage boy needs an average daily allowance of about 3,000 calories. This is his recommended daily dietary need. *The nutritionist's calorie is what a chemist calls a *kilocalorie*, and is equal to exactly 4,185 joules of energy.

Rules for good nutrition

- Eat a variety of foods at regular hours.
- Avoid too many fats and sugars.
- Regularly eat green vegetables and raw fruit.
- Eat slowly and chew well.
- Relax after meals.

Well-balanced meals

These consist of a variety of foods that supply enough, but not too much, energy-containing nutrients (carbohydrates, proteins and fats). It is the balance between these nutrients that is very important for our health. Balanced meals also contain necessary vitamins and minerals.

Below is an example of the 'daily dietary allowance' for a teenage boy using about 3,000 calories a day.

Quantities of food providing the same amount of energy

250g (8.8oz) vegetables, salad
220g (7.8oz) grapefruit
orange, lemon
170g (6.1oz) apple, pear
150g (5.1oz) milk
110g (3.9oz) potatoes
100g (3.5oz) bananas

26g (0.9oz) sugar
22g (0.8oz) biscuits
19g (0.7oz) chocolate
13g (0.5oz) butter
11g (0.4oz) oil

28g (1.0oz) noodles
31g (1.1oz) rice
34g (1.2oz) cream cheese
34g (1.2oz) honey
40g (1.4oz) white bread
48g (1.7oz) ice-cream
54g (1.9oz) lean meat
43g (1.5oz) egg

Examples of well-balanced meals

Breakfast	Lunch	Dinner
1 cup of whole milk 28g (1oz) of wheat flakes ½ cup of orange juice 2 slices of toast 1 tablespoon of jam 1 teaspoon of butter or margarine	Tuna fish salad: 85g (3oz) of tuna fish, 1 hard-boiled egg, 1 small stalk of celery, 1 teaspoon of lemon juice, 2 tablespoons of salad dressing, 1 large leaf of lettuce, 2 slices of wholewheat bread 1 teaspoon of butter or margarine 1 large bunch of grapes 1 cup of whole milk	85g (3oz) of roast beef 3 tablespoons of gravy 170g (6oz) of mashed potatoes 85g (3oz) of buttered green peas 2 small rolls 1 teaspoon of butter or margarine fruit salad: ½ orange, ½ apple, ½ banana 2 biscuits

Blood: the Stream of Life

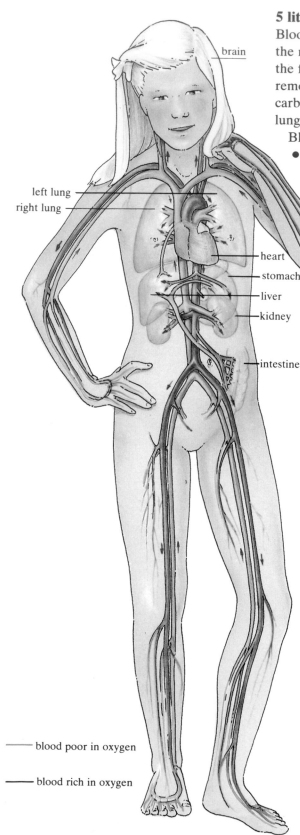

brain

left lung

right lung

heart

stomach

liver

kidney

intestine

blood poor in oxygen

blood rich in oxygen

5 litres (8.8 pints) of a most important liquid
Blood circulates in all parts of the body. It supplies the necessary energy (oxygen, digested food) for the functioning of the various parts of the body and removes waste products from them, in particular carbon dioxide, which is carried by the blood to the lungs, where it is exhaled.

Blood consists chiefly of:

- *red blood cells,* which are very numerous and give blood its red colour
  - *white blood cells*
  - a light-coloured liquid medium called *plasma.*

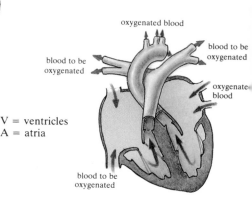

oxygenated blood

blood to be oxygenated

blood to be oxygenated

oxygenated blood

blood to be oxygenated

V = ventricles
A = atria

Blood rich in oxygen is bright red, whereas blood containing carbon dioxide is dark red.

A muscle that never sleeps

The heart is a very strong muscle located slightly to the left in the chest cavity. Like a pump, it draws up blood and forces it back, providing a continuous circulation.

The heart consists of two similar parts that are well separated but function together. One receives the blood rich in oxygen, the other receives blood carrying carbon dioxide.

At rest, the heart beats about *70 times per minute:* that is over *100,000 times per day.*

At every heartbeat, blood rich in oxygen leaves the heart and travels to all our organs; blood carrying carbon dioxide flows towards the lungs to be re-oxygenated. Physical effort, high

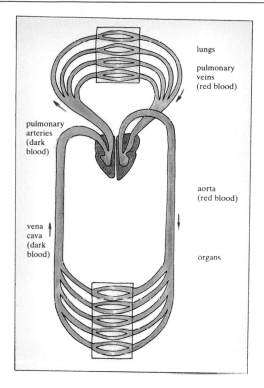

lungs

pulmonary veins (red blood)

pulmonary arteries (dark blood)

aorta (red blood)

vena cava (dark blood)

organs

100,000 miles of blood vessels

Blood circulates in a great number of vessels:
- *arteries* carry blood from the heart to the organs
- *veins* return it to the heart
- *capillaries,* as thin as hair, connect arteries to veins. They are the most numerous kind of vessel.

What is a haemorrhage?

A haemorrhage is a great loss of blood that may be fatal.

When is a blood transfusion needed?

A blood transfusion is needed after a haemorrhage that is due to an accident during work or on the road, or during long surgery. The lost blood is replaced by that of a donor.

temperatures or fear accelerate heartbeats. They may reach 100 to 180 per minute.

Heart disease is one of the world's leading causes of death. Bad diet, lack of physical exercise and heredity are all factors leading to heart disease.

Do we all have the same blood?

Not exactly. There are several blood types. A transfusion can only be made with identical blood. Blood tests are therefore necessary to determine the blood type needed. If the blood types do not match, the patient could suffer a serious reaction.

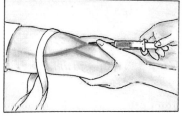

Blood donor

Between the ages of 18 and 60, people are able to donate blood. This can help to save lives.

Donating blood is not painful and the small quantity of blood taken is rapidly replaced by the body.

Taking the pulse

In order to count the number of heartbeats per minute, place two fingers – the index and the middle finger – on the inside of the wrist. This is the site of an artery and the pulsing of the blood can be felt.

Blood types

There are four major blood types: **A, B, AB** and **O**. They are inherited and transmitted.

What is in 1 cubic mm of blood?
- 5,000,000 red blood cells
- 7,000 white blood cells
- 250,000 platelets (which are the first to stop bleeding).

How long does it take blood to flow through the entire body?
A little less than a minute!

What is the average heartbeat of animals?
Below are the numbers of heartbeats per minute of four mammals and one bird:

elephant 18
dog 100
cat 180
mouse 240
pigeon 300

Seeing

How do we see?
The image is formed on the retina and is inverted (upside-down).

The optic nerve sends the message to the brain. At the rear of the eye are visual cells. When we look at an object, these cells transmit the message to the brain. The brain understands the message and gives the meaning of it.

The eyesight of an eagle!
Birds have eyesight that is much better than ours because their eyes have a larger number of visual cells. With the eyes of an eagle, we could read newspaper headlines from a distance of 1.6km (0.25 miles)!

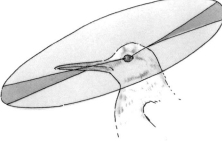

The position of the eyes determines the *field of vision*, which is about 180 degrees for humans.

Woodcock

Barn owl

This field can be very much *smaller* or *greater*.

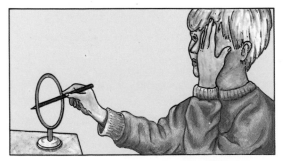

Why do we need two eyes?
With one eye closed, try to put a pencil through a ring. It is not easy. Now try it with both eyes open.

Binocular (with two eyes) vision makes it possible to estimate distances and to see objects in three dimensions.

To see and to remember

Every day, our brain records thousands of images. Only a few are selected and stored in our memory (the features of a friend, details of a landscape or of an object).

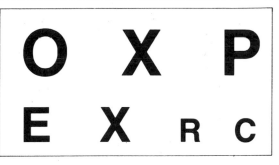

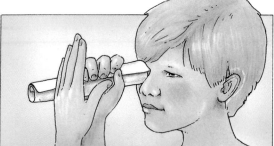

In 1315 glasses were first used to correct eyesight.

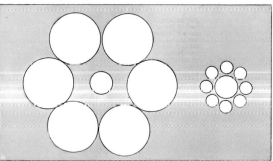

Our eyes are deceiving us!

The binocular vision in this example gives us the illusion that the hand is pierced by a hole.

Testing vision

Place your book at a distance of 6m (20ft) and try to read these letters by closing the right eye and then the left eye. Eyesight is measured in twenties – 20/20 corresponds to perfect vision. Only an optician can test vision properly.

An optical illusion

Which one of the two circles in the middle of the two patterns is larger?

Answer: The two circles are equal.

A white rabbit comes out of the hat!

Stare at the eye of the small black rabbit for about one minute. Then look just above the hat. After a few seconds, you will see the white rabbit appear.

Tasting, Smelling and Hearing

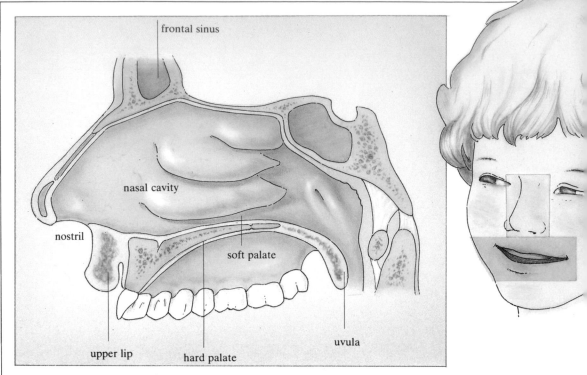

frontal sinus

nasal cavity

nostril

soft palate

upper lip

hard palate

uvula

Sense of smell

The olfactory system or *sense of smell* is located in the upper part of the nasal cavity. Odorous gases are carried by the air we breathe. Their message is transmitted to the brain by the *olfactory nerve*.

The sense of smell is very acute. It does not play a major role in humans but is highly developed in animals, and humans can make use of animals' senses. For example, dogs are often used for detecting explosives, finding persons buried in avalanches, or detecting hidden drugs.

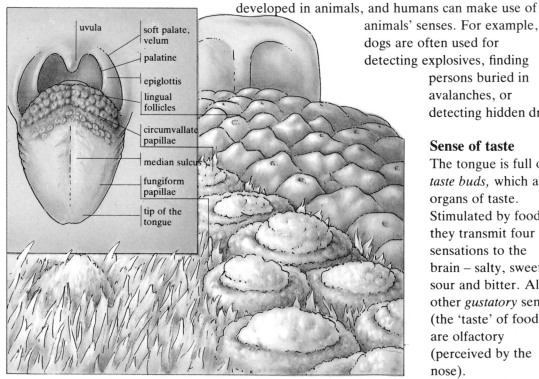

uvula

soft palate, velum

palatine

epiglottis

lingual follicles

circumvallate papillae

median sulcus

fungiform papillae

tip of the tongue

Sense of taste

The tongue is full of *taste buds,* which are organs of taste. Stimulated by food, they transmit four sensations to the brain – salty, sweet, sour and bitter. All other *gustatory* senses (the 'taste' of food) are olfactory (perceived by the nose).

Hearing

The ear is a receptor organ that responds to vibrations of the air – sound waves. These sounds, transformed into nerve impulses, follow the auditory nerve and reach the brain, which interprets them.

The ear is divided into three parts:

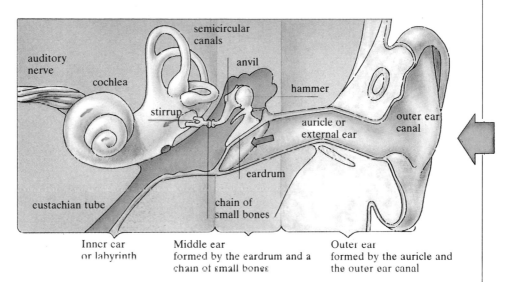

| Inner ear or labyrinth | Middle ear formed by the eardrum and a chain of small bones | Outer ear formed by the auricle and the outer ear canal |

A centre of balance

The semicircular canals of the inner ear give the sense of balance. They tell the brain the position of the head and how it is moving.

To emit a sound is to emit vibrations. When we talk, air expelled from the lungs passes by the vocal cords, which start to vibrate and produce sounds. The number of vibrations per second (*hertz*) is the frequency of the sound.

The human ear is tuned to frequencies between 16 and 18,000 hertz and hears the sound of a harp or a saxophone as well as the song of a bird. However, the sounds emitted by bats or dolphins are generally not heard by humans because their frequencies are too high.

What do animals perceive?

Although animal sense organs are different from ours, they also see, hear and smell. Very often, their perception of

Function of the ear

Sound vibrations, caught by the outer ear, travel down the auditory canal, strike the eardrum and make it vibrate.

The *hammer, anvil* and *stirrup* start to vibrate and transmit vibrations to the *cochlea* of the inner ear, where they reach the *cilia*. These cells produce a message that is sent to the brain by the auditory nerve.

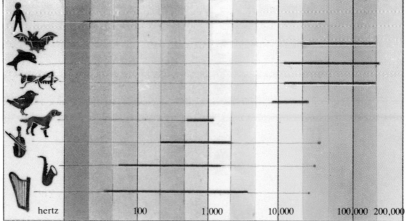

the world is dictated by one especially well-developed sense.

For instance, the *falcon*, whose eyesight is ten times more powerful than ours, can spot his prey from great distances.

The *dolphin* has an extraordinary hearing capacity.

The *fox* has excellent eyesight and a highly developed sense of smell.

The Sense of Touch

A very thin but resistant covering

Our skin covers and protects our entire body.

The thickness (from 1mm to 4mm) of our skin varies according to its location on the body. It is thicker on the palms and soles and thinner on our eyelids and lips.

Skin is very elastic and allows movement. It provides a protective barrier against physical injuries, humidity, cold and heat.

Skin wears down with repeated rubbing; however, it is constantly being renewed.

The skin surface of an average human being is between 1.4 and 1.9 sq m (between 15 and 20 sq ft).

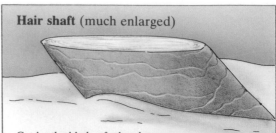

Hair shaft (much enlarged)

Cut by the blade of a hand razor

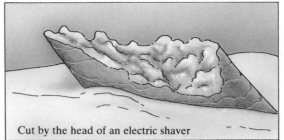

Cut by the head of an electric shaver

Structure of human skin

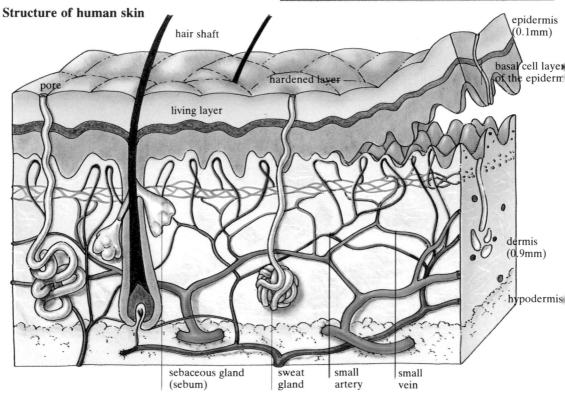

hair shaft

pore

living layer

hardened layer

epidermis (0.1mm)

basal cell layer of the epidermis

dermis (0.9mm)

hypodermis

sebaceous gland (sebum)

sweat gland

small artery

small vein

The organ of touch

The skin gives us five kinds of sensation: pressure, heat, cold, pain and touch.
The skin consists of two distinct layers:

- an upper layer called the epidermis
- a lower layer with five kinds of nerve terminals through which we perceive the various sensations: the dermis.

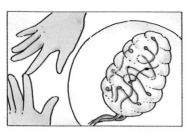

Meissner corpuscle (tactile)

Krause's corpuscle (cold)

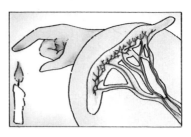

Ruffini's corpuscle (heat)

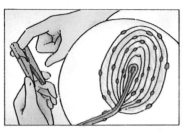

Pacinian corpuscle (pressure)

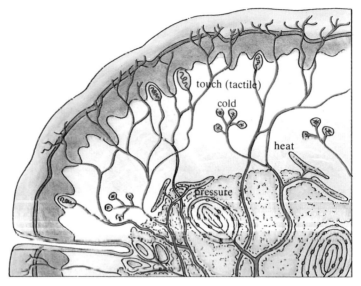

Epidermis and dermis. Various receptor organs of sensations can be observed.

Pain

The sensitive areas

The nerve terminals transmit sensations to the brain by way of the *spinal cord*.

These terminals are different according to what they transmit (cold, heat, pain) and they are randomly distributed in the skin. Therefore, certain skin zones are more or less sensitive to cold or to pain.

There are *600,000 receptors* that perceive sensation caused by contact of an object with the skin. These receptors are most numerous at the fingertips or on our lips.

There are *200,000 receptors* that perceive sensations of heat and cold.

Over *one and a half million receptors* perceive sensations of pain!

Taking care of skin

Skin is a remarkable material that protects our bodies and can renew itself if damaged, but it is important to take care of it. Skin should be kept clean and not exposed to too much sun if it is to remain elastic and healthy.

What are skin pores?

These are small openings through which wastes are continuously eliminated from the body.

On average, every day we eliminate one litre (2.2 pints) of sweat through our skin.
One sq cm of skin has thousands of pores.

Hair and nails are produced by the epidermis.

The skin is a thermostat

Evaporation of sweat allows the skin to act as a thermostat.

Evaporation helps to maintain a constant temperature in the body when the body is heated by a hot outside temperature or by physical exertion. Sweat evaporating causes a cooling effect.

The Body in Motion

A precise and solid framework

The *skeleton* is formed by 206 *bones*. It gives strength and shape to the body.

The bones provide protection (the bones of the skull, the rib cage) and support (the spine).

They are formed by living matter nourished by the blood. Long bones, such as those of the thigh, contain *bone marrow*, in which red and white blood cells are formed.

Articulated joints to let the body move

A *joint* is a place where two bones come together. If the bones can move with respect to one another, the joint is said to be *articulated*. At an articulated joint, the bones are held together by tough cords, called *ligaments*. A pad of *cartilage* between the bones absorbs shocks.

For instance, a hand is particularly flexible because of 26 very small bones that have articulated joints between them.

Some body parts have no joints. The skull, for example, is formed by eight flat *fused* bones.

The motors of movement

There are over 500 *muscles* that allow the skeleton to move.

Muscles are attached to the bones by *tendons*. When a muscle contracts, its tendon pulls on the bone and makes it move.

There are *smooth muscles,* found in the digestive tract, reproductive organs, bladder, arteries and veins.

Skeleton
skull
face
clavicle
shoulder blade
sternum
ribs
humerus
vertebral column (spine)
vertebrae
ulna
radius
wrist bone
pelvic girdle
metacarpals
phalanges (finger bones)
femur
kneecap (patella)
tibia
fibula
tarsus
metatarsals
phalanges (toes)

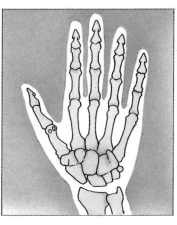

The 26 articulated bones of the hand

There are also *striated muscles*, located in the legs, arms, back and torso.

Most muscles are controlled by the *brain*. These are the *voluntary* muscles (those of the hand, the arms, the legs).

Other muscles, such as the heart, the muscles of the stomach and the thorax, work without our intervention.

These are *involuntary* muscles, which are not connected to bones.

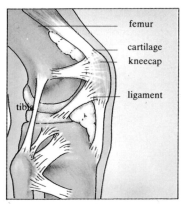

femur
cartilage
kneecap
ligament
tibia

Articulated joint of the knee

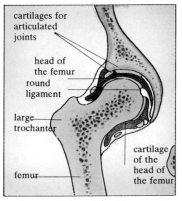

cartilages for articulated joints
head of the femur
round ligament
large trochanter
cartilage of the head of the femur
femur

Articulated joint of the hip (section)

Impaired functioning of muscles

Violent shocks (bicycle or skiing accidents) or sudden efforts sometimes cause bone and muscle injuries that may require temporary immobilization (rest).

Fracture

When a bone is broken it is immobilized in a plaster cast while the bony material heals the fracture together.

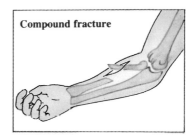

Compound fracture

Sprain

A common site for a sprain is at the ankle. It is a stretching or tearing of the ligaments that hold the bone in place.

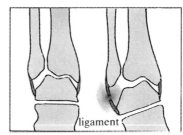

ligament

Articulated joint in place   Sprain

Laceration

A laceration, or tear, happens to the entire muscle. Pain is severe and immobilization lasts a long time.

Muscle pull

Sometimes, because of too great an effort, part of a muscle can be torn.

Anatomy
(drawing of a person without skin to show the muscles)

Contraction of biceps: triceps relaxed

Biceps relaxed: contraction of triceps

Which is the smallest bone?

The smallest bone in the human body is called the *stirrup*.
  It is located in the middle ear and measures between 2.5 and 3.8mm (0.1 and 0.15in). It weighs between 2 and 4.3mg.

How many bones are there in our faces?

There are *14* bones of which only one can be moved   the lower jaw.

Are there several kinds of muscles?

Not all muscles are alike. They may be long, short, thin, flat, or in the form of rings.
  Actions of muscles can involve *contraction* or *relaxation*. Muscles often work in pairs. You can see how they do this in the picture of upper arm muscles on the left.

How many muscles work when walking?

About *100* different muscles are used simply for walking.

What is lactic acid?

When working, a muscle produces a waste product, *lactic acid*, which is eliminated by oxygen during breathing.

Rickets

Calcium and phosphorus play an important role in the making of bones in children. Vitamin D is necessary to provide calcium. A lack of this vitamin leads to impairment of growth – rickets.

Did you know?

A bone soaked in hydrochloric acid for 24 hours loses two-thirds of its weight and becomes soft.

The Nervous System

The central nervous system

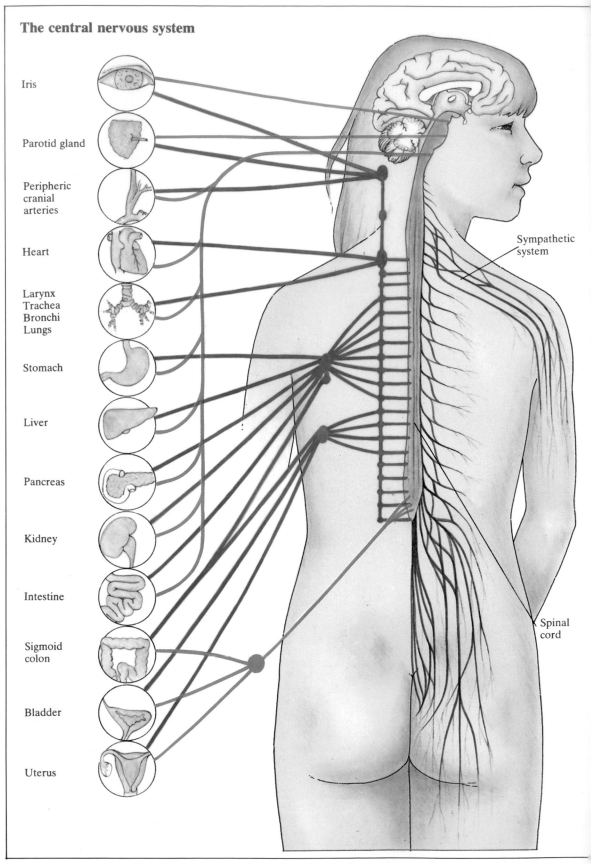

Iris

Parotid gland

Peripheric cranial arteries

Heart

Larynx
Trachea
Bronchi
Lungs

Stomach

Liver

Pancreas

Kidney

Intestine

Sigmoid colon

Bladder

Uterus

Sympathetic system

Spinal cord

A well-organized and well-protected system

The major part of the nervous system, the *cerebrum* or brain, is protected by the skull.

The brain consists of the *cerebrum*, the *cerebellum* and the *medulla*.

The brain itself is connected to the long *spinal cord*.

The spinal cord is protected by the bones of the *spine*.

The brain and spinal cord make up the central nervous system.

Among all the organs, the brain has the greatest complexity and not all the functions of its parts are understood.

The brain accounts for about 2% of the weight of the human body – about 1.4kg (3lb).

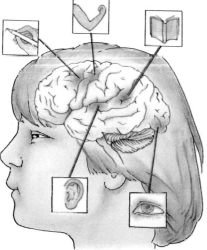

The control centre

All the nerves of the body are connected to the central nervous system. This is the control centre for all sensations, movement and more complex and poorly understood phenomena, such as intelligence, feelings, will and emotion.

Precise functioning

Sensations are transmitted by nerve cells to one part of the brain where they are interpreted. Orders can then be sent to the muscles by means of *motor neurons*.

This exchange of 'reception-emission'

takes place in the thin layer of *grey matter* at the surface of the brain. According to its location, the thickness varies from 1.3mm to 4.5mm.

If a nerve section is cut, the corresponding sensation is eliminated.

A communication network

There are 43 pairs of nerves, 12 of which leave from the brain, and 31 from the spinal cord. These have many branches, which connect the central nervous system with every part of the body.

Two kinds of nerves exist:

- those that transmit information of sensations, the *sensory nerves* (optic nerve, auditory nerve, olfactory nerve);
- those that transmit orders, the *motor nerves* (oculomotor nerve).

Most nerves contain motor and sensory neurons. They are called *mixed nerves*.

The brain

The brain is a soft organ located in the bony cage of the skull.

It is divided into many parts and every

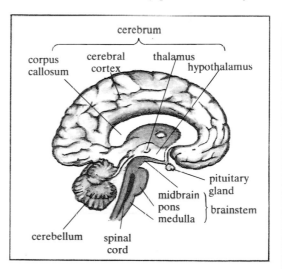

part has a different function – a centre for speech, for writing, etc.

Strangely enough, the right hemisphere of the brain gives orders to the left side of the body and the left hemisphere to the right side.

The Stresses of the Nervous System

The quality of the environment acts upon our nervous system. Excitement and commotions that are too intense tire our nervous system and create stress.

Noise

Too much noise may lead to nervous fatigue with loss of appetite and problems in balancing. It can sometimes impair a person's intellectual capacities.

Bright light

This is also a stimulant for the nervous system.

Alcohol

Even in small amounts, alcohol acts upon our nervous system.

It decreases the speed of our reflexes and causes us to be unco-ordinated.

It causes partial loss of memory.

With a large alcohol intake, cells are destroyed and a person's character can change (laziness, sadness, aggression, violence).

Alcoholism is quite a common kind of drug addiction. It causes many deaths from liver damage and car accidents.

Tobacco

Abuse of tobacco, smoking, also acts on the nervous system. Nicotine, a very toxic substance in tobacco (1 milligram per cigarette), is highly addictive. It leads progressively to loss of memory, very slow reflexes, an increase in uncoordinated movements, and circulatory disease. Other parts of tobacco smoke produce lung cancer.

Other drugs

Certain substances (heroin, morphine, cocaine) act directly upon the consciousness and change behaviour, progressively impairing health. Very rapidly, a drug addict becomes entirely dependent upon the drug used. Increase in drug consumption and serious related consequences in our modern society justify the war on drugs. Drug addicts are very sick people who must be helped and treated; they are a danger to themselves and to all society.

Drug abuse can also lead to other crimes, as addicts steal money to buy the expensive drugs they crave.

Drug abuse treatment centres are available in all areas of the country, but the war on drugs has yet to be won.

Sleep

Sleep is absolutely necessary for the benefit of the nervous system and hence the body's health.

The need for sleep varies according to age. Up to three months, a baby sleeps between 14 and 16 hours a day. At 15, a teenager sleeps about 10 hours.

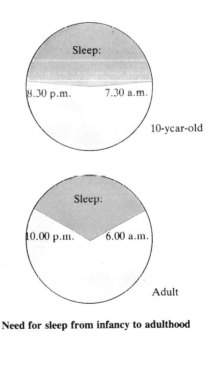

Sleep:

8.30 p.m.   7.30 a.m.

10-year-old

Sleep:

10.00 p.m.   6.00 a.m.

Adult

Need for sleep from infancy to adulthood

Did you know?

In the entire world, 120 million people suffer from serious mental diseases.

There are many types of mental illness: schizophrenia, affective, anxiety and personality disorders.

People with mental illness can be helped by many different kinds of treatment.

Viruses and Microbes

What are microbes?

Microbes are microscopic living things found everywhere. They live in the air, in the ground, in water, in human and animal bodies and in plants.

The are not visible to the naked eye.

Their existence was discovered in the 17th century, thanks to the invention of the microscope.

Microbes multiply rapidly. For instance, in a small quantity of fresh milk they increase in a few hours from some thousands to several millions! (The milk curdles.)

1665
Single-objective model

Microscope

eyepiece lens

mirrors

intermediate lenses

objectives on revolving turret

path of light beam

objective lens
stage clip
thin section
stage

coarse and fine adjustment knobs

switch

light source

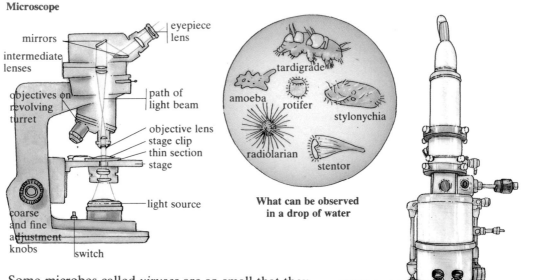

What can be observed in a drop of water

tardigrade

amoeba   rotifer

stylonychia

radiolarian

stentor

Some microbes called *viruses* are so small that they cannot be observed with an ordinary microscope. Their size is of the order of *millimicrons*, that is, a *millionth of a millimetre!* We can see them only with the electron microscope.

electron microscope

measles virus

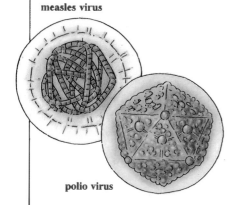

polio virus

Friends or enemies?

Microbes are known for causing diseases. Indeed, more than *1,000 infectious diseases* are caused by viruses in humans, animals and plants.

The common cold, measles, chicken pox and polio are viral diseases.

Nevertheless, many microbes are useful to humans.

moulds + bacteria for dairy products

yeast for bread and alcohol

Microbes get rid of waste products such as dead leaves, excrement, stagnant water and refuse of all kinds.

Some microbes are used for *fermentation* (the making of cheese, vinegar and yeasts).

They also play an important role in the transformation of foods during digestion.

Natural defence system

The skin provides an efficient barrier against microbes. If this barrier is broken (a wound, for example) there is risk of infection. When microbes enter the body, *white blood cells* try to destroy them. This battle often results in fever.

If the infection continues or becomes more serious, microbes are the victors over white blood cells. Then the organism needs help to defend itself.

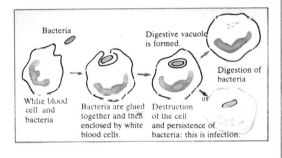

Bacteria

Digestive vacuole is formed.

Digestion of bacteria

White blood cell and bacteria

Bacteria are glued together and then enclosed by white blood cells.

Destruction of the cell and persistence of bacteria: this is infection.

Artificial defence

Very hot or cold temperatures kill most of the microbes (water is boiled to make it safe for drinking and food is preserved in a freezer). Certain *medicines* help the body to fight against microbial invasion and to stop it. *Antibiotics* such as *penicillin* are very efficient.

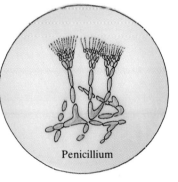

Penicillium

How does vaccination help?

A vaccine is not a medicine. It is a means of helping the body to mobilize its defence weapons against serious diseases.

With vaccination, some diseases (diphtheria, whooping cough and tuberculosis) have almost completely disappeared.

What is in a vaccine?

A vaccine contains a very weak dose of the disease against which the body needs protection.

The body responds by making defences that protect it against a more powerful invasion of the disease.

Why is Pasteur famous?

He discovered that microbes cause disease. He also discovered the vaccine against rabies, a viral disease that attacks the brain. The disease occurs mostly among animals, but it can be given to humans by a bite.

Pasteur also discovered that microbes in milk could be killed by heating the milk to a high temperature. This is why it is called pasteurized milk.

Vertebrates I

Classification

There are many animal species. To distinguish between them, they were first divided into two large groups: *vertebrates* (those with a vertebral, or spinal, column) and *invertebrates* (those without a vertebral column).

These two groups have been subdivided into smaller groups and classified according to their dominant characteristics. These are the groups of vertebrates:

Mammals

Reproduction
They are viviparous. Eggs develop inside the female's uterus. They nourish their young with milk.

Protection of the body
The skin is generally covered with hair.

Environment
They live on land and sometimes in water. A few can fly.

Respiration
They breathe with lungs. Even those living in water breathe air.

Birds

Reproduction
They lay eggs and incubate them. These eggs, protected by a shell, contain a food supply for the developing chick.

Protection of the body
The body is covered with feathers.

Environment
They live on land, on the surface of water, and in the air.

Respiration
They breathe with lungs.

Other characteristics
They have a beak, two legs covered with scales, and two wings.

Reptiles

Reproduction
They lay eggs on the ground but do not incubate them. These eggs are protected by a shell containing food supplies for the developing young.

Protection of the body
The body is covered with welded protective scales.

Environment
They live on the ground and/or in water.

Respiration
They breathe with lungs.

Other characteristics
Some have four legs.

Amphibians

Reproduction
They lay eggs without shells, usually in water. Tadpoles undergo metamorphosis (change of shape).

Protection of the body
The skin is naked and always wet.

Environment
They live on land and in water.

Respiration
Tadpoles breathe in water with gills. Adults breathe with lungs.

Other characteristics
They have four legs

Fish

Reproduction
They lay eggs without shells in water. These eggs are often abandoned.

Protection of the body
The body is generally covered with scales that can be removed one by one.

Environment
They live in fresh or sea water.

Respiration
They breathe with gills, taking dissolved oxygen out of the water.

Other characteristics
They have fins.

Vertebrates II

Mammals

camels

elephant

kangaroo

rhinoceros

lion

bat

gorilla

zebra

horse

sheep

cow

dog

hare

seal and seal cub

bear

whale

dolphin

Birds

swallows

vultures

pelicans

ostrich

goose

owl

cockerel

turkey

pheasants

swan

Amphibians

newt

frog

Fish

carp

pike

tuna

trout

perch

shark

eel

Invertebrates

Numerous animal species belong to this group. They are subdivided into smaller groups and classified according to their characteristics.

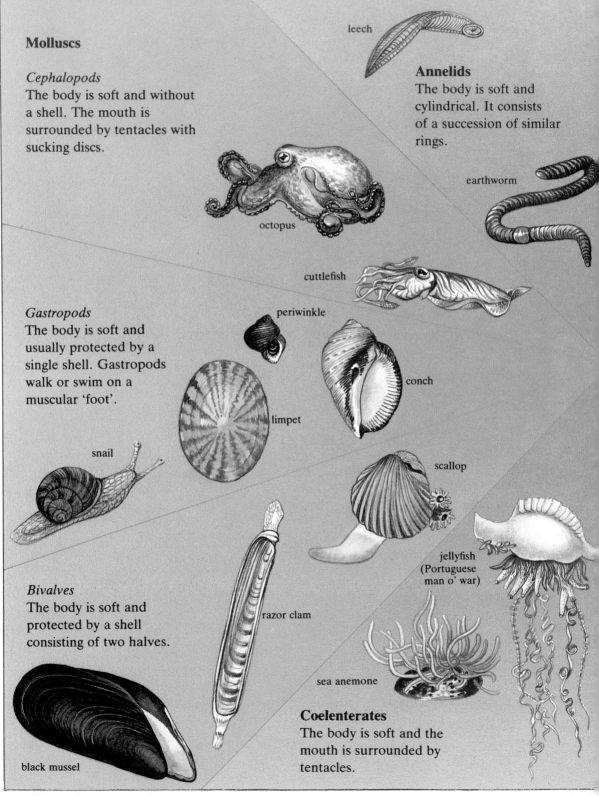

Molluscs

Cephalopods
The body is soft and without a shell. The mouth is surrounded by tentacles with sucking discs.

octopus

cuttlefish

Gastropods
The body is soft and usually protected by a single shell. Gastropods walk or swim on a muscular 'foot'.

periwinkle

limpet

conch

snail

scallop

Bivalves
The body is soft and protected by a shell consisting of two halves.

razor clam

black mussel

Annelids
The body is soft and cylindrical. It consists of a succession of similar rings.

leech

earthworm

jellyfish (Portuguese man o' war)

sea anemone

Coelenterates
The body is soft and the mouth is surrounded by tentacles.

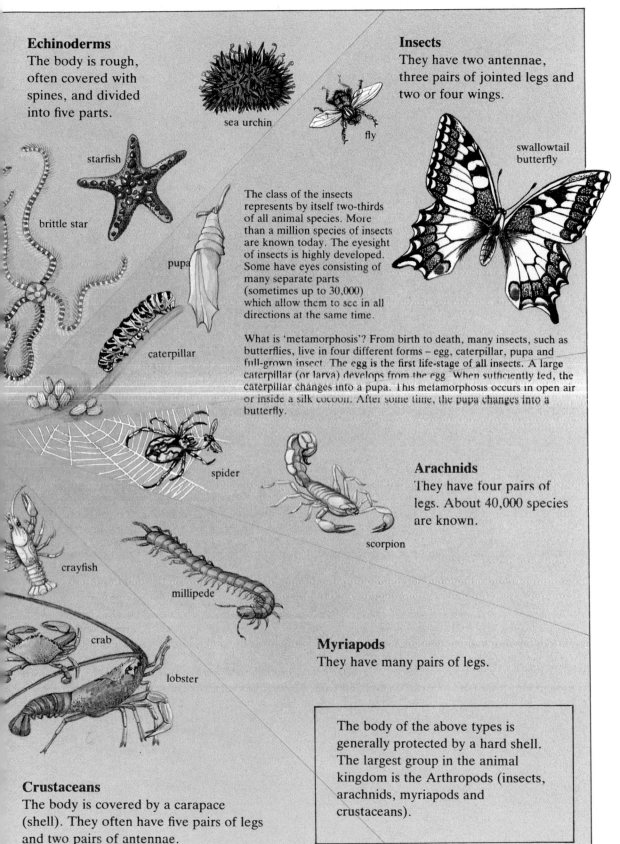

Echinoderms

The body is rough, often covered with spines, and divided into five parts.

sea urchin

starfish

brittle star

pupa

caterpillar

Insects

They have two antennae, three pairs of jointed legs and two or four wings.

fly

swallowtail butterfly

The class of the insects represents by itself two-thirds of all animal species. More than a million species of insects are known today. The eyesight of insects is highly developed. Some have eyes consisting of many separate parts (sometimes up to 30,000) which allow them to see in all directions at the same time.

What is 'metamorphosis'? From birth to death, many insects, such as butterflies, live in four different forms – egg, caterpillar, pupa and full-grown insect. The egg is the first life-stage of all insects. A large caterpillar (or larva) develops from the egg. When sufficiently fed, the caterpillar changes into a pupa. This metamorphosis occurs in open air or inside a silk cocoon. After some time, the pupa changes into a butterfly.

spider

scorpion

Arachnids

They have four pairs of legs. About 40,000 species are known.

crayfish

millipede

crab

lobster

Myriapods

They have many pairs of legs.

The body of the above types is generally protected by a hard shell. The largest group in the animal kingdom is the Arthropods (insects, arachnids, myriapods and crustaceans).

Crustaceans

The body is covered by a carapace (shell). They often have five pairs of legs and two pairs of antennae.

Animals in their Environment

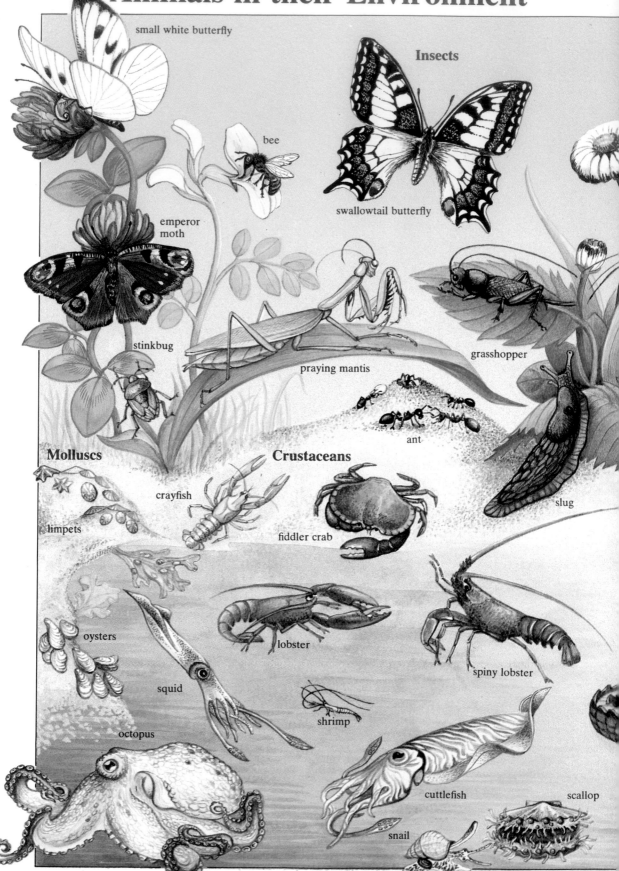

small white butterfly

Insects

bee

swallowtail butterfly

emperor moth

stinkbug

praying mantis

grasshopper

ant

slug

Molluscs

Crustaceans

crayfish

limpets

fiddler crab

oysters

lobster

spiny lobster

squid

shrimp

octopus

cuttlefish

scallop

snail

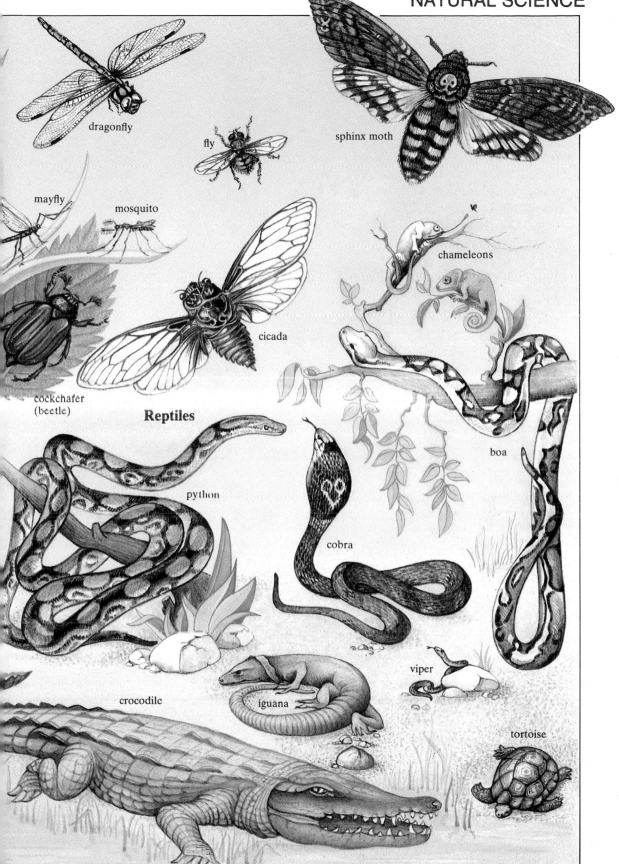

dragonfly

sphinx moth

fly

mayfly

mosquito

chameleons

cicada

cockchafer
(beetle)

Reptiles

boa

python

cobra

viper

crocodile

iguana

tortoise

The Food Chain

Energy from food

The animal and plant kingdoms supply food for every living creature on Earth. Plants get their energy from the Sun and this energy is passed on to whatever animal eats the plants. That animal in turn may be eaten by another animal, and so the energy is passed on again.

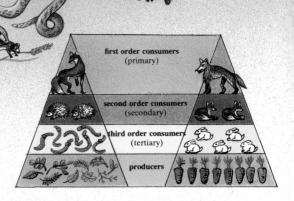

A sequence of eating
Here is one example of a food chain. At the beginning is a plant eaten by a rodent. The rodent is the prey of a snake, which in turn is caught by a hawk.

first order consumers
(primary)

second order consumers
(secondary)

third order consumers
(tertiary)

producers

Like the links of a chain

These diagrams show simple *food chains*. Every species is food for the following one and is part of the food chain. There is a transfer of food from one link to the other. *Decomposers* (insects, worms, microbes) transform organic matter (plants and dead animals) into minerals used by green plants, which are at the beginning of the food chain.

Some examples of a food chain

The number of links can vary from one chain to the other. The *pyramidal* shape shows that at any level there are more food organisms than eaters.

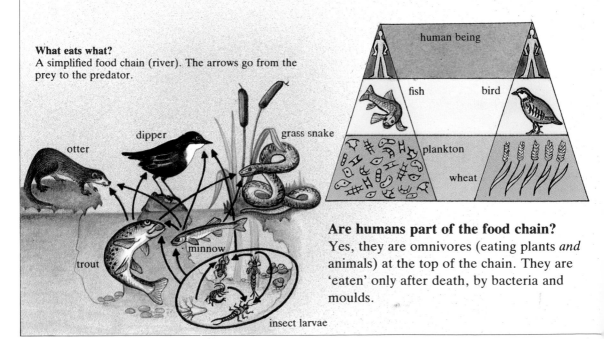

What eats what?
A simplified food chain (river). The arrows go from the prey to the predator.

otter   dipper   grass snake

trout   minnow   insect larvae

human being

fish   bird

plankton   wheat

Are humans part of the food chain?

Yes, they are omnivores (eating plants *and* animals) at the top of the chain. They are 'eaten' only after death, by bacteria and moulds.

When a chain is broken

Disorders in a food chain may rapidly lead to the disappearance of certain species and, at the same time, cause proliferation (increase) of certain other species.

If one kind of plant or animal becomes more or less numerous, the balance of the food chain becomes upset.

Destruction of the food chain by the use of insecticides. The dangerous chemical is carried into rivers by rainwater

Humans are sometimes responsible for this imbalance. The killing of many birds of prey has caused proliferation among various rodents.

Killing wolves in North America led to the proliferation of so many deer that much vegetation was destroyed and the deer starved.

Introduction of the missing link

To avoid the proliferation of certain species, humans have introduced, sometimes on purpose, certain predators or diseases (the missing link in the chain).

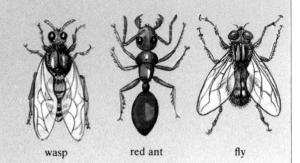

wasp   red ant   fly

Predators of the pine caterpillar introduced by humans.

For example, to exterminate pine caterpillars, insects that destroyed European forests, humans introduced particular predators in these forests – flies, red ants and wasps – which eat either eggs, or caterpillars, or harmful butterflies. Care had to be used here to control reproduction of these predators so that they developed less rapidly and less abundantly than their prey. If such care is not taken, in trying to improve one imbalance, another may be caused.

Three examples of devastating proliferations

1 The setting free of a few rabbits in Australia ended in disaster. Rabbits, which reproduce rapidly, soon became wild and, in about 10 years, numbered several hundred million, causing great damage to agriculture.

With an artificially induced contagious disease, *myxomatosis*, the population of wild rabbits was eventually controlled in Australia. However, the disease itself spread over all the continents and attacked domestic rabbits.

2 The mongoose was introduced into some Caribbean islands to control the rats in sugar-cane fields. The mongooses became pests because they became too numerous and, also, because they eat chickens.

3 A pair of muskrats was imported from America to destroy large vegetations in swamps in central Europe. The muskrats proliferated and invaded areas in Germany, Belgium, the Netherlands and France.

Muskrats are animals which dig underground tunnels at the foot of dams, causing great damage. They also prevent the normal development of other species.

The Plant Kingdom

Animal life is possible only because green plants and algae make food. Plants and algae are the first link in every food chain.

Algae and fungi

These organisms are stationary, like plants, but they are without roots, stems, leaves or a *vascular system* (system for taking water from the soil).

Lichens are a combination of algae and fungi. They live and develop in very harsh environments, such as high altitudes, deserts or rocks.

Without chlorophyll: mushrooms and other fungi

With chlorophyll: algae

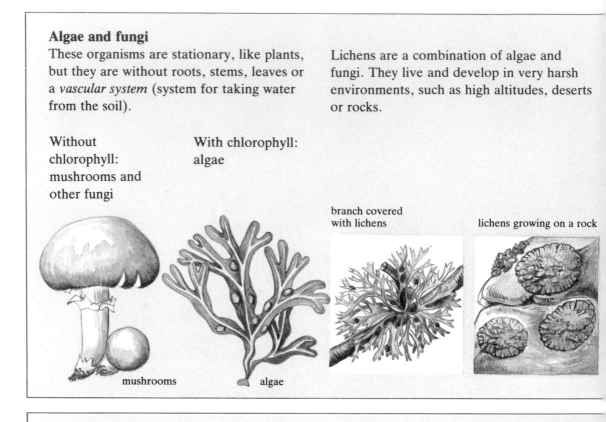

branch covered with lichens

lichens growing on a rock

mushrooms

algae

Plants that form seeds

These plants consist of stems, leaves, roots, a vascular system and seeds.

Gymnosperms

The seeds of these plants are exposed. They are not enclosed in an ovary, but are borne in cones (pine, fir, spruce).

Angiosperms

The seeds of these plants are enclosed in an ovary, which becomes a fruit (pea, bean, buttercup, cherry tree).

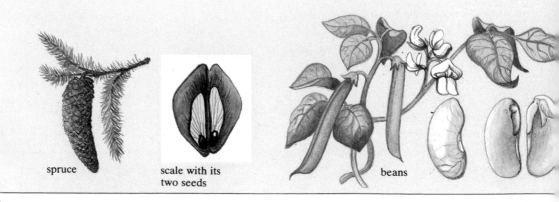

spruce

scale with its two seeds

beans

Primitive plants

Plants with roots, stems, leaves and vessels – ferns and horsetails.

Plants without roots or vessels but with leaved stems – moss.

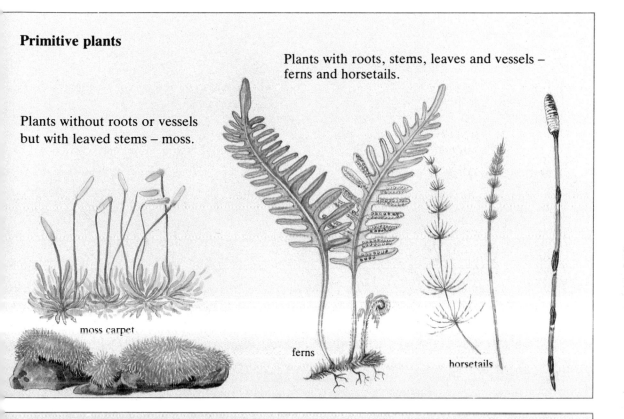

moss carpet

ferns

horsetails

Angiosperms are divided into:

Monocots
- The leaves often have parallel veins.
- The seed has a single cotyledon (seed leaf). Wheat, rice, lily of the valley and palm trees are examples of monocots.

Dicots
- Leaves have branching veins.
- Flowers have either free petals (poppy), welded petals (sage) or no petals (oak, beech).
- The seed has two seed leaves (is divided in two).

lily of the valley

section of the flower

poppy

sage

section of the flower

Discovering the Forest

The history of forests

The extent of forests has changed through the centuries. Originally, most European countries were covered by forests. However, over the years, many of these forests have been cleared for farms, towns and cities. In Britain, huge numbers of trees were cut down in the 16th century to build ships for the navy.

Today, especially in northern countries, forestry is an important industry. Forests – usually of evergreen conifers – are planted every year to be harvested in 30 or 40 years' time.

Forests supply timber for building, wood pulp for making paper, and wood fibres for materials such as rayon.

The different levels of vegetation

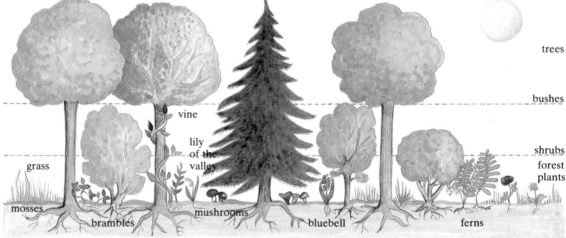

A well-organized community

Each plant in a forest occupies a certain level or height. Ferns, shrubs, bushes and trees are well-arranged in tiers.

In a forest, trees have a different growth pattern from when they grow on their own. Generally, their trunks grow higher because their lower branches, deprived of light, dwindle and die. *Forestry techniques* promote the growth of tall, straight trees suitable for use as timber.

Life span of trees

Life span varies according to the type of tree:

Cluster pine	40 – 80 years
Scots pine	60 – 100 years
Fir	120 – 150 years
Spruce	150 – 180 years
Oak	150 – 225 years

Each climate has its forest

Some forests consist of deciduous trees (oaks, birches, beeches).

Mountain forests and forests in northern countries consist of evergreen conifers (pines, firs, spruces).

Tropical rain forests have hundreds of different kinds of trees, some of them deciduous in the dry season.

What role do forests play?

Forests are very important for the equilibrium of the natural environment.

They protect the soil from erosion.
The tree roots hold the earth and sand and prevent soil erosion by rain and wind.

Eroded and gullied soil is no longer fertile (nothing will grow in it).

They purify the air.
Trees renew the atmosphere through the release of oxygen and thus are necessary for human life.

They affect the climate.
Trees draw from the ground a good deal of water, which they release into the atmosphere as water vapour. This contributes to the formation of clouds.

Soil erosion along a motorway

They shelter a world of animals.
Mammals (rabbits, squirrel, deer), birds (thrushes, warblers, owls) and many, many insects live in forests.

They prevent floods.
The soil holds a great deal of water. Forest trees can use up this water quickly.

When water overflows a river bank, it can often be absorbed before it does damage.

A wealth worth protecting

Forests are exploited because they provide a source of revenue. Wood is a very valuable product. It is a raw material suitable for numerous uses (building, furniture, fuel, paper pulp).

However, wood is not an inexhaustible resource. It has to be harvested carefully.

The enemies of the forest

Humans
They are responsible for:
- over-exploitation
- non-replanting of cut trees
- lack of conservation
- forest fires

Fire
Forest fires destroy many acres of valuable forest land.

Different uses of wood

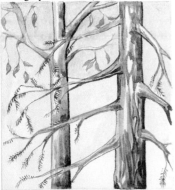
Another enemy: acid rain (water falling through polluted air)

Insects
Insects often cause considerable damage by chewing leaves or boring into bark. Whole forests can be destroyed by insects.

Wood damaged by insects

The age of a tree

The age of a cut tree can be found by counting the number of rings visible on a cross-section of the trunk – one ring represents one year.

Oxygen and the forest

Each day, 93 sq m (1,000 sq ft) of forest produces up to 1,200 litres (1,057 quarts) of oxygen.

Coniferous and Deciduous Trees

There are two main groups of trees –
coniferous and *deciduous*.

Resinous or coniferous trees
Their narrow leaves are actually *needles* or *scales*,
which are not shed in winter (with the exception of
the larch).

Their fruits are *cones*, which is why they are
called 'conifers'. Their sap is called *resin*.

larch

fir tree

spruce

cypress

juniper

cluster pine

Scots pine

stone pine

yew

Deciduous trees

The leaves of deciduous trees are shed in the autumn. In spring new leaves grow. Leaves may be *simple* or *compound*. Compound leaves are divided into a number of leaflets, as horse chestnut leaves are. Trees that keep their leaves in winter are called *evergreen*.

oak

horse chestnut

chestnut

birch

poplar

elm

beech

ash

plane tree

hornbeam

231

Edible Fruits and Exotic Trees

strawberry

white currant

raspberry

blackberry

fig

olive

orange

lemon

quince

apple

pear

hazel

peach

grape

cherry

banana

cacao (cocoa)

coffee

Palm trees

There are about 4,000 species. They are important commercial and agricultural resources in tropical regions. The best known are the coconut palm and the date palm.

Giant trees

The *eucalyptus* originates from Australia. There are many kinds, and some reach a height of over 90m (300ft).

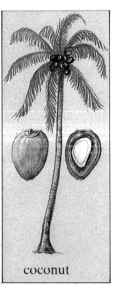

coconut

palm tree

date

eucalyptus

sequoia

baobab

The *sequoia* originates in North America. It is one of the largest and longest-living trees in the world (between 1,500 and 2,500 years). It may reach a height of 107m (350ft). It is a conifer.

The *baobab* grows in equatorial Africa. Its trunk may measure up to 46m (150ft) in circumference.

Fungi

Mushrooms and toadstools are *fungi* of various shapes with the characteristics of having neither flowers, nor leaves, nor chlorophyll. Certain species are edible, while others are poisonous, and some are deadly.

While mushrooms are a favourite type of food, collecting them requires great care. The collector must be able to recognize many species so as to avoid any potential danger by choosing poisonous ones.

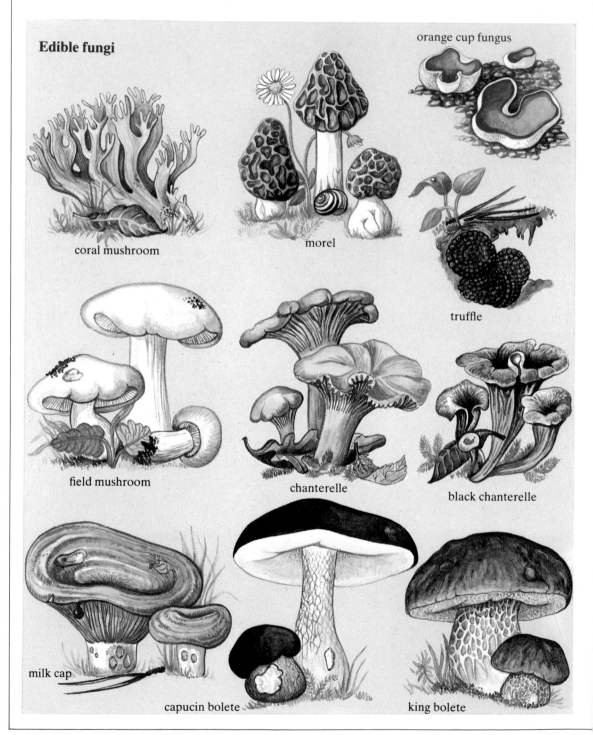

Edible fungi

orange cup fungus

coral mushroom

morel

truffle

field mushroom

chanterelle

black chanterelle

milk cap

capucin bolete

king bolete

The families of fungi

Agaricaceae (amanita *psalliotis*)

Polyporaceae (of the woods)

Polyporaceae (polypora) birch polypora

Hydnaceae (hydnum)

Thelephoraceae (craterellus)

Morchellaceae (morel)

Lycoperdaceae (puff ball)

Helvellaceae (helvella)

Clavariaceae (coral mushroom)

Tuberaceae (truffle)

Pezizaceae (orange cup fungus)

Red clathrus

Deadly fungi

destroying angel

spring death cup

deadly amanita

Poisonous fungi

rabbit ear mushroom

devil's bolete

amanita aspera

fly amanita

Wild and Garden Flowers I

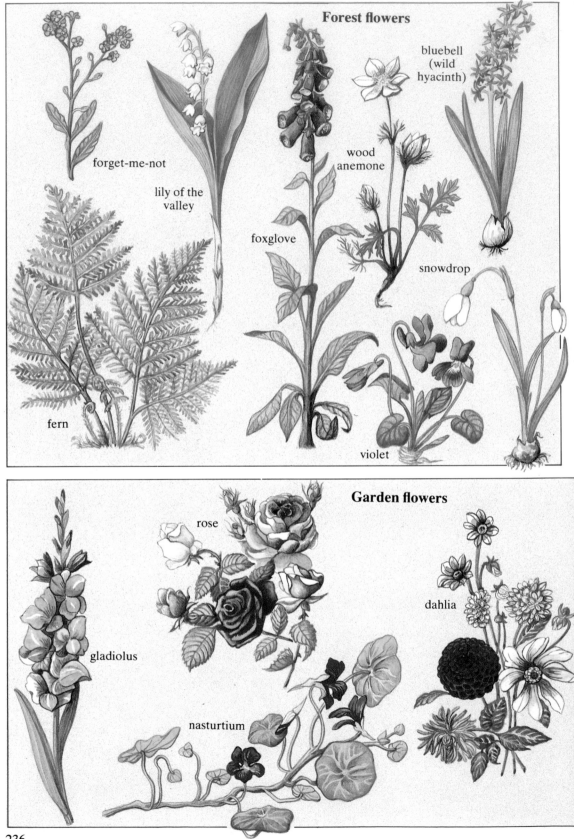

Forest flowers

forget-me-not

lily of the valley

foxglove

wood anemone

bluebell (wild hyacinth)

snowdrop

fern

violet

Garden flowers

rose

gladiolus

nasturtium

dahlia

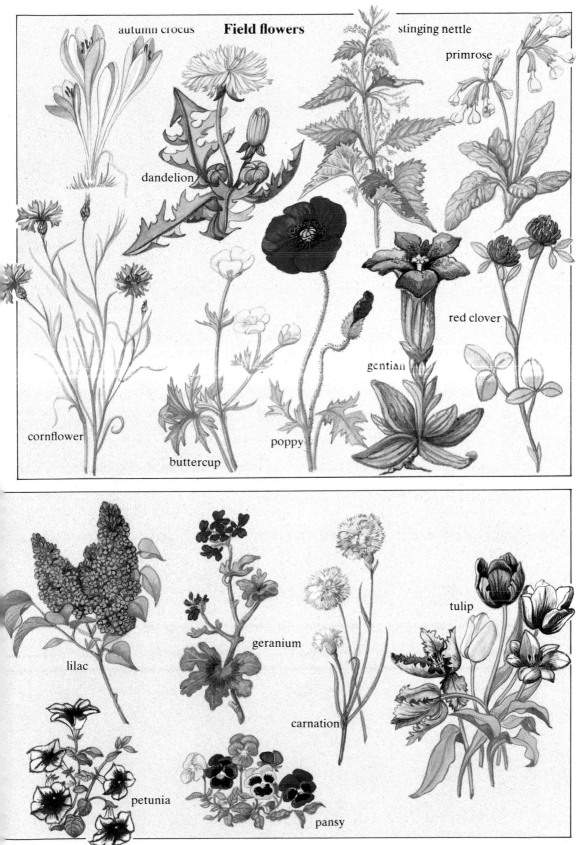

autumn crocus

Field flowers

stinging nettle

primrose

dandelion

cornflower

buttercup

poppy

gentian

red clover

lilac

geranium

petunia

pansy

carnation

tulip

Wild and Garden Flowers II

Climbing plants

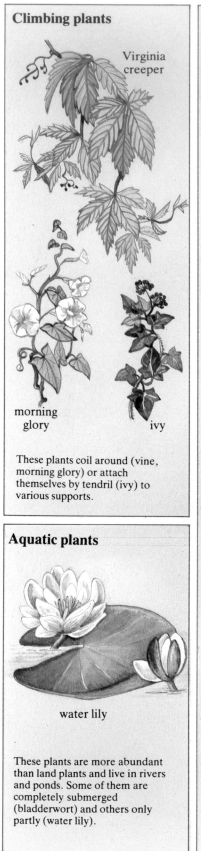

Virginia creeper

morning glory

ivy

These plants coil around (vine, morning glory) or attach themselves by tendril (ivy) to various supports.

Aquatic plants

water lily

These plants are more abundant than land plants and live in rivers and ponds. Some of them are completely submerged (bladderwort) and others only partly (water lily).

Vegetables

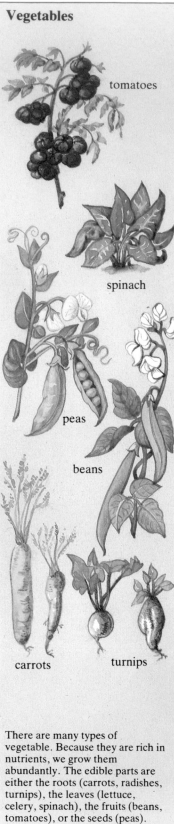

tomatoes

spinach

peas

beans

carrots

turnips

There are many types of vegetable. Because they are rich in nutrients, we grow them abundantly. The edible parts are either the roots (carrots, radishes, turnips), the leaves (lettuce, celery, spinach), the fruits (beans, tomatoes), or the seeds (peas).

Herbs

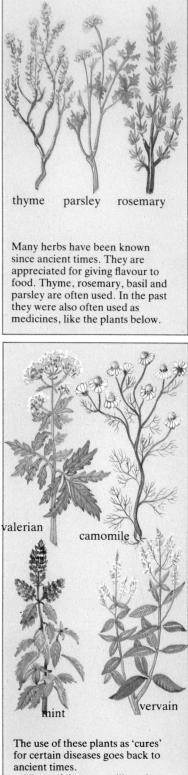

thyme   parsley   rosemary

Many herbs have been known since ancient times. They are appreciated for giving flavour to food. Thyme, rosemary, basil and parsley are often used. In the past they were also often used as medicines, like the plants below.

valerian

camomile

mint

vervain

The use of these plants as 'cures' for certain diseases goes back to ancient times.
Many of them are still used today in various forms.

Poisonous plants

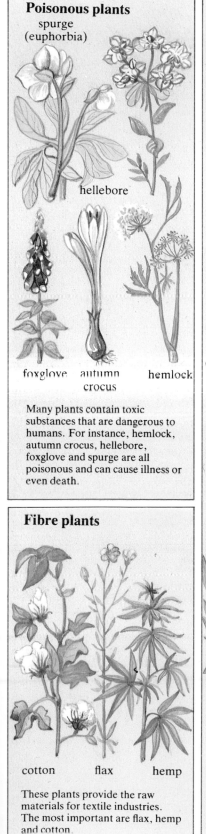

spurge
(euphorbia)

hellebore

foxglove autumn hemlock
crocus

Many plants contain toxic substances that are dangerous to humans. For instance, hemlock, autumn crocus, hellebore, foxglove and spurge are all poisonous and can cause illness or even death.

Fibre plants

cotton flax hemp

These plants provide the raw materials for textile industries. The most important are flax, hemp and cotton.

Cereals and fodder plants

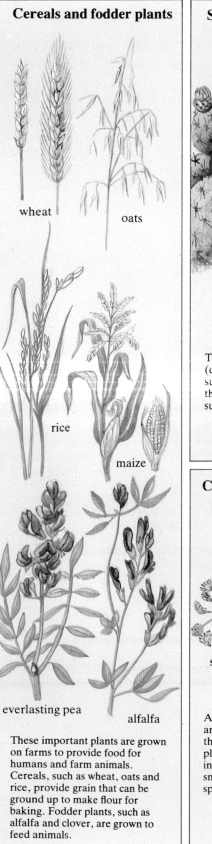

wheat oats

rice

maize

everlasting pea alfalfa

These important plants are grown on farms to provide food for humans and farm animals. Cereals, such as wheat, oats and rice, provide grain that can be ground up to make flour for baking. Fodder plants, such as alfalfa and clover, are grown to feed animals.

Succulents

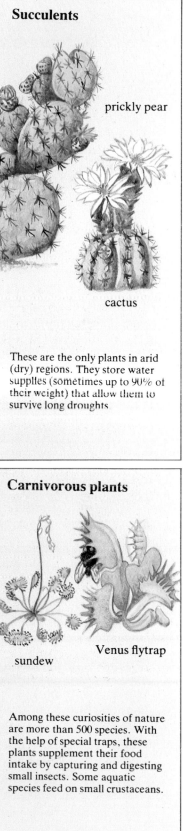

prickly pear

cactus

These are the only plants in arid (dry) regions. They store water supplies (sometimes up to 90% of their weight) that allow them to survive long droughts.

Carnivorous plants

Venus flytrap

sundew

Among these curiosities of nature are more than 500 species. With the help of special traps, these plants supplement their food intake by capturing and digesting small insects. Some aquatic species feed on small crustaceans.

239

SOS Pollution!

Nature is threatened. Our environment is in danger. Will we be able to act before it is too late?

Pollution has existed ever since the first cities were founded. With industrial civilization and the increase in world population, pollution has reached an alarming level.

And it gets worse every day. The environment is deteriorating. The survival of humans and numerous animal and plant species is endangered.

Today, many nations are beginning to make use of new and efficient measures to fight the dangers of pollution. However, these measures are expensive and require organization, determination and co-operation among the nations of the world.

We must be aware, however, that the battle for the environment has just begun.

Air pollution

The burning of fossil fuels (oil and coal) by factories, homes and vehicles, causes toxic gases to be released into the air. Rain contaminated by these gases falls as *acid rain* and damages plants and trees.

Governments have passed laws to try to prevent too much toxic gas being emitted. Cars, for example, can have catalytic converters fitted to cut down on fumes from exhausts.

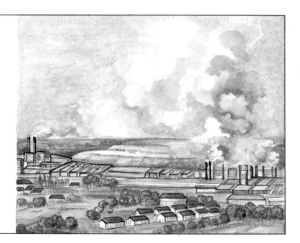

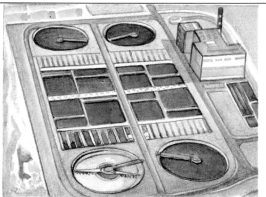

Water treatment plant. Water is 'cleaned' before being returned to the river.

Water pollution

The dumping into rivers of wastes from towns and cities (sewage) and from industry (toxic chemicals, such as sulphur, chlorine and mercury) causes dangerous pollution that can become a disaster when it reaches a high level. For example, many rivers in the United States are 'dying' because of pollution –

no plants. Also, there are nitrates from farm fertilizers which cause the overgrowth of plants, choking out the oxygen in the water.

Water treatment plants are designed to fight against this pollution. More and more plants are being built.

Nuclear waste materials are placed in sealed containers, but there is still argument about the safest place to store such containers.

Crops are sprayed with insecticides.

Ground pollution

Disposing of rubbish

Our cities produce thousands of tonnes of rubbish every day. Some of it is burned in incinerators. Much of it is piled up in landfill sites (waste ground), where it decays. People do not like to live near incinerators because they pollute the air, and space for landfills is getting scarce. Proper disposal of rubbish can be expensive, and a lot of illegal dumping is done to save money.

Insecticides and herbicides

Chemicals are often used to kill insects and weeds. But these chemicals can build up in the soil and damage the environment. Governments are trying to control their use more strictly.

Noise pollution

As machines become bigger and more powerful, they often make more noise. People are beginning to realize that this pollutes the environment too, making life difficult for animals and humans.

Accident!

When a disaster such as the wreck of an oil tanker at sea happens, special teams of experts rush to the area to try to prevent further damage.

A bird covered with crude oil.

The protection of nature

Oceans and seas are also heavily polluted by industrial waste products. Transportation of fuels has caused numerous catastrophes when oil tankers have been wrecked at sea causing massive oil spills. These 'black tides' have destroyed marine animals and birds and polluted beaches.

The black tide caused by the wreckage of the oil tanker 'Torrey Canyon' killed more than 100,000 sea birds of various species in 1967.

To preserve as much natural environment as possible, governments have established nature reserves and national parks. These help to ensure that some areas stay free of pollution.

The Mineral Kingdom

Rocks and minerals are components of the Earth's crust.
A rock is formed from one or several minerals clumped together.

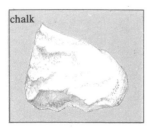

Chalk consists of
one single mineral –
95% is *calcium*.

Granite consists of
three minerals –
quartz, feldspar and
mica.

There are about 2,000 known minerals.

Geometrical structures

When a grain of salt is crushed, a hand lens
reveals that its fragments have the shape of
small cubes. Each one of these fragments
is a *crystal*.

Most rocks are made of small crystals
joined together. According to the kind of
mineral, the crystals have a different
geometrical structure (shape).

salt crystals

quartz crystals

sulphur crystals

Igneous rocks

These form when magma (liquid rock) cools and
crystallizes.

   The first minerals to crystallize are high in iron,
magnesium and calcium and low in silicon. *Basalt* is a
common igneous rock of this kind.

   The last minerals to crystallize are potassium
feldspar and quartz. Igneous rocks in which these two
minerals predominate are referred to as having a
granitic composition. Granite frequently forms the core
of eroded mountains, whereas basalt is found in many
volcanic eruptions.

basalt

Sedimentary rocks

These are rocks formed by debris detached from other rocks by mechanical and chemical weathering. Most of these sediments are deposited in lakes, rivers and seas.

Fossils are remains of former animals and plants found in sedimentary rocks.

The most common sedimentary rocks are *limestone*, *sandstone* and *shale*.

Oil and *coal* come from rocks where dead animals and plants were crushed together and over millions of years changed into fossil fuels.

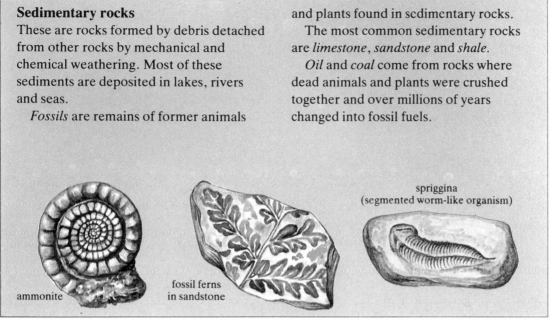

ammonite

fossil ferns in sandstone

spriggina
(segmented worm-like organism)

What are ores?

Ores are rocks that contain valuable and useful minerals occurring either in a native state or as mixtures (ores of iron, zinc, aluminium). After they are mined, ores have to be processed in some way to extract the useful mineral. For example, iron ore is heated to a high temperature.

Valuable minerals – precious stones

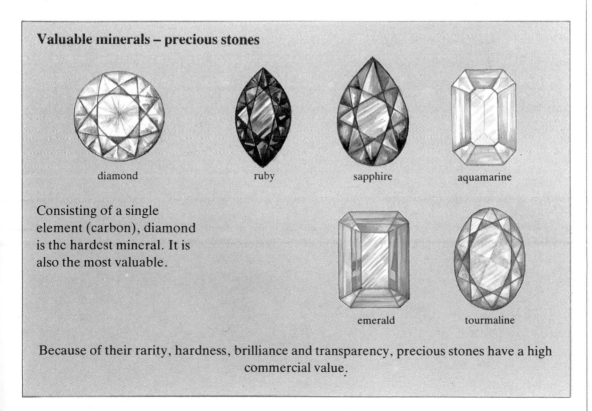

diamond   ruby   sapphire   aquamarine

emerald   tourmaline

Consisting of a single element (carbon), diamond is the hardest mineral. It is also the most valuable.

Because of their rarity, hardness, brilliance and transparency, precious stones have a high commercial value.

Sentences and Parts of Speech

What is a sentence?
A sentence is a group of words expressing a complete idea.

- 'The bank manager is friendly.' This *is* a sentence.

- 'A friendly bank manager' *is not* a sentence.

Four types of sentence
Anything we wish to say may be expressed in one of these types of sentence.

- 'Our goat, Blanche, is happy in the forest.'

This sentence is *declarative* because it makes a statement. Declarative sentences end with a full stop.

- 'Is Blanche happy in the forest?'

This is an *interrogative* sentence because it asks a question. Interrogative sentences end with a question mark.

- 'What an outstanding animal!'

This is an *exclamatory* sentence because it shows strong emotion. Exclamatory sentences often end with an exclamation mark.

- 'Blanche, come here at once!'

This is an *imperative* sentence. It commands or requests. Some imperative sentences end with a full stop ('Close the door, please.') while others are more forceful and end with an exclamation mark ('Be silent!').

Exercise
Are the following sentences *declarative, interrogative, exclamatory* or *imperative*?

1 Has the space shuttle landed yet?
2 What a heat wave!
3 My birthday is in October.
4 I'm getting a new bike.
5 Come here at once!
6 When is your birthday?
7 Get ready, get set, go!
8 My wallet is missing!

Answers

1 interrogative		5 imperative	
2 exclamatory		6 interrogative	
3 declarative		7 imperative	
4 declarative		8 exclamatory	

Sentences are made up of words, of course. Each of the words we use belongs to a different part of speech: a word is either a *noun, pronoun, verb, adjective, adverb, preposition, conjunction* or *article*.

Nouns

- There are *common nouns* that name persons (uncle), places (farm), or things (milk).

- Also, there are *proper nouns* that name a particular person (Adele), place (London) or thing (Coca-Cola).

Pronouns

These words take the place of nouns. Instead of repeating the name Adele in our sentences, for example, we may wish to use pronouns such as *she, her, hers*. Instead of always repeating London or Coca-Cola, we may at times use the pronoun *it*.

- The books were delivered to Adele. (or to *her*)

- I left the message at Adele's house. (or at *her* house)

- Adele is at the restaurant. (or *She* is)

- London is hot in July. (or *It*)

- I added ice to my Coca-Cola. (or to *it*)

Verbs

These are words that express action, that show what happens. When we say, 'My brother *hit* the ball', we are describing the action, telling what the subject of the sentence (brother) did.

Note the verbs (action words) in the following sentences:

- Ellis *left* the airport. (subject is *Ellis*)

- The minister *spoke* to the reporters. (subject is *minister*)

- Light *streamed* through the windows. (subject is *light*)

Some verbs do not show direct action as the ones in italics above. Instead, they tell us what the situation is. *To be* is a good example of such a verb. Some of its forms are:

I *am*
you *are*
he, she, it *is, was*

we *were*
they *will be, have been*, etc.

All of the words in italics above are different parts of the important verb *to be*. So, you see, while most verbs express action, some tell us about the *state of being, what the situation is*.

Sentences and Parts of Speech

Adjectives

These are words that describe nouns or pronouns. Is it a *new* car, a *red* car, a *flashy* car? Those three adjectives tell about the noun (*car*); they describe the kind of noun we are talking about.

If we say, 'He's *generous*', 'She's *kind*', 'They are *late*', we are using adjectives to describe pronouns.

In addition to describing *what kind*, adjectives can tell us *how many*.

> EXAMPLES
> We saw *three* sailors.
> Matthew has *two* pairs of trainers.
> Karen broke *six* of them.

Once again, adjectives are being used to describe nouns or pronouns, but in this case they also make the meaning more specific by telling us *how many*.

Words that answer the question *which one?* are adjectives.

> EXAMPLES
> She wants *that* pen. Which one? *That* one.
> Sally prefers *these* apples. Mark bought *this* hat.
> Take *any* card.

The words in italics are adjectives that are helping to describe nouns.

Adverbs

Adverbs *describe* (modify) verbs. We say that 'Marsha sang', but that simple act could be described even further. *When* did she sing? *Where* did she sing?

> EXAMPLES
> Marsha sang *yesterday*. (an adverb tells *when* she sang)
> Marsha sang *beautifully*. (an adverb tells *how* she sang)
> Marsha sang *here*. (an adverb tells *where* she sang)

Adverbs have another use – they modify adjectives.

> EXAMPLE
> The moon was *very* bright.

Moon is a *noun*. *Bright* is an *adjective* describing (modifying) the moon. *Very* is an *adverb* telling how bright.

> EXAMPLES
> The dentist is quite skilful. (adverb *quite* modifies adjective *skilful*)
> Cynthia is too excitable. (adverb *too* modifies adjective *excitable*)
> Arthur was seriously ill. (adverb *seriously* modifies *ill*)

Finally, adverbs also modify other adverbs.

> EXAMPLE
> The aeroplane flew too high.

Flew is a *verb*. High is an *adverb* modifying *flew*. *Too* is an *adverb* modifying the adverb *high*. How high? Too high.

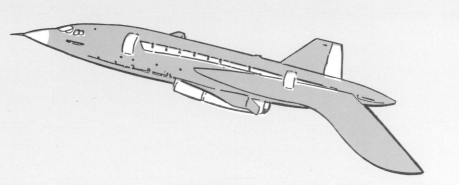

EXAMPLES

Brenda entered the room *very* cautiously. (adverb *very* modifies adverb *cautiously*)

We are *much too* clever for him. (adverb *much* modifies adverb *too*)

Victor did *especially well* in the test. (adverb *especially* modifies adverb *well*)

Prepositions

A preposition is a word that *points*. It shows the relationship between the noun (or pronoun) that follows it and some other word in the sentence. Here are 25 familiar prepositions:

about	between	in	since
above	by	into	to
among	down	of	under
at	except	off	until
before	for	on	up
behind	from	over	with
below			

We need these words to help make our sentences clearer, to show *relationships*.

EXAMPLES

I spoke *to* him.

We live *above* the shop.

This milk is *for* you.

The key is *on* the counter.

Notice in the sentences above that the prepositions are followed by nouns or pronouns.

Conjunctions

Conjunctions *join* related words or groups of words. Some of the most familiar conjunctions are:

and	for	or
but	neither	so
either	nor	whether

Sentences and Parts of Speech

Conjunctions join words:

> ham *and* eggs
> sad *but* true
> new *or* used toys

Conjunctions join *groups* of words:

- I sat down *and* wrote a letter to my parents.

- Be on time *or* you may lose your job.

- My sister had the measles *but* she recovered quickly.

Conjunctions may be used in pairs:

- *Neither* Edna *nor* Betty will be at the picnic.

- I can't say *whether* Sandy *or* David will be there.

- *Both* the chorus *and* the band will perform.

Articles
In addition to nouns, pronouns, verbs, adjectives, adverbs, prepositions and conjunctions, the English language has one other part of speech: *articles*. Articles are easy to identify because there are only three of them: *a, an, the*.

EXAMPLE
I never miss *an* opportunity to make *a* new friend in *the* school.

These three articles always act like adjectives; they modify nouns: *an* opportunity, *a* friend, *the* school.

Identifying parts of speech
Study the following sentence to make sure that you understand the part of speech of each word:

ARTICLE	ADVERB	ADJECTIVE	NOUN	VERB	ADVERB	PREPOSITION	ARTICLE	NOUN
The	very	brave	terrier	barked	angrily	at	the	burglar,

PRONOUN	VERB	CONJUNCTION	VERB	PREPOSITION	ARTICLE	NOUN
who	screamed	and	fled	into	the	night.

Tenses of Verbs

Note the verbs in these sentences:

- I *see* Eddie every day.
- I *saw* Eddie yesterday.

In the first sentence, the verb (*see*) is said to be in the *present* tense. In the second sentence, the past tense (*saw*) is used to show an action that took place earlier.

Each of our verbs can be used in a present or past form.

Present	Past
Bob *has*	Bob *had*
Bob *walks*	Bob *walked*
Bob *climbs*	Bob *climbed*
Bob *is*	Bob *was*

Other tenses

In English we can be very precise by using the proper tense of the verb. Knowing all of the tenses of a verb allows you to communicate your meaning effectively. This chart for the verb *to send* introduces you to the future, present perfect, past perfect, and future perfect tenses.

Present tense	
Singular	*Plural*
I send	we send
you send	you send
he, she, it sends	they send

Past tense	
Singular	*Plural*
I sent	we sent
you sent	you sent
he, she, it sent	they sent

Exercise

What is the correct form of the verb in each of the following sentences?

(see)	1	Yesterday we _____ Prince in concert.
(think)	2	I had _____ of that idea last November.
(learn)	3	Beverly is _____ how to skate.
(be)	4	Cary _____ our previous team captain.
(drive)	5	My mother has _____ me to school every day this year.

Answers   1 saw   2 thought   3 learning   4 was   5 driven

Tenses of Verbs

Future tense
(*shall* or *will* + the present)

Singular	Plural
I shall send you will send he, she, it will send	we shall send you will send they will send

Perfect tense
(*have* or *has* + the past participle)

Singular	Plural
I have sent you have sent he, she, it has sent	we have sent you have sent they have sent

Simple past tense

Singular	Plural
I sent you sent he, she, it sent	we sent you sent they sent

Pluperfect tense
(*had* + the past participle)

Singular	Plural
I had sent you had sent he, she, it had sent	we had sent you had sent they had sent

(This tense is used to express an action that was completed in the past *before* some other past action: 'We had written to them before we heard about the accident.')

Future pluperfect tense
(*shall have* or *will have* + the past participle)

| I shall have sent
you will have sent
he, she, it will have sent | we shall have sent
you will have sent
they will have sent |

(This tense is used to express an action that will be completed in the future before some other future action: 'By the time you receive this letter, we shall have landed in Baltimore.')

Two other tenses

You should also be familiar with the *present participle* and *past participle* forms of verbs.

Present participle examples: *writing, living, drawing*. Present participles always end in *ing*.

EXAMPLES
Ron is *sending* us an invitation.
Rhonda is *entering* the contest.
Ricky is *dreaming* of a white Christmas.

Past participle examples: *walked, wished, rained*.

EXAMPLES
I have *raced* around this track many times.
Charles had *turned* the corner when I saw him.
She has *eaten* in that restaurant every Monday for years.

(Past participles are usually used with a helping word – some form of the verb *to have*, such as *has, had, have* or *having*.)

Regular verbs

Some verbs are called *regular* verbs. They form their simple past tense and past participle by adding **d** or **ed**.

Present tense	Simple past tense	Past participle
stretch	stretched	stretched
breathe	breathed	breathed
snow	snowed	snowed

Irregular verbs

Some verbs are called *irregular* verbs. Instead of adding **d** or **ed** as the regular ones do, they form their simple past tense and past participle in other ways.

Present tense	Simple past tense	Past participle
do	did	done
eat	ate	eaten
go	went	gone
see	saw	seen
sing	sang	sung

Plural forms of nouns

Regular plurals

Changing singular nouns to plurals generally means adding an **s** to the singular:

Singular	Plural
boy	boys
lamp	lamps
table	tables

But nouns that end in **s**, **sh**, **ch** or **x** add **es** to form the plural.

Plural Forms of Nouns

Singular	Plural
box	boxes
church	churches
glass	glasses
sash	sashes

Nouns that end in **y** and have a vowel before the **y** form their plural by adding an **s**:

Singular	Plural
day	days
donkey	donkeys
toy	toys

When a consonant (a letter other than a vowel) comes before the final **y**, however, we change the **y** to **i** and add **es**:

Singular	Plural
baby	babies
diary	diaries
lady	ladies

When a noun ends in **f** or **fe**, usually an **s** is added to form the plural:

Singular	Plural
chief	chiefs
proof	proofs
safe	safes

However, there are some nouns ending in **f** or **fe** that form their plurals by changing the **f** to **v** and then adding **es**:

Singular	Plural
half	halves
self	selves
wife	wives

Irregular plurals

Most nouns form their plurals in a regular way, following the rules explained above, but other nouns, *irregular* ones, do not obey those rules. Here are some examples:

Singular	Plural
child	children
foot	feet
goose	geese
ox	oxen
tooth	teeth

Exercise

Do you know the plurals of these words?

1 knife 2 mouse 3 country 4 woman 5 calf
6 party 7 valley 8 patch 9 flash 10 fireman

Answers
1 knives 2 mice 3 countries 4 women 5 calves
6 parties 7 valleys 8 patches 9 flashes 10 firemen

Agreement of subjects and verbs

If the noun or pronoun that is the subject of the sentence is *singular*, then the verb that agrees with that subject must be *singular* too. In such cases, we say that the subject and verb agree in *number*.

- *She* (subject-singular) *is* (verb-singular) always on time.

- *Marty* (subject-singular) *works* (verb-singular) in the laundry.

When the subject of the sentence is plural, then the verb that agrees with that subject must be plural too:

- *They* (subject-plural) *were* (verb-plural) at the park.

- *Our athletes* (subject-plural) *have to be* (verb-plural) in good condition.

Exercise

Pick the correct verb forms to match the subjects in these sentences:

1 Mr Spencer, the teacher in charge of the buses, (is, are) my cousin.
2 Joshua and Maria (know, knows) how to play chess.
3 We (doesn't, don't) want to surrender.
4 Biologists (study, studies) animals.
5 They (has, have) no chance of succeeding.

Answers
1 is 2 know 3 don't 4 study 5 have

Different Types of Sentences

Simple, compound and complex sentences

Simple sentences

A group of words can be considered a *simple sentence* if (1) they have a subject and verb, and (2) the words make a complete thought.

EXAMPLE

Swimming   *is*   great fun.
subj.   verb

Compound sentences

Two simple sentences can be combined to make a *compound sentence* by using a conjunction such as *and*, *but*, *or*.

EXAMPLE

Swimming *is* great fun, and *I* *recommend* it to you.
subj.   verb   subj.   verb

Complex sentences

Complex sentences have two or more *clauses* (groups of words containing a subject and verb).

EXAMPLE

The children gathered in the playground,
1st clause

where the teacher spoke to them.
2nd clause

The *main clause* expresses the main idea in the sentence. A second, *subordinate clause* gives more information about the main clause or modifies it in some way.

EXAMPLE

We knew that the weather would change
main clause

if we remained patient.
subordinate clause

A *complex sentence* may have two or more *main clauses* and one or more *subordinate clauses*.

EXAMPLE

Mary went to the cinema and Denise decided to go too because it was raining.
main clause   main clause   subordinate clause

Remember
- Simple sentences consist of one clause (subject-verb combination).
- Compound sentences consist of two or more clauses of equal importance joined by a conjunction.
- Complex sentences consist of two or more clauses joined in such a way as to make one clause the main clause and the others subordinate.

Use of Pronouns

In order to understand English grammar, you must know how pronouns are used. Pronouns take the place of nouns, and some personal nouns are used as subjects: *I, you, he, she, it, we, they*. Those personal pronouns that serve as subjects are said to be in the *nominative case*.

There is a matching set of personal pronouns that serve as objects and are in the *objective case*: *me, him, her, us, them*.

Basic sentence patterns in English are *subject-verb-object*.

- I   went   home.
  subj.   verb   object

- We   sold   lemonade.
  subj.   verb   object

In speaking or writing, the proper pronouns must be used in sentences. If a sentence requires an object, a nominative pronoun cannot be used. Similarly, the subject of a sentence may not be an objective pronoun.

Right:	Harriet sent *me* to the shop.
Wrong:	Harriet sent *I* to the shop.

Right:	Lloyd and *I* are old friends.
Wrong:	Lloyd and *me* are old friends.

Right:	Jane and *I* went to the cinema.
Wrong:	*Me* and Jane went to the cinema.

Study this chart:

Person	*Nominative*	*Objective*
Singular first	I	me
second	you	you
third	he, she it	him, her, it
Plural first	we	us
second	you	you
third	they	them

Use of Pronouns

Relative pronouns

Another type of pronoun is the *relative pronoun*. It has five forms: *that, which, who, whom, whose*.

In the sentence: 'Here is the trophy *that* I won.' the word *that* serves two purposes. It replaces trophy as the object of *won*, and it relates the statement *I won the trophy* to *Here is the trophy*.

Important: In using the relative pronouns *who* and *whom*, remember that *who* is in the *nominative case*, to be used when it is the *subject* of your sentence. When an *objective case* relative pronoun is needed, you must use *whom*.

EXAMPLES
Keith is the player *who* scored the most points.
(*who* is in the nominative case, the subject of the verb *made*)

Where is the violinist *whom* you told me about?
(*whom* is in the objective case, the object of the verb *told*)

Interrogative pronouns

The pronouns *who, whom, whose, which, what* that introduce questions are *interrogative pronouns*. *Who, whom* and *whose* indicate that the answer will refer to a person; *what* indicates that the answer will refer to a thing; *which* may be used for either persons or things.

EXAMPLES

Who was the singer?	Answer: Mary
What was she carrying?	Answer: A book
Which boy went home?	Answer: Justin

Exercise
Select the correct pronouns:

1　The doctor spoke to Barney and (I, me).
2　(We, Us) know how to bake a cake.
3　It's Matthew (who, whom) we invited.
4　(They, Them) should know better.
5　(Who, Whom) did you vote for?
6　The headmaster scolded Vivian and (I, me) for coming late.
7　I'll never forget (she, her) and Marjorie.
8　It's you (who, whom) are responsible.
9　The caretaker, a man (who, whom) we admire, was fired.
10　Just between you and (I, me), the home team will win.

Useful hint: When a pronoun is the object of a verb or the subject of a preposition, it is in the *objective case*.

Answers

1 me　2 We　3 whom　4 They　5 Whom
6 me　7 her　8 who　9 whom　10 me

256

Punctuation

As you read in the section on types of sentences, every sentence ends with some kind of punctuation mark: either a full stop (.), a question mark (?), or an exclamation mark (!).

Full stops come at the end of a *declarative* sentence or statement: 'We were guests of Mr and Mrs Kramer.' You will also find full stops after abbreviations of some places, dates and academic degrees.

Place	*Academic degree*	*Month*	*Name*
R. Thames	Ph.D.	Feb.	R. L. Smith

Question marks, of course, come at the end of interrogative sentences. 'When does the game start?' When we ask a question *directly*, the question mark follows the complete question.

EXAMPLES
'Why did you decide to leave?'
'Why,' she asked, 'did you decide to leave?'

If the exact words of a question are not used (an *indirect* question, that is), no question mark is needed.

EXAMPLES
She asked him why he decided to leave.
Ellen wanted to know when the show would start.

Exclamation marks follow words or statements that express strong feelings or emotions:

EXAMPLES
Fire!
'Watch out!' Marsha screamed.

Commas must be used properly or your sentences will be incorrect and confusing.

EXAMPLES
The mayor said the governor is a complete fool.
or
'The mayor,' said the governor, 'is a complete fool.'

Commas help to make meanings clear.

EXAMPLE
After shaving Barry went to the party.

We can make better sense out of those words by using a comma that shows a pause is necessary.

EXAMPLE
After shaving, Barry went to the party.

When to use commas
● Between the name of a town or city and county:

EXAMPLES
Yarmouth, Isle of Wight
Norwich, Norfolk

Punctuation

- In an introductory expression:

  EXAMPLES
  Well, let's go.
  Oh no, I'm against it.

- In the opening of a letter:

  EXAMPLES
  Dear Marilyn,
  My dear friends,

- In the close of a letter:

  EXAMPLES
  Yours truly,
  Yours sincerely,

- To separate words in a series:

  EXAMPLES
  I bought shirts, ties, socks and gloves.
  Beth is bright, modest, loyal and amusing.

- Before the conjunction *and* when the sentence might otherwise be confusing:

  EXAMPLE
  I like cakes and biscuits, and I always eat too many of them.
  The rains came and we were soaked. (Comma not needed.)
  The coach sent for Peter, and Bert came along. (Comma needed.)

- To separate the person to whom the speaker is talking from the rest of the sentence:

  EXAMPLES
  'Dad, may I have my pocket money?'
  'Listen, Laura, this is important for you.'
  'Is it time to leave, Miss Taylor?'

- To separate interruptions in a sentence from the main clause of the sentence:

  EXAMPLES
  The fireworks, in my opinion, were superb.
  It's your turn, however, to make a contribution.

- To set off *appositives* (nouns that are placed next to other nouns to explain or identify them):

  EXAMPLES
  Bruce, the club's treasurer, gave his report.
  The twins, Joanna and Jeremy, came along for the ride.

Notice how the commas are used in this paragraph:

It was 6.10 in the evening, Sunday, 6 July 1975, and about 35,000 people were present when the Derby winner, Foolish Pleasure, stepped on to the track at Epsom, Surrey, for the first race. Joining him was the filly Ruffian, who was alert, edgy and eager to run. The winner, certain to be in racing's Hall of Fame, would receive £225,000, with £125,000 going to the loser.

Semicolons (;) indicate a stronger pause than a comma and a weaker pause than a full stop:

EXAMPLES
Be sure to get there on time; the game starts promptly at six.
We sent many protests to the mayor; no answers were received.

A semicolon is used between the clauses of a compound sentence that are joined by adverbs such as *however, furthermore, in addition, moreover, as a result*, etc.

EXAMPLES
All the winners received cash prizes; in addition they were taken to dinner.
Friday's game is an important one; therefore, we must do our best.

(*Note*: Never end a sentence with a semicolon.)

Colons are used to:

- Introduce lists:

EXAMPLE
The president pledged to do the following: reduce taxes, balance the budget, create new jobs and maintain the peace.

- Introduce explanations:

EXAMPLE
The purpose of the experiment was clear: to find a cure for baldness.
It could only be one person: the butler.
There can only be one explanation: a complete lack of concentration.

- Precede long quotations:

EXAMPLE
Winston Churchill wrote: 'We shall fight on the beaches, on the land, in the air . . .'

Punctuation

Apostrophes

Ownership. We show ownership by using certain pronouns:

EXAMPLES
This is *her* dress.
His number was called.

There are other ways to show possession, however.

EXAMPLES
This is *Helen's* dress.
The *boy's* number was called.

Not only is an **s** added to *Helen* and *boy*, but also the punctuation mark called an apostrophe
(') is added. That apostrophe shows ownership, and we use it to indicate possession by one
noun:

EXAMPLES
These are *Helen's* dresses.
The *boy's* numbers were called.

To show possession by *more than one noun*, add an **s** and then add the apostrophe:

EXAMPLES
These are the *girls'* dresses.
The *boys'* numbers were called.

When a plural noun does not end in **s** (such as *men*), we add an apostrophe and an **s** to show
ownership (*men's*):

EXAMPLES
children's toys
mice's tails
geese's feathers

Contractions. Apostrophes are also used to show that letters have been left out in order to
form a contraction:

EXAMPLES
is not − isn't
we will = we'll
he had = he'd
she would = she'd

(*Note:* Do not use an apostrophe in the possessive form of personal pronouns such as *ours*,
yours, his, hers, its, theirs. For example, *it's* must always stand for *it is* or *it has*.)

Quotation marks. We use quotation marks before and after someone's exact words:

EXAMPLES

The patriot said, 'I regret that I have but one life to give for my country.'
Roger asked, 'When will dinner be served?'
'You,' my brother exclaimed, 'are a pain in the neck!'

Notes:
- The final punctuation mark of a quotation is placed *inside* the quotation marks.
- The first word of a quotation usually has a capital letter.
- Separate the quotation from the rest of the sentence by commas.

Direct and indirect quotations. When we give the speaker's exact words, we are using a *direct quotation.*

But when the speaker's words are changed by whoever is reporting them, we are using an *indirect quotation*; no quotation marks are needed for indirect quotations.

Direct: Eloise said, 'I'm going to visit my aunt this weekend.'
Indirect: Eloise said that she would be visiting her aunt this weekend.

Quotation marks in titles. We use quotation marks around the titles of short forms of writing such as magazine articles, songs, short poems, short stories and book chapters:

EXAMPLES

We had to memorize 'Daffodils' by William Wordsworth.
Poe's 'The Tell-Tale Heart' frightened me.
Chapter Four, 'Crossing the Road', in *The Grapes of Wrath* is marvellous.

Addition

Concept of the operation

To add is to join together, to gather, to group elements in order to calculate the *sum*, the *total*.

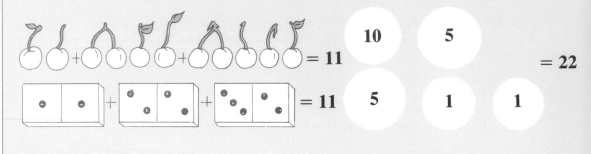

Addition properties

Addition is *commutative*. The sum of two or more numbers is not affected by reversing their order. Therefore: 8 + 12 = 12 + 8 = 20

Addition is *associative*:
Therefore:

$$26 + (4 + 10) = (26 + 4) + 10$$
$$26 + 14 = 30 + 10$$
$$40 = 40$$

Addition of whole numbers

4 + 743 + 33 + 5,237 =
(base 10)

th	h	t	u
5	2	3	7
	7	4	3
		3	3
+			4
6	0	1	7

We read:
six thousand and seventeen.

We operate by placing each digit in the appropriate column and adding from the right.

When a column adds up to more than 10, we put the units in the column we are adding and carry the tens to add into the next column to the left.

Exactly the same happens when adding in other bases.

101,101 + 1,011 =
(base 2)

```
    101,101
+     1,011
    111,000
```

We read:
one, one, one, zero, zero, zero.

Addition of decimals

4.234 + 12.316

```
     4.234
+   12.316
    16.550
```

We add the decimal part, and then the whole numbers. The decimal points of numbers and sum must be lined up correctly, one beneath the other.

2.3715 + 23.04

```
     2.3715
+   23.04
    25.4115
```

262

Addition of whole numbers and decimals

$34 + 5.25 + 16.153 =$

$0.205 + 153 + 0.030 =$

```
    34.              34.000
     5.25     or      5.250
+   16.153          + 16.153
   ───────          ────────
    55.403            55.403
```

```
     0.205              0.205
   153.        or     153.000
+    0.030          +   0.030
   ───────          ────────
   153.235            153.235
```

The decimal point is placed between the last digit of the whole number (units) and the first digit of the decimal part (tenths). By adding zeros after the decimal point of whole numbers, you can keep to the right columns more easily.

At a glance

Without performing any calculations:
1) Point out which sums are equal to the given amount.

54	125	800	46.5
17 + 27	90 + 45	350 + 450	33.25 + 13.25
38 + 16	80 + 45	525 + 275	24. + 12.5
19 + 35	92 + 23	630 + 270	18.5 + 18.
29 + 15	72 + 53	460 + 240	34.5 + 12.

2) Which one is the correct answer?

$24.9 + 34.2$	$=$	78.1	538.1	59.1	58.1
$114.25 + 8.025$	$=$	1,112.75	122.275	122.75	122.50

The addition table

The sum of an addition is found at the *intersection* of the row and column that begin with the numbers you want to add. So $7 + 5 = 12$.

0	1	2	3	4	5	6	7	8	9
1	2	3	4	5	6	7	8	9	10
2	3	4	5	6	7	8	9	10	11
3	4	5	6	7	8	9	10	11	12
4	5	6	7	8	9	10	11	12	13
5	6	7	8	9	10	11	12	13	14
6	7	8	9	10	11	12	13	14	15
7	8	9	10	11	12	13	14	15	16
8	9	10	11	12	13	14	15	16	17
9	10	11	12	13	14	15	16	17	18

Find the missing digits

```
                        --
     6─4        2─4       6─.─8
+     ─9─   +   ─61   +  ─3.25
   ───────    ──────    ──────
    1,081     1,209      82.9─
```

Answers

Subtraction

Concept of the operation

To subtract is to *take away* one number from another.
Subtraction is the opposite of addition.

If $a - b = c$, then $b + c = a$
c is the *difference* that, when added to the smaller number, gives the larger.

$$\begin{array}{r} 60in. \\ -50in. \\ \hline 10in. \end{array}$$

10 in. is the difference between Mark's and Sophie's size.

Mark *Sophie*
60in. *50in.*

In the box there is room for 8 more eggs. 8 is the *difference* between 21 and 13.
$21 - 13 = 8$ $13 + 8 = 21$

Properties of subtraction

Subtraction is *not commutative.*
$21 - 13$ is different from $13 - 21$

Subtraction is not *associative.*
$21 - 5 - 3 = (21 - 5) - 3$
$= 16 - 3 = 13$

is different from

$21 - (5 - 3)$
$= 21 - 2 = 19$

Subtraction of whole numbers

$2,943 - 1,767 =$
(base 10)

$1,101 - 110 =$
(base 2)

We operate by placing each digit in the appropriate column. If there are not enough units, you can change a 10 into 10 units and so on, always working from right to left.

th	h	t	u
2	$^8 9$	$^{13}4$	$^1 3$
1	7	6	7
1	1	7	6

$$\begin{array}{r} ^0 1,^{10}1^1 0\,1 \\ 1\,1\,0 \\ \hline 1\,1\,1 \end{array}$$

Successive subtraction procedure

$35 - 12 - 7\ =$
$35 - (12 + 7) =$
$35 - 19\qquad = 16$

$35 - (12 + 7)$
$35 - 19$
16

$346 - 25 - 13 - 5\ =$
$346 - (25 + 13 + 5) =$
$346 - 43\qquad\quad = 303$

Subtraction of decimals

14.286 − 2.479 =

$$\begin{array}{r} 1^34.^12^78^16 \\ -\ \ 2.479 \\ \hline 11.807 \end{array}$$

The numbers are placed in such a way that decimal points are lined up correctly, one beneath the other. Again, work from the right and change a number into tens if it is too small to take away from.

3.049 − 0.79 =

$$\begin{array}{r} ^2 3.^90^14\ 9 \\ -\ 0.790 \\ \hline 2.259 \end{array}$$

Subtraction of whole numbers and decimals

216.075 − 183 =

$$\begin{array}{r} ^12^16.075 \\ -\ 183. \\ \hline 33.075 \end{array}$$ or $$\begin{array}{r} ^12^16.075 \\ -\ 183.000 \\ \hline 33.075 \end{array}$$

243 − 0.075 =

$$\begin{array}{r} 24^23.^90^90^90 \\ -\ \ \ \ 0.075 \\ \hline 242.925 \end{array}$$

The decimal point is placed between the last digit of the whole number (units) and the first of the decimal part (tenths). Add zeros after the decimal point.

At a glance

Without performing any calculations:

1) Which differences are equal to the given amounts?

14	105
138 − 124	310 − 205
96 − 72	562 − 467
148 − 114	800 − 695
75 − 61	440 − 315

0.25	1.50
15.5 − 15	15.75 − 14
0.75 − 0.50	105.75 − 104.25
1.50 − 1.25	18 − 16.5
3.25 − 2.00	13.5 − 10.5

2) Find the missing numbers.

$$0.25\ +\ \dots\ =\ 1$$
$$0.60\ +\ \dots\ =\ 1$$
$$9.9\ +\ \dots\ =\ 10$$
$$34.50\ +\ \dots\ =\ 40$$
$$45.75\ +\ \dots\ =\ 50$$
$$99.6\ +\ \dots\ =\ 100$$

3) Find the missing digits

$$\begin{array}{r} -,-3- \\ -\ \ 2,3-5 \\ \hline 1,451 \end{array}\qquad \begin{array}{r} --- \\ -\ \ 17.4 \\ \hline 24.8 \end{array}$$

$$\begin{array}{r} -,-37 \\ -\ \ 2,3-4 \\ \hline 4,82- \end{array}\qquad \begin{array}{r} 7.-85 \\ -\ \ 4.3-- \\ \hline -.50- \end{array}$$

Answers

7.885 − 4.38 = 3.505
42.2 − 17.4 = 24.8
7,137 − 2,314 = 4,823
3,836 − 2,385 = 1,451

3) *Missing digits*

0.10	0.4
0.40	4.25
0.75	5.50

2) *Missing numbers*

to 1.50   105.75 − 104.25; 18 − 16.5
to 0.25   0.75 − 0.50; 1.50 − 1.25
to 105:   310 − 205; 800 − 695
to 14:   138 − 124; 75 − 61

1) *Equal differences*

Multiplication

A substitute for addition

The calculation of the addition of the same numbers over and over again can be shortened by using *multiplication*.

The numbers of flowers in all these bunches are:

$$4 + 4 + 4 + 4 + 4 + 4 = 24$$

or

$$4 \quad \times \quad 6 \quad = 24$$

Properties of multiplication

Multiplication is *commutative:*

$$4 \times 6 = 6 \times 4 = 24$$

Multiplication is *associative:*

$$24 \times 5 = (12 \times 2) \times 5 = 12 \times (2 \times 5) = 12 \times 10 = 120$$

Multiplication is *distributive* over addition:

$$5 \times (20 + 4) = (5 \times 20) + (5 \times 4) = 100 + 20 = 120$$

Multiplication of whole numbers

$$
\begin{array}{r}
234 \\
\times\ 105 \\
\hline
1\ 1,7,0 \\
23\ 400 \\
\hline
24,570
\end{array}
\qquad
\begin{array}{l}
= 234 \times 5 \\
= 234 \times 100
\end{array}
$$

Multiplication by 10, 100, 1,000 simply involves adding the correct number of zeros.

$$45 \times 10 = 450 \qquad 45 \times 100 = 4,500 \qquad 45 \times 1,000 = 45,000 \qquad 45 \times 10,000 = 450,000$$

Multiplication of decimals

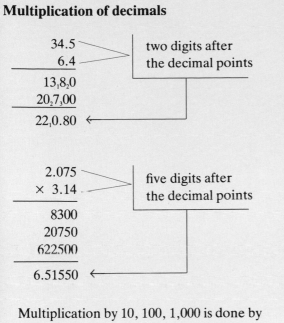

```
  34.5
   6.4          two digits after
              the decimal points
  13,8,0
 20,7,00
 22,0.80  ←
```

```
  2.075
× 3.14          five digits after
              the decimal points
  8300
 20750
622500
 6.51550  ←
```

Multiplication by 10, 100, 1,000 is done by moving the decimal point to the right.

```
24.75 × 10    = 247.5
24.75 × 100   = 2,475.0
24.75 × 1,000 = 24,750.0
```

Multiplication table

$5 \times 4 = 20$
$7 \times 6 = 42$

Reading across one row gives you the times table for the number at the beginning of the row.

1	2	3	4	5	6	7	8	9	10
2	4	6	8	10	12	14	16	18	20
3	6	9	12	15	18	21	24	27	30
4	8	12	16	20	24	28	32	36	40
5	10	15	20	25	30	35	40	45	50
6	12	18	24	30	36	42	48	54	60
7	14	21	28	35	42	49	56	63	70
8	16	24	32	40	48	56	64	72	80
9	18	27	36	45	54	63	72	81	90
10	20	30	40	50	60	70	80	90	100

Other ways of multiplying

You can multiply 28×16 by thinking of it as $(20 + 8)$ multiplied by $(10 + 6)$. $28 \times 16 = (20 + 8) \times (10 + 6)$. This means that 20 and 8 are *each* multiplied by 10 and 6 and all the products are added:

```
20 × 10 = 200
20 × 6  = 120
8 × 10  =  80
8 × 6   =  48
         448
```

Believe it or not, you can multiply any two numbers together knowing only the 2 times table.

Suppose we want 38×54. Divide 38 repeatedly by 2, throwing away remainders, until you can't divide any more. Multiply 54 by 2 as many times as you divided 38 by 2:

```
38 × 54
19 × 108
9 × 216
4 × 432
2 × 864
1 × 1,728
```

Now cross out all lines where there is an even number in the 38 column. Add what is left in the 54 column:

```
38 ×    54
19 ×   108
 9 ×   216
 4 ×   432
 2 ×   864
 1 × 1,728
     2,052
```

Division

What do we mean by division?

Division is

the process of dividing an amount into a number of equal parts in order to determine *the value of one part*.

looking for *the number of equal parts* contained in a certain amount when the value of a part is known.

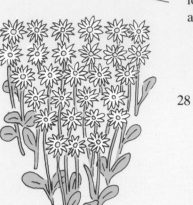

28 flowers

to make 4 bunches 28 ÷ 4 = 7
7 flowers per bunch

7 flowers per bunch 28 ÷ 7
4 bunches

Division is the opposite of multiplication.

$28 \div 4 = 7 \rightarrow \quad 4 \times 7 = 28$
$28 \div 7 = 4 \rightarrow \quad 7 \times 4 = 28$

Properties of division

Division is *not commutative:*
28 ÷ 4 is different fom 4 ÷ 28

Division is not *associative:*
(32 ÷ 8) ÷ 2 = 2 is different from 32 ÷ (8 ÷ 2) = 8

Certain calculations may be simplified by breaking them up:
$426 \div 2 = (400 \div 2) + (20 \div 2) + (6 \div 2)$
$\quad\quad = \quad\quad 200 \quad + \quad 10 \quad + \quad 3 \quad\quad = 213$

Dividing whole numbers

Dividing by a number less than 10 is easy if you know your times tables.

To divide 243 by 9, write the numbers as they are below and divide each digit by 9. Start from the left and carry forward any remainders as shown. Write the answer at the top as you go along.

$$9 \overline{)\, 23^{5}8^{4}5} \quad \begin{array}{c} 265 \end{array}$$

In the division above, the first digit, 2, cannot be divided by 9. Leave a space above the 2 and divide the first two digits, 23, by 9 instead. 23 ÷ 9 = 2 with 5 left over. Put the 2 at the top and write the 5 against the next digit: 8. You then divide 58 by 9, and so on to the end of the sum.

Division of whole numbers by 10, 100, 1,000 . . .

$$64 \div 10 \div 6.4$$
$$64 \div 100 \div 0.64$$
$$64 \div 1,000 \div 0.064$$
$$64 \div 10,000 \div 0.0064$$

The decimal point is moved to the left as many places as there are zeros in the number you are dividing by.

Division of decimal numbers by 10, 100, 1,000 . . .

$$64.5 \div 10 \quad = 6.45$$
$$64.5 \div 100 \quad = 0.645$$
$$64.5 \div 1,000 = 0.0645$$

Divisibility

It is possible to tell whether a number is exactly divisible without working it out. A number can be divided exactly:

by 2 If it is an even number, ending in **0, 2, 4, 6, 8.**
124 and 46,278 are divisible; 231 and 1,275 are not.

by 3 If the sum of its digits is *equal* to **3, 6,** or **9** (keep adding until you have a single digit).
210 and 12,435 are divisible; 125 and 12,743 are not.

by 5 If the *ending* digit is **0** or **5.**
1,250 and 34,245 are divisible; 342 and 624 are not.

by 6 If the number is *divisible,* at the same time, by **2** (even number) and by **3** (the sum of the digits is 3, 6, 9). 108 and 21,330 are divisible; 453 and 4,538 are not.

by 9 If the sum of its digits is *equal* to **9.**
450 and 26,145 are divisible; 345 and 1,270 are not.

At a glance
Without performing any calculation find out by which numbers (2,3,5,6,9) the following numbers are divisible:

216   540   135

Answers

135 is divisible by 3,5,9.

540 is divisible by 2,3,5,6,9.

216 is divisible by 2,3,6,9.

Fractions

Look back to page 129 for a reminder of how fractions work.

Addition

Fractions can only be added together if they have the same *denominator*. If they do, you simply add the *numerators* together to get the answer.

$$\frac{3}{7} + \frac{5}{7} = \frac{8}{7}$$

If the fractions to be added do not have the same denominator, they must be changed to a common denominator before adding.

The fraction $\frac{1}{2}$ is the same as $\frac{2}{4}$ or $\frac{8}{16}$ or even $\frac{350}{700}$

A fraction stays the same if the numerator and the denominator are both multiplied or divided by the same number.

So to find a common denominator for two fractions to be added together, the easiest thing is to multiply both parts of each fraction by the denominator of the other.

$$\frac{3}{4} + \frac{5}{6} =$$

$$\frac{3 \times 6}{4 \times 6} + \frac{5 \times 4}{6 \times 4} = \frac{18}{24} + \frac{20}{24} = \frac{38}{24}$$

The final answer should always be as simple as possible. This means that it should have as small a denominator as possible. Look at your answer to see if both parts of the fraction can be divided by the same number. In this case they can both be divided by 2, so the final answer is:

$$\frac{3}{4} + \frac{5}{6} = \frac{19}{12}$$

Fractions and decimals

Adding together a fraction and a decimal number is simple if you remember that a decimal number is divided into tens or *tenths*.

So $2.3 = \frac{23}{10}$ and $7.345 = \frac{7345}{1000}$

Example

$$2.3 + \frac{3}{4} = \frac{23}{10} + \frac{3}{4} = \frac{23 \times 4}{10 \times 4} + \frac{3 \times 10}{4 \times 10} = \frac{92}{40} + \frac{30}{40} = \frac{122}{40} = \frac{61}{20}$$

Subtraction

Subtraction of fractions works in the same way as addition. The important thing to remember is that both fractions must have the same denominator.

$$\frac{7}{5} - \frac{4}{5} = \frac{3}{5}$$

If there is a whole number in the sum, then this must be made into a fraction with the same denominator before you subtract.

$$9 - \frac{3}{5} = \frac{45}{5} - \frac{3}{5} = \frac{42}{5} = 8\frac{2}{5} \text{ or } 8.4$$

If the denominators are different, you can get a common denominator by multiplying just as for addition.

$$\frac{4}{5} - \frac{2}{3} = \frac{4 \times 3}{5 \times 3} - \frac{2 \times 5}{3 \times 5} = \frac{12}{15} - \frac{10}{15} = \frac{2}{15}$$

Fractions and decimals are treated in just the same way as for addition, by turning the decimal into a fraction.

Multiplication

Multiplying fractions is easy. You simply multiply the two denominators together and the two numerators together. Again, you must look at your result to see if the fraction can be simplified.

$$\frac{3}{5} \times \frac{4}{3} = \frac{12}{15} = \frac{4}{5} \text{ or } 0.8$$

To multiply a whole number and a fraction together, remember that a whole number can be written as a fraction too.

$$6 = \frac{6}{1} \qquad \text{So } 6 \times \frac{3}{4} = \frac{6}{1} \times \frac{3}{4} = \frac{18}{4} = \frac{9}{2} = 4\frac{1}{2} \text{ or } 4.5$$

Division

Dividing by a fraction is quite simple too. Simply turn the fraction you are dividing by upside down and multiply instead.

$$\frac{3}{4} \div \frac{5}{6} = \frac{3}{4} \times \frac{6}{5} = \frac{18}{20} = \frac{9}{10} \text{ or } 0.9$$

Test your skills

Which fraction represents the largest amount ?
The smallest?

1) $\frac{1}{3}, \frac{1}{5}, \frac{1}{2}, \frac{1}{8}, \frac{1}{4}, \frac{1}{6}$

2) $\frac{2}{3}, \frac{1}{4}, \frac{5}{6}, \frac{3}{4}, \frac{1}{5}, \frac{4}{5}$

Answers   1) largest: $\frac{1}{2}$ smallest: $\frac{1}{8}$ 2) largest: $\frac{5}{6}$ smallest: $\frac{1}{5}$

Measuring Time

Counting in 60s

60 seconds = 1 minute   60 minutes = 1 hour = 3,600 seconds

Base 60 is used for measuring time.

Therefore, 75 seconds = 60 seconds + 15 seconds   65 minutes = 60 minutes + 5 minutes
= 1 minute 15 seconds   **1 hour 5 minutes**

Abbreviations

second = sec
minute = min
hour = hr
day = da

Calculations

A)   To find the number of seconds represented by 3hr 12min 20sec:

3hr = 3,600sec × 3 =	10,800sec
12min = 60sec × 12 =	720sec
20sec =	20sec
	11,540sec

B)   To find the number of hours, minutes and seconds in 7,348sec:

a) Divide the seconds by 60 to give the number of minutes (and leftover seconds).

b) Divide the minutes by 60 to give the numbers of hours (and leftover minutes).
= 2hr 2min 28sec.

Divisions of a day

A day is divided into 24hr.
1da = 24hr

=   60 × 24 = 1,440min
=   3,600 × 24 = 86,400sec

Divisions of a year

A year has **365** or **366** days. There is an additional day in February every four years (leap year). 1992 was a leap year.

A year is divided into:
12 months or
52 weeks.
A century lasts 100 years.
A millennium lasts 1,000 years.

Addition of units of time

3hr 25min 38sec + 1hr 37min 43sec =

$$
\begin{array}{r}
3\text{hr } 25\text{min } 38\text{sec} \\
+\ 1\text{hr } 37\text{min } 43\text{sec} \\
\hline
4\text{hr } 62\text{min } 81\text{sec}
\end{array}
$$

We take away 60sec that we replace by adding 1min to the minutes column.

$$4\text{hr } 63\text{min } 21\text{sec}$$

We take away 60min that we replace by adding 1hr to the hours column.

$$5\text{hr }\ \ 3\text{min } 21\text{sec}$$

Subtraction of units of time

1) 3hr 25min 12sec − 1hr 48min 27sec =

$$
\begin{array}{r}
3\text{hr } {}^{24}\!\!\not{25}\text{min } {}^{72}\!\not{12}\text{sec} \\
-\ 1\text{hr }\ \ 48\text{min }\ \ 27\text{sec}
\end{array}
$$

We cannot subtract 27sec from 12sec.

We take away 1 min (60sec) from 25min; we add these 60sec to the 12sec: 12sec + 60sec = 72sec.

$$
\begin{array}{r}
{}^{2}\!\not{3}\text{hr } {}^{84}\!\not{24}\text{min }\ \ 72\text{sec} \\
-\ 1\text{hr }\ \ 48\text{min }\ \ 27\text{sec} \\
\hline
1\text{hr } 36\text{min } 45\text{sec}
\end{array}
$$

We cannot subtract 48min from 24min. We take away 1hr (60min) from 3hr; we add these 60min to the 24min: 24min + 60min = 84min.

2)
$$
\begin{array}{r}
1\text{da } 12\text{hr } 15\text{min } 25\text{sec} \\
-\ \ \ \ \ \ \ \ 24\text{hr } 10\text{min } 50\text{sec} \\
\hline
\end{array}
$$

We cannot subtract 50sec from 25sec. We take away 1min (60sec) from the 15min; we add these 60min to the 25: 25sec + 60sec = 85sec.

$$
\begin{array}{r}
1\text{da } 12\text{hr } 14\text{min } 85\text{sec} \\
-\ \ \ \ \ \ \ \ 24\text{hr } 10\text{min } 50\text{sec} \\
\hline
\end{array}
$$

We cannot subtract 24hr from 12hr; consequently we convert one day to hours (24), which we add to the 12hr: 12hr + 24hr = 36hr.

$$
\begin{array}{r}
\mathbf{36\text{hr } 14\text{min } 85\text{sec}} \\
-\ \ \ \ 24\text{hr } 10\text{min } 50\text{sec} \\
\hline
12\text{hr }\ \ 4\text{min } 35\text{sec}
\end{array}
$$

Using a Calculator

As a general rule a simple pocket calculator is able to perform:

a) addition (+)
   subtraction (−)
   multiplication (×)
   division (÷)
b) square root ($\sqrt{}$) calculations
c) percentage (%) calculations.

It also has:

- a correction key   CE
- a key   M+   addition to the number in the memory
- a key   M−   subtraction from the number in the memory
- a key   MR   to recall from the memory
- a key   MC   to erase the memory
- a key   C   total erasure

Display capacity: 8 digits.

To perform addition

of whole numbers

245 + 431 =
We punch:

245 + 431 = 676

of decimals
136.2 + 282.5 =
We punch:

136 . 2 + 282 . 5 = 418.7

Use of the correction key
25 + 14 =

We punch:

25 + 15 CE 14 = 39

To perform subtraction

1) 621 − 196 =
2) 196 − 621 =

We punch:

1) 621 − 196 = 425

2) 196 − 621 = −425

Repeated calculations

To add the same number several times:
35 + 18 + 18 + 18 =

We punch:

35 + 18 = = = 89

To subtract:
38 − 4 − 4 − 4 =

We punch:

38 − 4 = = = 26

In other calculators 35 + 18 + 18 + 18 must be performed by punching:

18 M+ M+ M+ MR + 35 = 89

To perform multiplication or division

1) 263.4 × 48 =
2) 624 ÷ 3 =

We punch:

1) 263 . 4 × 48 = 12643.2

2) 624 ÷ 3 = 208

ARITHMETIC

Mixed calculations

9 + 4 − 4.5 =

We punch:

9 [+] 4 [−] 4 [.] 5 [=] 8.5

2 − 9 + 3 =

We punch:

2 [−] 9 [+] 3 [=] −4

(8 × 3) ÷ 2 =

We punch:

8 [×] 3 [÷] 2 [=] 12

Using the memory

(30 × 20) + (40 × 25) + (60 × 15) =

We punch:

30 [×] 20 [M+]

40 [×] 25 [M+]

60 [×] 15 [M+]

We punch: [MR] 2500

Calculation of square roots

5 is the square root of 25, because 5 × 5 = 25.

We write $\sqrt{25} = 5$ (square root of 25 is 5).

The calculator enables us to find immediately the square root of any number.

We punch the number, then we punch the key

[$\sqrt{}$]

EXAMPLE

224 [$\sqrt{}$] 14.966629

152 [$\sqrt{}$] 12.328828

Calculation of a percentage

How much is 25% of 235?
We punch:

235 [×] 25 [%] 58.75

How much is 85% of 15?
We punch:

15 [×] 85 [%] 12.75

Calculation of an amount with an added percentage

350+20%−

We punch:

350 [×] 20 [%] [+] [=] 420

Calculation of an amount with a percentage subtracted (discount)

350 − 20% =

We punch:

350 [×] 20 [%] [−] [=] 280

Some tests

1) 1246.58 + 398.75=

2) 284.5−719.25−

3) (48 × 24) + (37.5 × 19.3)
    + (172.02 × 91.75) =

4) $\sqrt{288}$ =

5) 35% of 6948 =

Answers

1) 1645.33   2) −434.75   3) 17658.585   4) 16.970562   5) 2431.8

275

Periods of History

Historical periods are often referred to by the name of the person reigning at that time. In the lists below, the years given are for the beginning and end of each reign.

Roman emperors

27 BC–AD 14	Augustus (Octavian)
14–37	Tiberius
37–41	Caligula (Gaius)
41–54	Claudius
54–68	Nero
68–69	Galba
69	Otho
69	Vitellius
69–79	Vespasian
79–81	Titus
81–96	Domitian
96–98	Nerva
98–117	Trajan
117–38	Hadrian
138–61	Antoninus Pius
161–80	Marcus Aurelius
161–69	Lucius Aurelius Verus
180–82	Commodus
193	Pertinax
193	Didius Julian
193–211	Septimius Severus
211–17	Caracalla
217–18	Macrinus
218–22	Elagabalus
222–35	Alexander Severus
235–38	Maximinus
238	Gordian I
238	Gordian II
238	Pupienus
238	Balbinus
238–44	Gordian III
244–49	Philip ('the Arab')
249–51	Decius
251–53	Gallus
253	Aemilian
253–59	Valerian
259–68	Galienus
268–70	Claudius II
270–75	Aurelian
275–76	Tacitus
276	Florian
276–82	Probus
282–83	Carus
283–84	Numerian and Carinus
284–85	Carinus
284–305	Diocletian
286–305	Maximian
305–06	Constantius I
305–11	Galerius
311–37	Constantine I (the Great)
337–61	Constantine II
337–50	Constans
361–63	Julian (the Apostate)
363–64	Jovian
364–75	Valentinian I (in the West)
364–78	Valens (in the East)
375–83	Gratian (in the West)
375–92	Valentinian II (in the West)
379–95	Theodosius the Great (in the East, and after 394 in the West)
383–88	Maximus (in the West)
392–94	Eugenius (in the West)
395–408	Arcadius (in the East)
395–423	Honorius (in the West)
421	Constantius III (co-emperor in the West)
408–50	Theodosius II (in the East)
425–55	Valentian III (in the West)
450–57	Marcian (in the East)
455	Petronius (in the West)
455–56	Avitus (in the West)
457–61	Majorian (in the West)
457–74	Leo I (in the East)
461–65	Severus (in the West)
467–72	Anthemius (in the West)
472	Olybrius (in the West)
473	Glycerius (in the West)
473–75	Julius Nepos (in the West)
473–74	Leo II (in the East)
474–91	Zeno (in the East)
475–76	Romulus Augustulus (in the West)

Kings and Queens of England

Saxons

827–39	Egbert
839–58	Ethelwulf
858–60	Ethelbald
860–66	Ethelbert
866–71	Ethelred I
871–99	Alfred (the Great)
899–924	Edward (the Elder)
924–39	Athelstan
939–46	Edmund
946–55	Edred
955–59	Edwy
959–75	Edgar
975–78	Edward (the Martyr)
978 1016	Ethelred II (the Unready)
1016	Edmund Ironside

Danes

1016–35	Canute
1035–40	Harold I (Harefoot)
1040–42	Hardicanute

Saxons

1042–66	Edward (the Confessor)
1066	Harold II

House of Normandy

1066–87	William I (the Conqueror)
1087–1100	William II
1100 35	Henry I
1135–54	Stephen

House of Plantagenet

1154–89	Henry II
1189–99	Richard I
1199–1216	John
1216–72	Henry III
1272–1307	Edward I
1307–27	Edward II
1327–77	Edward III
1377–99	Richard II

House of Lancaster

1399–1413	Henry IV
1413–22	Henry V
1422–61	Henry VI

House of York

1461–83	Edward IV
1483	Edward V
1483–85	Richard III

House of Tudor

1485–1509	Henry VII
1509–47	Henry VIII
1547–53	Edward VI
1553–58	Mary I
1558–1603	Elizabeth I

Kings and Queens of Scotland

1005–34	Malcolm II
1034 40	Duncan I
1040–57	Macbeth
1057–93	Malcolm III (Canmore)
1093–94	Donald Bane
1094	Duncan II
1094–97	Donald Bane (restored)
1097–1107	Edgar
1107–24	Alexander I
1124–53	David I
1153–65	Malcolm IV
1165–1214	William (the Lion)
1214–49	Alexander II
1249–86	Alexander III
1286–90	Margaret of Norway
1290–92	*Interregnum – many people claim the throne*
1292–96	John Balliol
1296–1306	*Interregnum*
1306–29	Robert I (Bruce)
1329–71	David II

House of Stuart

1371–90	Robert II
1390–1406	Robert III
1406–37	James I
1437–60	James II
1460–88	James III
1488–1513	James IV
1513–42	James V
1542–67	Mary (Queen of Scots)
1567–1625	James VI (later James I of Great Britain)

Periods of History

Kings and Queens of Great Britain

House of Stuart

1603–25	James I
1625–49	Charles I
1649–59	*Commonwealth*
1660–85	Charles II
1685–88	James II
1689–94	William III and Mary II
1694–1702	William III
1702–14	Anne

House of Hanover

1714–27	George I
1727–60	George II
1760–1820	George III
1820–30	George IV
1830–37	William IV
1837–1901	Victoria

House of Saxe-Coburg

1901–10	Edward VII

House of Windsor

1910–36	George V
1936	Edward VIII
1936–52	George VI
1952–	Elizabeth II

British Prime Ministers

C = Coalition, Con = Conservative, Lab = Labour, Lib = Liberal, P = Peelite, T = Tory, W = Whig.

1721–42	Sir Robert Walpole (W)
1742–43	Earl of Wilmington (W)
1743–54	Henry Pelham (W)
1754–56	Duke of Newcastle (W)
1756–57	Duke of Devonshire (W)
1757–62	Duke of Newcastle (W)
1762–63	Earl of Bute (T)
1763–65	George Grenville (W)
1765–66	Marquess of Rockingham (W)
1766–67	Earl of Chatham (W)
1767–70	Duke of Grafton (W)
1770–82	Lord North (T)
1782	Marquess of Rockingham (W)
1782–83	Earl of Shelbourne (W)
1783	Duke of Portland (C)
1783–1801	William Pitt (T)
1801–04	Henry Addington (T)
1804–06	William Pitt (T)
1806–07	Lord Grenville (W)
1807–09	Duke of Portland (T)
1809–12	Spencer Perceval (T)
1812–27	Earl of Liverpool (T)
1827	George Canning (T)
1827–28	Viscount Goderich (T)
1828–30	Duke of Wellington (T)
1830–34	Earl Grey (W)
1834	Viscount Melbourne (W)
1834–35	Sir Robert Peel (T)
1835–41	Viscount Melbourne (W)
1841–46	Sir Robert Peel (T)
1846–52	Lord John Russell (W)
1852	Earl of Derby (T)
1852–55	Earl of Aberdeen (P)
1855–58	Viscount Palmerston (Lib)
1858–59	Earl of Derby (Con)
1859–65	Viscount Palmerston (Lib)
1865–66	Earl Russell (Lib)
1866–68	Earl of Derby (Con)
1868	Benjamin Disraeli (Con)
1868–74	William Gladstone (Lib)
1874–80	Benjamin Disraeli (Con)
1880–85	William Gladstone (Lib)

1885–86	Marquess of Salisbury (Con)
1886	William Gladstone (Lib)
1886–92	Marquess of Salisbury (Con)
1892–94	William Gladstone (Lib)
1894–95	Earl of Rosebery (Lib)
1895–1902	Marquess of Salisbury (Con)
1902–05	Arthur Balfour (Con)
1905–08	Sir Henry Campbell-Bannerman (Lib)
1908–15	Herbert Asquith (Lib)
1915–16	Herbert Asquith (C)
1916–22	David Lloyd-George (C)
1922–23	Andrew Bonar Law (Con)
1923–24	Stanley Baldwin (Con)
1924	Ramsay MacDonald (Lab)
1924–29	Stanley Baldwin (Con)
1929–31	Ramsay MacDonald (Lab)
1931–35	Ramsay MacDonald (C)
1935–37	Stanley Baldwin (C)
1937–40	Neville Chamberlain (C)
1940–45	Winston Churchill (C)
1945	Winston Churchill (Con)
1945–51	Clement Attlee (Lab)
1951–55	Sir Winston Churchill (Con)
1955–57	Sir Anthony Eden (Con)
1957–63	Harold Macmillan (Con)
1963–64	Sir Alec Douglas-Home (Con)
1964–70	Harold Wilson (Lab)
1970–74	Edward Heath (Con)
1974–76	Harold Wilson (Lab)
1976–79	James Callaghan (Lab)
1979–90	Margaret Thatcher (Con)
1990–97	John Major (Con)
1997–	Tony Blair (Lab)

Periods of History

Presidents of the United States of America

D = Democrat, DR = Democratic Republican, F = Federalist, R = Republican, U = Union,
W = Whig.

1789–97	George Washington (F)	1885–89	Grover Cleveland (D)
1797–1801	John Adams (F)	1889–93	Benjamin Harrison (R)
1801–09	Thomas Jefferson (DR)	1893–97	Grover Cleveland (D)
1809–17	James Madison (DR)	1897–1901	William McKinley (R)
1817–25	James Monroe (DR)	1901–09	Theodore Roosevelt (R)
1825–29	John Quincy Adams (DR)	1909–13	William H. Taft (R)
1829–37	Andrew Jackson (D)	1913–21	Woodrow Wilson (D)
1837–41	Martin Van Buren (D)	1921–23	Warren G. Harding (R)
1841	William H. Harrison (W)	1923–29	Calvin Coolidge (R)
1841–45	John Tyler (W)	1929–33	Herbert C. Hoover (R)
1845–49	James K. Polk (D)	1933–45	Franklin D. Roosevelt (D)
1849–50	Zachary Taylor (W)	1945–53	Harry S. Truman (D)
1850–53	Millard Fillmore (W)	1953–61	Dwight D. Eisenhower (R)
1853–57	Franklin Pierce (D)	1961–63	John F. Kennedy (D)
1857–61	James Buchanan (D)	1963–69	Lyndon B. Johnson (D)
1861–65	Abraham Lincoln (R)	1969–74	Richard M. Nixon (R)
1865–69	Andrew Johnson (U)	1974–77	Gerald R. Ford (R)
1869–77	Ulysses S. Grant (R)	1977–81	James E. Carter (D)
1877–81	Rutherford B. Hayes (R)	1981–89	Ronald Reagan (R)
1881	James A. Garfield (R)	1989–	George Bush (R)
1881–85	Chester A. Arthur (R)		

Secretaries General of the United Nations

1946–53	Trygve Lie (Norway)
1953–61	Dag Hammarskjöld (Sweden)
1961–72	U Thant (Burma)
1972–81	Kurt Waldheim (Austria)
1982	Javier Perez de Cuellar (Peru)

Index

Moon: first man on, 13; phases of, 183
Morse code, 198
Moses, 30
Mosques, 31
Multiplication, 266–267
Muscles: energy source, 170; facts about, 208–209
Mushrooms: types of, 234–235
Music: basic instruments, 122; historical view, 122
Muslims: Holy Wars, 31, 33, 40–41
Mussolini, Benito, 62
Myriapods, 221
Mystery plays, 43, 118

N

Nagasaki, 63, 172
National Assembly: France, 51
Nation states: medieval period, 38–39
Native Americans, 45
Navy flag: signals, 98
Nazism, 62
Neolithic period: villages, 16–17
Nervous system: brain, 211; environmental influences on, 212–213; facts about, 210–211
New Amsterdam, 49
Newspapers, 112–113
New Stone Age: villages, 16–17
Newton, Isaac, 47, 180
Niepce, Nicéphore, 190
Nile River, 18
Noise pollution, 241
Nomads: prehistoric humans, 15
Normandy, 33
Normans, 33, 35, 100
North Pole, 95
Nouns, 245; plurals, 251–253
Novel, 108

Nuclear energy, 70–71, 171; nuclear power plant, 165, 173; arguments for and against, 173; production of, 172
Nuclear weapons, 67, 172
Numbers: counting methods, 126–131; large, powers, 134–135; types of, 128–129; *see also* Mathematics
Nutrition: calories, 199; classification of food, 198; well-balanced diet, 196, 198, 199

O

Oceania: countries of, 94; facts about, 94
Oceans, 78; depth, 79; energy source, 171
Old English, 100
Oligarchy, 22
Olympic Games, 23
Omnivores, 224
Optical illusions, 203
Organ transplants, 70
Oviparous, 193

P

Pagoda, 28
Paper: invention of, 44
Papyrus of Rhind, 124
Parthenon, 12
Parts of speech, 245–248
Pasteur, Louis, 215
Pearl Harbour attack, 63
Peloponnesian War, 23
Pendulum, 187
Penicillin, 215
Penn, William, 49
Percentages, 154–155; calculations of, 154–155;

graphic representations of, 155
Peter the Great, 39
Pharaoh, 18, 19
Photography: camera, 190; film development, 191; historical view, 190
Pictographs, 97
Pictures and communication, 98–99; 114–115
Pilgrims, 48
Plans: graphics representations, 152
Plants: algae, 226–227; exotic plants, 223; fertilizers, 197; flowers, 236–239; fruit-bearing plants, 232–233; fungi, 226–227; nourishment for, 197; reproduction, 193; respiration, 195; seed-forming plants, 226–227; trees, 228–231; types of 238–239
Platform weighing machines, 179
Plurals, 251–253
Poetry: historical view, 110–111
Polar lands: facts about, 95
Polar zone, 80
Pollution: types of, 240–241
Polynesia, 94
Population of Earth, 74, 84–85
Power station: electricity, 169
Precious stones, 243
Precision balance, 179
Pregnancy, 193
Prehistoric times: art in caves, 14; cave dwellers, 14–15; fire, discovery of, 15; life on Earth during, 10–11; timeline of, 12–13; tools and weapons, 14, 15; villages, 16–17
Prepositions, 247
Primates: prehistoric, 10
Prime meridian, 76

Printing press, 12; invention of, 44, 97

Pronouns, 245; use of, 255–256

Psychrometer, 166

Pterodactyl, 11

Ptolemy, 202

Pulley, 178

Punctuation, 257–261

Puritans, 49

Pyramids, 19

Q

Quotation marks: use of, 261

R

Rabelais, François, 47

Racism, 72

Radio activity, 172

Radio broadcasting, 113

Railways: fastest trains, 71; earliest, 54, 189

Rainbow, 180

Rain forests, 66, 68

Rain gauge, 167

Ramses II, 19

Red Cross, 73

Reference books, 111

Refugees, 67

'Reign of Terror', 51

Religion: major religions, 30–31

Religious art, 120

Rembrandt van Rijn, 46

Renaissance, 46–47; art and science in, 46–47; beginning of, 46; mathematics, 125; poetry, 110

Reproduction: egg-layers, 193; human, 192–193; plants, 193

Reptiles: facts about, 216;

prehistoric times, 11; types of, 223

Respiration: fish, 195; humans, 194–195; plants, 195

Richter scale, 83

Roads: Roman, 24

Robotics, 70

Rocks: minerals, 242–243

Roman empire: fall of, 26, 32; size of, 24; emperors of, 276

Romania, 64–65

Romantic era: poetry, 109; theatre, 119

Rome (ancient), 24–25; mathematics, 125, 127, 135

Romulus and Remus, 24

Rousseau, Jean-Jacques, 50

S

Sahara Desert, 86

Satellites: type and uses of, 71

Satire, 108

Saxons, 32, 33

Scale: common scale, 179; graphic representations, 152–153

Science: in fifteenth century, 47; in Renaissance, 47

Seasons: changes, 75

Seed-forming plants, 226–227

Seesaw, 179

Seismographs, 83

Semicolons, use of, 259

Senate, 52

Senses: hearing, 205; sight, 202–203; smell, 204; taste, 204; touch, 206–207

Sentences, 244, 254; subject – verb agreement, 253; types of, 244, 254

Serbia, 60

Serfs, 37, 41

Shakespeare, William, 47, 108, 110, 118

Ships: invention of, 189

Short story, 110

Sight: facts about, 202–203

Signals: for communication, 98–99

Sign language, 98

Skeletal system: bones, 208; muscles, 208–209

Skin: sensation and, 206–207; structure of, 206

Sky: facts about, 182–183

Slavery: American Civil War, 57

Sleep, 213

Smell: facts about, 204

Solar energy, 171

Solar System, 182–183

Sonar, 174, 175

Sound: facts about, 174–175

Sound barrier, 175

Sound signals, 89

South Pole, 95

Space exploration, 71

Space shuttle, 71

Spain: absolute monarchs, 39

Spanish-American War, 59

Sparta, 23

Speed: sound and, 175

Sperm, 192

Spoken communication, 96

Stars, 182, 183; star charts, 204–205

Steamboat: invention of, 189

Steam engine, 13; invention of, 54

Steelyard: balance, 179

Stethoscope, 174

String telephone, 174

Subtraction, 264–265

Sumer (ancient), 20; written language, 97

Sundial, 186

Supersonic planes, 175

Symbols for communication, 98–99

Synonyms, 103